PAPAL PRIMACY

PAPAL PRIMACY AND THE UNIVERSAL CHURCH

Edited by
Paul C. Empie and T. Austin Murphy

Lutherans and Catholics in Dialogue V

Augsburg Publishing House
Minneapolis, Minnesota

PAPAL PRIMACY AND THE UNIVERSAL CHURCH

CONTENTS

PREFACE

The value of dialogue between theologians of different Christian traditions is linked to the extent to which insights gained can be communicated to, and are deemed credible by, the constituencies of the churches involved. This fact of life was recognized from the start when representatives of the Roman Catholic Bishops' Commission for Ecumenical and Interreligious Affairs and those from the USA National Committee of the Lutheran World Federation and of the Lutheran Church—Missouri Synod formulated the sequence of topics of their discussions. Initial studies, related to the role of the Nicene Creed as dogma and to baptism, were followed by consideration of the eucharist as sacrifice and the character and function of the Ministry, thus beginning with subjects in which it was surmised that agreements substantially outweighed differences, proceeding thereafter to more formidable issues. Readers will observe that the contents of this volume proceed out of the discussion on the Ministry published in *Lutherans and Catholics in Dialogue IV: Eucharist and Ministry*.

Some observers felt that prudence had been thrown to the winds when the group ventured to grapple with the dogma on papal primacy. "What can you hope to accomplish regarding an issue so thorny and neuralgic during four centuries of Lutheran-Roman Catholic polemics?" it was asked. "The emotional factor by itself is so strong that any agreement is doomed to be regarded from both sides as either compromise or betrayal of truth!"

It is indeed a hazardous undertaking, but Christian integrity requires that it be faced, not evaded. The reader of this volume will discover the belief that the common ground from which any forward steps may come is likely to be the deep concern held alike by each tradition for the unity of the church—its inner reality and its public manifestation.

No easy solutions are offered here. Much hard work remains to be done. The participants, however, were encouraged by clarifications which emerged and are convinced that the questions raised, together with the tentative suggestions put forward, open up avenues for significant steps toward a resolution of the issue, and should be seriously pursued by the churches themselves. It must be understood that the views expressed in the papers and the summaries are those respectively of the authors and the participants, not necessarily reflecting official positions of their churches.

As in the preceding sessions, the guidance of the Holy Spirit was sought and, we hope, received in this search for ways to surmount this divisive issue which would combine fidelity to the apostolic witness with obedience to Christ and his will for his church. We record our gratitude for the experienced blessings of such Christian fellowship engaged in mutual search for truth in love.

Paul C. Empie
U.S.A. National Committee
Lutheran World Federation

T. Austin Murphy
Bishop's Committee
    for Ecumenical and
    Inter-religious Affairs

1

DIFFERING ATTITUDES TOWARD PAPAL PRIMACY

Part I
Common Statement

Introduction

In the discussions conducted in the United States between Roman Catholic and Lutheran theologians, we have found broad areas of agreement on the Nicene Creed and the christological center of the faith as well as on baptism, the eucharist, and the Ministry of word and sacrament.[1] In the most recent sessions of our dialogue, we have moved to the problems of how that Ministry might best nurture and express the unity of the universal church for the sake of its mission in the world. It is within this context that we have considered papal primacy.

Visible unity in the church has from earliest times been served by several forms of the Ministry. Some of these forms, such as that exercised in the ecumenical councils,[2] have not been the subject of major disputes between Catholics and Lutherans. By contrast the role of the papacy has been the subject of intense controversy, which has generated theological disagreements, organizational differences, and psychological antagonisms.

In discussing the papacy as a form of Ministry within the universal church we have limited ourselves to the question of papal primacy. No attempt has been made to enter into the problem of papal infallibility. While this issue must be faced in the discussions between our churches, we believe that this limitation of the scope of our present discussion is justified, since papal primacy was a doctrinal issue long before papal infallibility became a major problem.

In these sessions, we have once again found common ground. There is a growing awareness among Lutherans of the necessity of a specific Ministry to serve the church's unity and universal mission, while Catholics increasingly see the need for a more nuanced understanding of the role of the papacy within the universal church. Lutherans and Catholics can now begin to envision possibilities of concord, and to hope for solutions to problems that have previously seemed insoluble. We believe that God is calling our churches to draw closer together, and it is our prayer that this joint statement on papal primacy may make some contribution to that end.

The Setting of the Problem

(1) The church as reconciled and reconciling community cannot serve God's purpose in the world as it should when its own life is torn by divisions and disagreements. The members of the church, wherever they are found, are part of a single people, the one body of Christ, whose mission is to be an anticipatory and efficacious sign of the final unification of all things when God will be all in all. In order to bear credible witness to this coming kingdom, the various Christian bodies must mutually assist and correct each other and must collaborate in all matters which concern the mission and welfare of the church universal. Even within the same Christian communion, local churches or units must be related to the church universal, so that pluralism and pluriformity do not undermine oneness, and unity and uniformity do not destroy a desirable diversity.

(2) As we Lutheran and Roman Catholic theologians turned in our discussions to the need for visible unity in the church universal, we were assisted by the fundamental accord stated in an earlier report on the doctrine of ministry. We there agreed that, by the will of God 1) the general ministry of proclaiming the gospel devolves upon the whole people of God, and 2) "the Ministry of word and sacrament" serves to unify and order the church for its mission in and to the world.[3]

Our previous discussions had centered on the service rendered to the local communities by the Ministry. Now we focus on the unifying and ordering function of this Ministry in relation to the universal church—on how a particular form of this Ministry, i.e., the papacy, has served the unity of the universal church in the past and how it may serve it in the future.

(3) Catholics and Lutherans have in part recognized and employed similar means for fostering the unity of the universal church. Christians of the various communities have been bound together by one baptism and by their acceptance of the inspired scriptures. Liturgies, creeds, and confessions have also been unifying factors. For both traditions the councils of the church have had a significant unifying role. The Reformers affirmed the value of councils; and this has been implicitly acknowledged in a different form by most contemporary Lutheran churches through their formation of the Lutheran World Federation and, on a wider scale, by participation in the World Council of Churches. On the Catholic side, the importance of the conciliar principle has been reasserted by Vatican II in its exercise of conciliar functions, as well as in its emphasis on the collegial structure of the church.

(4) Precisely because large areas of agreement exist on such means of unifying the church, we have focused our attention in this discussion on another unifying factor on which there has been disagreement, namely, the role of particular persons, offices, or officeholders in exercising responsibility for the unity of the universal church. In describing this specific Ministry and its exercise by a person we were naturally drawn, in the light of centuries of development, to the image of Peter.[4] Among the companions of Jesus, he is given the greatest prominence in the New Testament accounts of the origins of the church. He is spoken of in the Gospels in terms relating him to the founding of the church, to strengthening his brethren, to feeding the sheep of Christ. He is a prominent figure in some of the Pauline letters, in Acts, and for two of the Catholic Epistles—a fact which suggests that he was associated with a wide-ranging ministry. Subsequent church history made him the image of a pastor caring for the universal church. And so, although we are aware of the danger of attributing to the church in New Testament times a modern style or model of universality, we have found it appropriate to speak of a "Petrine function," using this term to describe *a particular form of Ministry exercised by a person, officeholder, or local church with reference to the church as a whole.* This Petrine func-

tion of the Ministry serves to promote or preserve the oneness of the church by symbolizing unity, and by facilitating communication, mutual assistance or correction, and collaboration in the church's mission.

(5) Such a Petrine function has been exercised in some degree by various officeholders, for example by bishops, patriarchs, and church presidents. However, the single most notable representative of this Ministry toward the church universal, both in duration and geographical scope, has been the bishop of Rome. The Reformers did not totally reject all aspects of the papal expression of the Petrine function, but only what they regarded as its abuses. They hoped for a reform of the papacy precisely in order to preserve the unity of the church. Melanchthon held that "for the sake of peace and general unity among Christians" a superiority over other bishops could be conceded to the pope.[5] For many years Lutherans hoped for an ecumenical council that would reform the papacy. They continued to concede to the pope all the legitimate spiritual powers of a bishop in his diocese, in this case, Rome. They even granted the propriety of his exercising a larger jurisdiction by human right over communities that had by their own will placed themselves under him.[6]

The Issues

(6) Nevertheless, the pope's claims to primacy and his exercise of it have occasioned violent disagreements. Lutherans and others have even gone so far as to call the papacy "antichrist."

The disputes have centered, first, on the question whether the papacy is biblically warranted. Roman Catholics have read the New Testament as indicating that Jesus conferred on Peter a unique role of leadership in the whole church for all times and in this sense provided for successors in the Petrine function, the bishops of Rome. In this view, the papacy has remained substantially the same through succeeding centuries, all changes being accidental.

Lutherans, in contrast, have minimized Peter's role in the early church and denied that this role continued in the church in later periods or that the Roman bishops could be considered his successors in any theologically significant sense.

(7) Closely linked to this historical question regarding the institution of the papacy by Christ is the theological issue

whether the papacy is a matter of divine law (*ius divinum*).[7] Roman Catholics have affirmed that it is and consequently have viewed it as an essential part of the permanent stucture of the church. Lutherans have held, in opposition to this, that the papacy was established by human law, the will of men, and that its claims to divine right are nothing short of blasphemous.

(8) A third area of controversy centers on the practical consequences drawn from these prior disagreements. Roman Catholics have tended to think of most major aspects of papal structure and function as divinely authorized. The need or possibility of significant change, renewal, or reform has generally been ignored. Most important, it has been argued that all ministry concerned with fostering unity among the churches is subject—at least in crisis situations—to the supervision of the bishop of Rome. His jurisdiction over the universal church is in the words of Vatican I, "supreme," "full," "ordinary," and "immediate."[8] This authority is not subject to any higher human jurisdiction, and no pope is absolutely bound by disciplinary decisions of his predecessors.[9] This view of the exercise of papal power has been vehemently repudiated by Lutherans and viewed by them as leading to intolerable ecclesiastical tyranny.

In the course of our discussions, however, we have been able to gain helpful and clarifying insights regarding these points of controversy.

Focus on the New Testament Question

(9) Any biblical and historical scholar today would consider anachronistic the question whether Jesus constituted Peter the first pope, since this question derives from a later model of the papacy which it projects back into the New Testament.[10] Such a reading helps neither papal opponents nor papal supporters. Therefore terms such as "primacy" and "jurisdiction" are best avoided when one describes the role of Peter in the New Testament. Even without these terms, however, a wide variety of images is applied to Peter in the New Testament which signalizes his importance in the early church.[11]

(10) It is well to approach the question of Peter's role in the church by recognizing that the New Testament writings describe various forms of Ministry directed toward the church as a whole. These writings show a primary concern for local communities of believers (the churches). There is

also ample evidence of concern for groups of churches, for relationships between churches of different areas or backgrounds, and also for *the* church as the one body of Christ. Paul sometimes holds up one local church as an example to another; he seeks to retain fellowship between the Gentile and the Jewish churches; he collects from the churches he has founded for the support of the church in Jerusalem. Both the letter to the Galatians and the book of Acts describe a meeting in Jerusalem among church leaders to settle a major problem facing various communities, namely, the circumcision of the Gentiles. The First Epistle of Peter, the Pastoral Letters, and the Revelation (the Apocalypse), show concern for groups of churches. Colossians and Ephesians speak of the church as the body of Christ, and Ephesians in particular stresses the unity of the body. In the description of the Pentecost scene in Acts, there is a global vision of the Spirit-filled community reaching men of every land and tongue. In the Fourth Gospel, Jesus speaks of the day when there will be one flock and one shepherd.

(11) What role does Peter play in this Ministry directed to the church at large? There is no single or uniform New Testament outlook on such a question. The New Testament books, written by men of different generations and varying outlooks, living in widely scattered churches, see Peter in a diversity of ways.[12] There are certain features common to or underlying these different pictures of Peter. He is listed first among the Twelve; he is frequently their spokesman; he is the first apostolic witness of the risen Jesus; he is prominent in the Jerusalem community; he is well known to many churches. Yet it is not always easy to tell to what extent he exercises a function in relation to the church as a whole and to what extent his influence remains regional. For instance, Galatians 2:7 attributes to Peter a special role in relation to the gospel addressed to the Jews, while Paul has a similar role in relation to the gospel addressed to the Gentiles. Moreover, the relative silence of the New Testament about the career of Peter after the Jerusalem meeting (ca. A.D. 49) makes it difficult to find a biblical basis for affirmations about his continuing role in the church in his later years. There is increasing agreement that Peter went to Rome and was martyred there, but we have no trustworthy evidence that Peter ever served as the supervisor or bishop of the local church in Rome. From the New Testament, we know nothing of a succession to Peter in Rome. We cannot exclude

the possibility that other figures, such as Paul or James, also had a unifying role in relation to the whole church, although the available documents connect them primarily with individual churches or groups of churches.

(12) Although the New Testament gives us limited information about the historical career of Simon Peter, individual writings associate him with different aspects or images of Ministry which have relevance to the church as a whole. It is Peter among the Twelve who confesses Jesus as the Christ (Mark 8, Matthew 16, Luke 9) and as the Holy One of God (John 6); he is listed as the first apostolic witness to the risen Lord (1 Corinthians 15; Luke 24); he is the rock on which the church is to be founded and he is to be entrusted with the power of the keys (Matthew 16); he is the one who is to strengthen his brethren in faith (Luke 22); he is the one who, after confessing his love, is told to feed Jesus' sheep (John 21); he takes the initiative in filling the vacancy among the Twelve (Acts 1) and receives the first Gentile converts (Acts 10). He is also the one who denies Jesus in an especially dramatic way (all four Gospels); who sinks in the waves because of his lack of faith (Matthew 14); he is sharply rebuked by Jesus (Mark 8, Matthew 16), and later on by Paul (Galatians 2). The fact that these failures were so vividly remembered is perhaps also evidence of his prominence.

(13) How this view of Peter in the New Testament as developed by modern scholarship relates to the papacy might be summarized thus. Peter was very important as a companion of Jesus during Jesus' public ministry; he was one of the first of the disciples to be called and seems to have been the most prominent among the regular companions. This importance carried over into the early Palestinian church, as indicated in the record of an appearance of the risen Jesus to Peter (probably the first appearance to an apostle). Clearly he was the most prominent of the Twelve and took an active part in the Christian missionary movement. Peter had a key role in decisions that affected the course of the church. Thus one may speak of a prominence that can be traced back to Peter's relationship to Jesus in his public ministry and as the risen Lord.

Of even greater importance, however, is the thrust of the images associated with Peter in the later New Testament books, many of them written after his death. While some of these images recall his failures (e.g., Peter the weak and sinful man), Peter is portrayed as the fisherman (Luke 5, John 21), as the shepherd of the sheep of Christ (John 21), as a presbyter who addresses other presbyters (1 Peter 5:1); as proclaimer of faith in Jesus the Son of God (Matthew 16:16-17); as a receiver of special revelation (Acts 10:9-16); as one who can correct those who misunderstand the thought of a brother apostle, Paul (2 Peter 3:15-16); and as the rock on which the church was to be built (Matthew 16:18). When a "trajectory" of these images is traced, we find indications of a development from earlier to later images. This development of images does not consitute papacy in its later technical sense, but one can see the possibility of an orientation in that direction, when shaped by favoring factors in the subsequent church. The question whether Jesus appointed Peter the first pope has shifted in modern scholarship to the question of the extent to which the subsequent use of the images of Peter in reference to the papacy is consistent with the thrust of the New Testament.

Historical and Theological Questions

(14) Historical studies have opened new perspectives not only on the New Testament writings but also on other problems. It is now clear that the question of papal primacy cannot adequately be treated in terms of proof passages from scripture or as a matter of church law, but must be seen in the light of many factors—biblical, social, political, theological—which have contributed to the development of the theology, structure, and function of the modern papacy.

(15) In the period following the New Testament era, two parallel lines of development tended to enhance the role of the bishop of Rome among the churches of the time. One was the continuing development of the several images of Peter emerging from the apostolic communities, the other resulted from the importance of Rome as a political, cultural, and religious center.

The trajectory of the biblical images of Peter continued in the life of the early church, enriched by the addition of other images; missionary preacher, great visionary, destroyer of heretics, receiver of the new law, gatekeeper of heaven, helmsman of the ship of the church, co-teacher with Paul, co-martyr with Paul in Rome.[13] These images had a theological significance even before they were associated with the bishop of Rome.

(16) A parallel line of development occurred through the early church's accommodation to the culture of the Graeco-Roman world, when it adopted patterns of organization and administration prevailing in the area of its missionary work. Churches identified themselves according to the localities, dioceses, and provinces of the empire. The prestige and centrality of Rome as the capital city, combined with the wealth and generosity of Roman Christians, quite naturally led to a special prominence of the Roman church. Moreover this church enjoyed the distinction of having been founded, according to tradition, by Peter and Paul, and of being the site where these martyrs were buried.

(17) In the controversy with the gnostics, episcopal sees of apostolic foundation served as a gauge or standard of orthodoxy, and the Roman church, associated with Peter and Paul, was especially emphasized in this respect by Western writers. During the first five centuries, the church of Rome gradually assumed a certain pre-eminence among the churches: it intervened in the life of distant churches, took sides in distant theological controversies, was consulted by other bishops on a wide variety of doctrinal and moral questions, and sent legates to faraway councils. In the course of time Rome came to be regarded in many quarters as the supreme court of appeal and as a focus of unity for the world-wide communion of churches.

(18) With Leo I the correlation between the bishop of the Roman church and the image of Peter, which had already been suggested by some of his predecessors, became fully explicit. According to Leo, Peter continues his task in the bishop of Rome, and the predominance of Rome over other churches derives from Peter's presence in his successors, the bishops of the Roman see. The Petrine function of the bishop of Rome is nothing less than the care for all the churches. It imposes upon other bishops the duty to obey his authority and apply his decisions. Thus Western theological affirmations of papal primacy found an early expression in the teaching of Leo I.

(19) The later development of these claims can now be seen by both Lutherans and Catholics to have had both positive and negative features. On the one hand, this development was furthered by the historical situation of the Middle Ages, when Rome no longer found itself in competition with the other major metropolitan sees in the long struggle against secular, and especially imperial, power. On

the other hand, the theoretical interpretation of primacy in the categories of canon law made rapid progress. Among others, Gregory VII and Innocent III, relying on such documents as the False Decretals, depicted the church as a papal monarchy in accordance with secular models available in their day. Documents such as Boniface VIII's *Unam Sanctam* (1302) embodied the claim that the pope had not only spiritual but also temporal dominion over the whole earth.[14] At the same time, some medieval theologians continued to see Rome as the center of unity in a world-wide communion of churches. Some accented the religious and charismatic, rather than the juridical and administrative, aspects of papal primacy.

In the high Middle Ages the mendicant orders and some of their prominent theologians, such as Bonaventure and Thomas Aquinas, tended to exalt the powers of the Roman see. Moreover, the growth of scholastic theology reinforced a pyramidal view of authority in the church. The powers diffused in the body of the faithful were seen to be concentrated in the order of bishops and still further in the one person of the bishop of Rome. Some theologians, for example the conciliarists, interpreted the powers as ascending from the body into the head, while others, for example the papal canonists, saw them as descending from the head into the body. The latter view reemerged with added emphasis after the Council of Basel (1431-37). The Council of Florence in its Decree of Union for the Greek and Latin churches (1439)[15] set forth the doctrine of papal primacy in terms that approximate those of Vatican I.

Within post-Tridentine Roman Catholicism, the polemics of the sixteenth century and the Counter-Reformation strengthened this trend. Several centuries of struggle against nationalistic movements, an upsurge of ultramontane centralism, and the desire to oppose nineteenth century liberalism created the climate for Vatican I. This council taught that the pope as successor of Peter has a primacy of jurisdiction over all individuals and churches. It declared that this jurisdiction is "full," "supreme," "ordinary" (that is, not derived by delegation from another), and "immediate" (that is, direct), and linked this primacy of jurisdiction with papal infallibility.[16]

(20) The theology of Vatican II developed the teaching of Vatican I, giving a more balanced account of the relations of the pope to the bishops and of the bishops to the

people of God. The bishop of Rome is head of the college of bishops, who share his responsibility for the universal church. His authority is pastoral in its purpose even when juridical in form. It should always be understood in its collegial context.[17]

(21) We thus see from the above that the contemporary understanding of the New Testament and our knowledge of the processes at work in the history of the church make possible a fresh approach to the structure and operations of the papacy. There is increasing agreement that the centralization of the Petrine function in a single person or office results from a long process of development. Reflecting the many pressures of the centuries and the complexities of a world-wide church, the papal office can be seen both as a response to the guidance of the Spirit in the Christian community, and also as an institution which in its human dimensions, is tarnished by frailty and even unfaithfulness. The Catholic members of this consultation see the institution of the papacy as developing from New Testament roots under the guidance of the Spirit. Without denying that God could have ordered the church differently, they believe that the papal form of the unifying Ministry is, in fact, God's gracious gift to his people. Lutheran theologians, although in the past chiefly critical of the structure and functioning of the papacy, can now recognize many of its positive contributions to the life of the church. Both groups can acknowledge that as the forms of the papacy have been adapted to changing historical settings in the past, it is possible that they will be modified to meet the needs of the church in the future more effectively.

Toward the Renewal of Papal Structures

(22) In considering how the papacy may better serve the church as a whole, our reflections will bear on basic principles of renewal, and on questions facing Roman Catholics and Lutherans in view of the possibilities of rapprochement.

A. Norms for Renewal

(23) *The Principle of Legitimate Diversity*
The ultimate source of authority is God revealed in Christ. The church is guided by the Spirit and is judged by the word of God. All its members share in this guidance and are subject to this judgment. They should recognize that the Spirit's guidance may give rise to diverse forms in piety,

liturgy, theology, custom, or law. Yet a variety of ecclesial types should never foster divisiveness. With humility and in self-criticism, Ministers in the church should therefore "test the spirits", and listen to the judgment which may be implied in "the signs of the times".[18] Even the exercise of the Petrine function should evolve with the changing times, in keeping with a legitimate diversity of ecclesial types within the church.

(24) *The Principle of Collegiality*

Collegial responsibility for the unity of the church, as emphasized by Vatican II, is of utmost importance in protecting those values which excessive centralization of authority would tend to stifle. No one person or administrative staff, however dedicated, learned, and experienced, can grasp all the subtleties and complexities of situations in a world-wide church, whose many communities live and bear witness in the variegated contexts of several continents and many nations. It is only through the contributions of many persons and groups that the problems which need urgent attention can be identified, and the talents necessary to deal with them be mustered. The collegial principle calls all levels of the church to share in the concern and responsibilities of leadership for the total life of the church.

(25) *The Principle of Subsidiarity*

The principle of subsidiarity is no less important. Every section of the church, each mindful of its special heritage, should nurture the gifts it has received from the Spirit by exercising its legitimate freedom. What can properly be decided and done in smaller units of ecclesial life ought not to be referred to church leaders who have wider responsibilities. Decisions should be made and activities carried out with a participation as broad as possible from the people of God. Initiatives should be encouraged in order to promote a wholesome diversity in theology, worship, witness, and service. All should be concerned that, as the community is built up and its unity strengthened, the rights of minorities and minority viewpoints are protected within the unity of faith.

B. Roman Catholic Perspectives

(26) The church's teaching office "is not above God's Word; it rather serves the Word."[19] Indeed this is true of all ecclesiastical authority. The gospel may require that church offices be exercised in very different ways to meet the needs of various regions and periods. New means of exercising

authority may have to be discovered to fit the cultural patterns arising out of the changing forms of education, communications, and social organization. The signs of the times point to the need for greater participation of pastors, scholars, and all believers in the direction of the universal church.[20]

(27) Further, it is an important political principle that authority in any society should use only the amount of power necessary to reach its assigned goal. This applies also to the papal office. A canonical distinction between the highest authority and the limited exercise of the corresponding power cannot be ruled out and needs to be emphasized. Such a limitation need not prejudice the universal jurisdiction attributed to the pope by Roman Catholic doctrine. Thus one may foresee that voluntary limitations by the pope of the exercise of his jurisdiction will accompany the growing vitality of the organs of collegial government, so that checks and balances in the supreme power may be effectively recognized.

C. Lutheran Perspectives

(28) If perspectives such as the foregoing prevail, papal primacy will no longer be open to many traditional Lutheran objections. As we have noted (see 3 above), Lutherans increasingly recognize the need for a Ministry serving the unity of the church universal. They acknowledge that, for the exercise of this Minisitry, institutions which are rooted in history should be seriously considered. The church should use the signs of unity it has received, for new ones cannot be invented at will. Thus the Reformers wished to continue the historic structures of the church.[21] Such structures are among the signs of the church's unity in space and time, helping to link the Christian present with its apostolic past. Lutherans can also grant the beneficial role of the papacy at various periods of history. Believing in God's sovereign freedom, they cannot deny that God may show again in the future that the papacy is his gracious gift to his people. Perhaps this might involve a primacy in which the pope's service to unity in relation to the Lutheran churches would be more pastoral than juridical. The one thing necessary, from the Lutheran point of view, is that papal primacy be so structured and interpreted that it clearly serve the gospel and the unity of the church of Christ, and that its exercise of power not subvert Christian freedom.

(29) Our discussions in this dialogue have brought to

light a number of agreements, among the most significant of which are:

• Christ wills for his church a unity which is not only spiritual but must be manifest in the world.

• promotion of this unity is incumbent on all believers, especially those who are engaged in the Ministry of word and sacrament;

• the greater the responsibility of a ministerial office, the greater the responsibility to seek the unity of all Christians;

• a special responsibility for this may be entrusted to one individual Minister, under the gospel.

• such a responsibility for the universal church cannot be ruled out on the basis of the biblical evidence;

• the bishop of Rome, whom Roman Catholics regard as entrusted by the will of Christ with this responsibility, and who has exercised his Ministry in forms that have changed significantly over the centuries, can in the future function in ways which are better adapted to meet both the universal and regional needs of the church in the complex environment of modern times.

(30) We do not wish to understate our remaining disagreements. While we have concluded that traditional sharp distinctions between divine and human institution are no longer useful, Catholics continue to emphasize that papal primacy is an institution in accordance with God's will. For Lutherans this is a secondary question. The one thing necessary, they insist, is that papal primacy serve the gospel and that its exercise of power not subvert Christian freedom (see section 28).

There are also differences which we have not yet discussed. We have not adequately explored to what extent the existing forms of the papal office are open to change in the future, nor have we yet touched on the sensitive point of papal infallibility, taught by Vatican Councils I and II.

(31) Even given these disagreements and points yet to be examined, it is now proper to ask, in the light of the agreement we have been able to reach, that our respective churches take specific actions toward reconciliation.

(32) Therefore we ask the Lutheran churches:

• if they are prepared to affirm with us that papal primacy, renewed in the light of the gospel, need not be a barrier to reconciliation;

• if they are able to acknowledge not only the legitimacy of the papal Ministry in the service of the Roman Catholic communion[22] but even the possibility and the desirability of the papal Ministry, renewed under the gospel and committed to Christian freedom, in a larger communion which would include the Lutheran churches;

• if they are willing to open discussion regarding the concrete implications of such a primacy to them.

(33) Likewise, we ask the Roman Catholic Church:

• if in the light of our findings, it should not give high priority in its ecumenical concerns to the problem of reconciliation with the Lutheran churches;

• if it is willing to open discussions on possible structures for reconciliation which would protect the legitimate traditions of the Lutheran communities and respect their spiritual heritage;[23]

• if it is prepared to envisage the possibility of a reconciliation which would recognize the self-government of Lutheran churches within a communion;

• if, in the expectation of a foreseeable reconciliation, it is ready to acknowledge the Lutheran churches represented in our dialogue as sister-churches which are already entitled to some measure of ecclesiastical communion.

(34) We believe that our joint statement reflects a convergence in the theological understanding of the papacy which makes possible a fruitful approach to these questions. Our churches should not miss this occasion to respond to the will of Christ for the unity of his disciples. Neither church should continue to tolerate a situation in which members of one communion look upon the other as alien. Trust in the Lord who makes us one body in Christ will help us to risk ourselves on the yet undisclosed paths toward which his Spirit is guiding his church.

Part II

Reflections of the Lutheran Participants

(28) Many Lutherans as well as Roman Catholics will be startled by the convergence on papal primacy recorded in the preceding joint statement. This issue is both more sensitive and more difficult than any of those previously dealt with in our national dialogue.[1] It is doubly necessary, therefore,

that the Lutheran participants explain their views to their fellow Lutherans more fully than was appropriate in the common statement (just as the Roman Catholic participants will address their fellow Roman Catholics in the third part of this report). We need to explain (1) why we have dealt with this issue (2) what seems to us the position of the Lutheran tradition on this matter, and (3) why we believe the time has now come for our churches to consider seriously the possibility of a role for the papacy such as is sketched in Part I.

(29) It would have been impossible to avoid the question of papal primacy in our discussions even if we had wished to do so. The purpose of the dialogue is:

First, to define as clearly as possible the extent and the limits of the common ground between Roman Catholics and Lutherans at this particular time in our respective histories.

Second, and more important, we are called as Christians to give a credible witness to our unity in Christ for the sake of our mission in the world (John 17:21; Ephesians 4:3-6). This unity is not an exclusively spiritual unity. It is true that we have a unity that our one baptism and our one faith in Christ bring about. At the same time Lutheran theologians have insisted that the church is not a Platonic republic that exists only in an ideal realm (Apology 7:20),[2] but that it is an empirical assembly of Christians among whom the gospel is proclaimed and heard and the sacraments are administered.

Third, we must deal not only with problems on which agreement is already visibly developing (such as the eucharist and eucharistic Ministry),[3] but also with such apparently intractable issues as the papacy.

In our previous discussions on the ministry, we had already encountered the issue of the papacy. In those discussions we repeated the traditional Lutheran affirmation that "as long as the ordained Ministry is retained, any form of polity which serves the proclamation of the gospel is acceptable."[4] We also observed that the Luthern confessional writings "do not exclude the possibility that the papacy might have a symbolical or functional value in a wider area as long as its primacy is seen as being of human right."[5] In addition, we joined with our Roman Catholic colleagues in declaring that "the ordained Ministry, through the proclamation of the word and the administration of the sacraments, serves to unify and order the church in a special way for its ministry."[6] We were thus challenged to develop more fully a Lutheran view of the papacy's possible role as a symbol and center of unity in the exercise of a Ministry on behalf of the church universal.

We have not, as our joint report repeatedly mentions, discussed papal infallibility. Our common statement is therefore by no means a complete treatment of the papacy. It addresses itself particularly to the issues of papal primacy. While this fact may be disappointing to some people, it is our conviction that it is by such a step-by-step procedure that we can most responsibly clarify our agreements and differences.

(30) In considering the historic Lutheran position on the papacy, we have become very much aware that the early Reformers did not reject what we have called the "Petrine function," but rather the concrete historical papacy as it confronted them in their day. In calling the pope the "antichrist," the early Lutherans stood in a tradition that reached back into the eleventh century.[7] Not only dissidents and heretics but even saints had called the bishop of Rome the "antichrist" when they wished to castigate his abuse of power. What Lutherans understood as a papal claim to unlimited authority over everything and everyone reminded them of the apocalyptic imagery of Daniel 11, a passage that even prior to the Reformation had been applied to the pope as the antichrist of the last days. The pope's willingness to derive advantage from doctrines and practices that seemed to them to contradict the gospel compelled them to resist such doctrines and practices as antichristian.[8]

The claim that probably rankled most was Boniface VIII's sweeping assertion in the bull *Unam sanctam* (1302) that it is necessary for all human beings for their salvation to be subject to the bishop of Rome.[9] This declaration would probably not have played the role that it did in the sixteenth century if Leo X had not reaffirmed it at the Fifth Lateran Council (1516).[10] Against this teaching Lutherans consistently denied that the bishop of Rome is the visible head of Christendom by divine right, that is, on the basis of the word of God.[11]

Further, the direct involvement of the late medieval papacy in the politics of Europe, the popes' frequent resort to war and to the sometimes devious devices of medieval statecraft made the bishop of Rome in Lutheran eyes only one more secular prince who was ready to use his spiritual authority to achieve political ends.[12] As such he could be resisted in the name of patriotism in the same way any other foreign potentate might be resisted, a principle which was also admitted by Catholic theologians of the period.

Because of these factors, from the 1520s on, Lutherans regarded themselves as in fact outside the pope's spiritual jurisdiction. They saw themselves as being on a par with those parts of the church, especially in the East, which did not recognize the jurisdictional primacy of the bishop of Rome. The Lutheran refusal to submit to the authority of the bishop of Rome was reinforced in succeeding centuries by some of the political strategies employed by the Counter Reformation, by what seemed the defensiveness of the Roman Catholic reaction to intellectual and political liberalism, and by the increasing trend toward centralization of power in the Roman see and the Roman curia. The setting forth of the teachings of universal papal jurisdiction and of papal infallibility in 1870 seemed in Lutheran eyes to make the gulf between the Roman Catholic Church and the heirs of the Reformation virtually unbridgeable.

During the same period Lutheranism had difficulties of its own. It suffered from subservience to state power. Its own ecclesiastical authorities have not always fostered Christian liberty and faithfulness to the gospel. It too reacted defensively to intellectual and cultural movements. Worst of all, in many places it came close to losing the vision of the unity of God's people. In view of this record, Lutherans have no ground for self-righteousness.

(31) Today, after over four centuries of mutual suspicion and condemnation, it is generally supposed that Lutherans have had no place for papal primacy in their thinking about the church. This is not true. We need to remember that the earliest Lutherans hoped for a reform of the papacy precisely for the sake of seeing the unity of the church preserved. Melanchthon held that "for the sake of peace and general unity among the Christians" a superiority over the other bishops could be conceded to the pope.[13] Many Lutherans kept hoping for an ecumenical council to reform the papacy. Despite their often violent antipapal polemics, Lutherans continued to concede to the pope all the legitimate spiritual powers of a bishop in his diocese, in this case, Rome. They even granted the propriety of his exercising a larger jurisdiction by *human* right over communities that had by their own will placed themselves under him.[14]

They were ready to grant that the rock on which Christ promised to build his community was Peter in his capacity as a minister of Christ.[15]

Even theologians of the era of classic Lutheran orthodoxy conceded that in the New Testament Peter possessed a preeminence among the Twelve as a leader (*coryphaeus*), spokesman (*os*), chief (*princeps*) and the one "who proposed what was to be done."[16] In rejecting the monarchical authority of the bishop of Rome in the church, they were careful not to exclude a primacy of Peter among the apostles based on honor, age, calling, zeal, or order, nor did they deny that in a broad sense Peter could be called a "bishop" of Rome, and that the leadership of the Roman see devolved upon episcopal successors as happened in other apostolic sees.[17]

Since they felt bound by the gospel to seek the unity of the church, many of our Lutheran forefathers over a period of nearly two centuries negotiated with representatives of the Roman Catholic Church, in spite of deep reservations.[18] Lutherans sent delegations to the second phase of the Council of Trent,[19] and even after the peace of Augsburg (1555) responsible Lutheran leaders were ready to enter into discussion with their Roman Catholic counterparts.[20] Irenic attempts continued late into the seventeenth century.[21] The vision of "one church of the future" was in the minds of a number of prominent Lutherans throughout the nineteenth century.[22] The willingness of Lutherans to engage in serious dialogue suggests that they believed that ultimately the Holy Spirit might point both sides to a solution even of the knotty problem of the papacy.

(32) Ours is an era of change in social structures, in technology, in science, in human knowledge. In some ways these changes have brought all Christians closer together. Furthermore, the return to the sources, particularly the Bible and the church fathers, has helped prepare the way for a greater common understanding of the heritage shared by all Christians.

From our Roman Catholic partners in dialogue we have received a vivid impression of dramatic changes within their church, changes which are throwing new light on the role of the papacy in Roman Catholic thought and life. For instance, Pope John XXIII, by his gesture of "opening the windows," has become for many Christians a new symbol of what the papacy might be. Our partners are careful to point out that for them the pope is neither a dictator, nor an absolute monarch. He does not replace Christ; he represents Christ. His role is primarily that of one who serves. He cannot act arbitrarily but is limited by the same gospel that provides the norm for the life of the total Christian community. The documents of Vatican II, they emphasize, understand the papacy from the point of view of the church, not the church from the point of view of the papacy. These documents also stress the collegial aspect of church leadership.

To be sure, in the texts from Vatican II, as well as in more recent documents,[23] there are also claims for exclusive papal power. During the council, Pope Paul VI reserved certain questions[24] for himself and he has continued to act independently to a degree that at times seems to compromise the principle of collegiality.

We Lutherans have to ask ourselves if the same factors that have contributed to the new situation in Roman Catholicism are not in fact also changing our own perspective on the papacy. In this day of intensified global communication and international cooperation, the concern for the unity of the entire empirical church is being keenly felt. Lutherans in the past have used documents such as those contained in the *Book of Concord* as a device for achieving a common identity within their confessional family. In recent decades the Lutheran World Federation has been increasingly used for this purpose. Lutheran participation in the World Council of Churches, which includes major churches of the East, is also evidence of the Lutheran concern for unity of faith and action among all Christians. We Lutherans consider the need for symbols and centers of unity to be urgent. We believe that we must try more energetically than we have in the past to give concrete expression to our concern for the unity of the whole empirical church. When we think of the question of the church's unity in relation to its mission we cannot responsibly dismiss the possibility that some form of the papacy, renewed and restructured under the gospel, may be an appropriate visible expression of the Ministry that serves the unity and ordering of the church.

(33) The results of biblical research and historical scholarship have placed in a new perspective many of the once intensely debated issues surrounding the papacy. The National Dialogue group has recognized the importance of these findings for a fresh approach to the question by commissioning two independant studies, one on "Peter in the

New Testament"[25] and another on "Roman primacy in the patristic era."[26]

The report of the biblical panel makes it clear that "no matter what one may think about the justification offered by the New Testament for the emergence of the papacy, this papacy in its developed form cannot be read back into the New Testament; and it will help neither papal opponents nor papal supporters to have the model of the later papacy before their eyes when discussing the role of Peter."[27] This report quite properly warns against an anachronistic interpretation of the New Testament. Instead, it points out the diversity of the images of Peter in the various strata of the New Testament materials and directs attention to the "trajectories"[28] of these images of Peter, and to their continuation and use in the early church. The view of Peter as the confessor, missionary, repentant sinner, and martyr is as much a part of this tradition as the view of Peter as the shepherd, pastor, teacher, and spokesman.

On the other hand, Lutherans too will find many of their cherished polemical readings of the texts challenged. Exegetically it is hard to deny that Peter enjoyed a preeminence among the apostles during Jesus' ministry as well as in the post-Easter church. He exercised in his time a function on behalf of the unity of the entire apostolic church. This we have chosen to designate the "Petrine function", even though its exercise was not restricted to Peter alone. This "Petrine function" is significantly connected with the images of Peter not only in the book of Acts and the two Petrine epistles but also, less directly, in the Pauline letters. Paul had his own understanding of his special role in and for the universal church, but at the same time room is left for a Petrine function for the sake of unity.[29]

Again, the report of the patristics panel indicates that there is no conclusive documentary evidence from the first century or the early decades of the second for the exercise of, or even the claim to, a primacy of the Roman bishop or to a connection with Peter, although documents from this period accord the church at Rome some kind of preeminence.[30] Both primatial claims and the Petrine trajectories went through a long history in which—as the Common Statement points out—not only religious-theological but also political, social, and cultural factors played a considerable role before these two trends finally merged in the third century. While we are aware of the variety of factors which contributed to this development, we as Lutherans are impressed by the fact that the bishops of Rome were nevertheless able to exercise a Ministry of unifying and ordering the church in the West. Sometimes, as in the contribution of Leo the Great to the resolution of the christological controversies at Chalcedon in 451, this Ministry was extended to the East as well.

Critical as we Lutherans have been in our evaluation of papal history, we can recognize that the existence of the papacy has in many ways been beneficial. While the civilization of the West was emerging, bishops of Rome did in fact express and nurture the visible unity of the church in a world threatened by non-Christian forces and divisive tendencies. Thus the Petrine function was fulfilled in a specific way. As other concrete examples over the centuries we might cite the leadership of Gregory the Great in the promotion and protection of the Christian mission in northern Europe; the medieval popes who successfully asserted the independence of the Western church against attempts to subjugate it to the will of emperors, kings, and princes; and the serious humanitarian concern exhibited by modern popes in the face of war and social injustice.

(34) To be sure, there is for Lutherans no single or uniquely legitimate form of the exercise of the Petrine function. At every stage, the Petrine function developed according to the possibilities available at that time. Councils, individual leaders, specific local churches, credal statements[31] and the papacy have all in various ways ministered to the unity of the church. Further, the papal form of the universal Ministry has not always involved the centralized, juridical apparatus which now exists, nor need we assume that it will always continue to do so. Even if it should be desirable that the Petrine function be exercised by a single individual, the question of his powers would still be open.

(35) This brings us to a thorny problem between Lutherans and Roman Catholics which the group has had to discuss. Whatever primacy the Lutheran reformers accorded to the bishop of Rome was seen as a matter of historical development, and therefore of human right (*de iure humano*), rather than something rooted in the teaching of the scriptures. Over against this position the Roman Catholic view of the papal primacy claimed divine sanction (*de iure divino*) for certain papal prerogatives. Lutherans and Roman Catholics alike have often doubted that a reconciliation of the two stand-

points would be possible. We have found in our discussion however, through a series of careful historical investigations, that the traditional distinction between *de iure humano* and *de iure divino* fails to provide usable categories for contemporary discussion of the papacy.[32] On the one hand, Lutherans do not want to treat the exercise of the universal Ministry as though it were merely optional. It is God's will that the church have the institutional means needed for the promotion of unity in the gospel. On the other hand, Roman Catholics, in the wake of Vatican II are aware that there are many ways of exercising papal primacy. Some are willing to consider other models for the exercise of the Petrine function. They recognize the dangers of ecclesiastical centralism, and realize the limitations of a juridical description of the Petrine function.[33]

Rather than using the traditional terminology of divine and human right, therefore, both Lutherans and Roman Catholics have been compelled by their historical studies to raise a different set of questions: In what way or ways has our Lord in fact led his church to use particular forms for the exercise of the Petrine function? What structural elements in the church does the gospel require for the ministry which serves the unity of the empirical church?

(36) Structures invested with powerful symbolic meaning cannot be created at will. Therefore we do not anticipate that a concrete Ministry of unity to serve the church of the future will be something completely new. It will have to emerge from the renewal and the restructuring of those historical forms which best nurture and express this unity. We recognize that among the existing signs or structures for the Ministry of unity in the whole church, the papacy has a long history marked by impressive achievements in spite of all the things we have regarded as faulty in it.

(37) Lutherans are convinced that the church lives by the gospel. Our Lutheran forefathers rejected the late medieval papacy precisely because in their judgment it was obstructing the gospel. With them we believe that it is the task of the church at all times to proclaim the gospel in its fulness and to affirm the freedom of the children of God for which Christ has set us free. This very freedom, however, means that for the sake of the gospel Lutherans today are free to examine with an open mind the opportunities for the exercise of the Petrine function which a renewed and restructured papal office might provide.

(38) Lutherans can see in the papacy both values and what appear to be defects. On the positive side Lutherans can appreciate the papacy's assertion of the church's right to be independent of state control, the serious social concern exhibited by modern popes,[34] the liberating insight into the way in which the Bible should be studied, as set forth in encyclicals such as *Divino Afflante Spiritu*,[35] and the efforts which modern popes from Benedict XV on have devoted to the cause of peace among the nations. Nevertheless, for Lutherans as well as for many Roman Catholics, the present mode of operation of the papacy and the Roman curia leaves much to be desired. It is evident, moreover, that the close tie at the present time between primacy and infallibility has consequences in Roman Catholicism which will need thorough investigation in our future discussions. Again, any form of papal primacy that does not fully safeguard the freedom of the gospel is unacceptable to Lutherans. Many Roman Catholics manifest similar concerns when they insist, for example, that the primacy of the Roman bishop should not compromise the principle of collegiality.

(39) Everything that we have said underlines the fact that the discussion of papal primacy between our two churches has entered a new phase. It is true that the best model for the exercise of the Petrine function through a papacy is an issue that remains to be determined. At the same time, many of the changes decided upon at Vatican II and since are at least in the process of implementation. As examples we could point to the new rules for the Roman curia, the abolition of the index of prohibited books, the creation of an international synod of bishops meeting at regular intervals, and the appointment of an international commission of theologians.

In spite of the delay in implementing other reforms that have been under discussion among Roman Catholics, we Lutherans must maintain our hope that the papacy will continue to be renewed. We owe it to our Roman Catholic brothers to make this optimism evident. We acknowledge our profound indebtedness to them for the insights into their own church that they have mediated to us. They need to know in turn, about our hopes and prayers for a truly evangelical universal Ministry in the church just as we need to know what they are hoping and praying for us. Only thus will we be able to help and encourage each other in our common search for fuller manifestations of the unity that we have in Christ.

(40) We are not prepared in this report to spell out what the Lutheran willingness to recognize the primacy of a renewed and restructured papacy might mean in practice for Lutheran-Roman Catholic relationships. We are keenly aware that we have been speaking of possibilities whose actualization remains in the future. In the meantime, however, we believe that it is important for Lutherans to work for the renewal of the papacy, not only for the sake of their Roman Catholic brothers, but also for their own.

(41) We ask our churches earnestly to consider if the time has not come to affirm a new attitude toward the papacy "for the sake of peace and concord in the church"[36] and even more for the sake of a united witness to Christ in the world. Our Lutheran teaching about the church and the Ministry constrains us to believe that recognition of papal primacy is possible to the degree that a renewed papacy would in fact foster faithfulness to the gospel and truly exercises a Petrine function within the church. If this is indeed what Lutherans hold, ought they not to be willing to say so clearly and publicly? We urge the church bodies that have appointed us to accord high priority to the discussion of this question.

Part III

Reflections of the Roman Catholic Participants

In our view as Roman Catholic members of the consultation, the Common Statement, while falling short of total agreement, represents a major advance in the ecumenical discussion of one of the most sensitive issues that have historically divided the Lutheran and Catholic churches.

The Common Statement has positive significance for us as Roman Catholics. Together with the reflections of the Lutheran Participants it embodies a clear recognition on the part of our Lutheran colleagues that the church needs unifying Ministry concerned with the worldwide apostolate, and that this Ministry may be effectively exercised by a renewed papacy, at least as a humanly constituted organ.

The Common Statement, however, does not fully reflect everything that we believe concerning the papacy. The acceptance of the papal office is for us imperative because we believe that it is willed by God for his church. The mission entrusted to the church by Christ is served by the papacy. In it God has given us a sign of unity and an instrument for Christian life and mission. Therefore we affirm the traditional Roman Catholic position that the papacy is, in a true sense, "divinely instituted."

In the course of our discussion in this consultation, we have been able to refine and nuance our own thinking on many points. One important point has been precisely the meaning of the traditional term "divine right" (*ius divinum*). In earlier centuries it was rather commonly thought that this term involved, first, institution by a formal act of Jesus himself, and second, a clear attestation of that act by the New Testament or by some tradition believed to go back to apostolic times. Since "divine right" has become burdened with those implications, the term itself does not adequately communicate what we believe concerning the divine institution of the papacy.

In the New Testament we have found many indications positively pointing in the direction of the papacy, especially the Petrine texts and the various images of Peter alluded to in paragraphs 12 and 13 of the Common Statement. We have not, however, found a clear and direct affirmation of the papacy itself. This fact does not surprise or disconcert us. We believe that the New Testament is given to us not as a finished body of doctrine but as an expression of the developing faith and institutionalization of the church in the first century.

In many respects the New Testament and the doctrines it contains are complemented by subsequent developments in the faith and life of the church. For example, the statements of faith in the early creeds, though they are in conformity with scripture, go beyond the words and thought-patterns of scripture. The church itself, moreover, had to take responsibility for the selection of the canonical books, no list of which appears in the scriptures themselves. Similarly, the church had to specify its sacramental life and to structure its ministry to meet the requirements and opportunities of the post-apostolic period.

As Roman Catholics we are convinced that the papal and episcopal form of Ministry, as it concretely evolved, is a

divinely-willed sequel to the functions exercised respectively by Peter and the other apostles according to various New
Testament traditions. In seeking to carry out its mission
throughout the Roman Empire the episcopate frequently
appealed to the theological judgment and unifying influence
of the chair of Peter (*cathedra Petri*) at Rome, where
Peter and Paul were believed to have been martyred. Thus
the Petrine function, already attested in New Testament
times, was increasingly taken up by the bishop of Rome.

In the section of the Common Statement sketching the
subsequent historical developments of the papacy, we have
singled out the dogmatic teaching of Vatican Council I as
especially important. The teaching of this council should be
understood according to the context of the times in which it
was formulated and the intention of the council fathers. To
this end we may now call attention to some principles recently articulated by the Congregation for the Doctrine of
the Faith with regard to the historical conditioning of dogmatic formulations. In a declaration dated June 24, 1973,
the following four factors are set forth:

- a) The meaning of the pronouncements of faith depends partly upon the expressive power of the language used at a certain point in time and in particular
  circumstances.
- b) Sometimes a dogmatic truth is first expressed in-
  completely, but not falsely, and later more fully and
  perfectly in a broader context of faith and human
  knowledge.
- c) When the church makes new pronouncements, it
  not only confirms what is in some way contained in
  scripture or previous expressions of tradition; usually it also has the intention of solving specific questions or removing specific errors.
- d) Sometimes the truths the church intends to teach
  through its dogmatic formulations may be enunciated in terms that bear traces of the changeable
  conceptions of a given epoch.[1]

In confronting the specific problems and errors of its time,
Vatican Council I sensed that a concentration on the papacy
was crucially important, in order to safeguard the church's
evangelical freedom from political pressures and its universality in an age of divisive national particularism. Yet the
council tended to accent the juridical aspects of the papacy
more than church needs would require in the broader con-

text of our times. It has become apparent that the papal Ministry, as a spiritual and evangelical task, can and needs to find a "fuller and more perfect expression"[2] than was possible at Vatican Council I. Vatican Council II has already begun this process.

Since we have been cautioned by the holy see to recognize the conditioning imposed on church pronouncements by "the language used at a certain point of time and in particular circumstances," we must carefully interpret adjectives such as "full," "supreme," "ordinary," and "immediate," used by Vatican Council I to describe the pope's power of jurisdiction. Similar care must be exercised in detecting the historical conditioning of the affirmation of Vatican Council I with respect to the conferral of a primacy of "true and proper jurisdiction"[3] upon Peter by Christ. This affirmation must be understood in a way that allows for the complex process of gospel development explained in *Dei Verbum*, 19.

A general directive was given by Christ to his disciples: "Earthly kings lord it over their people . . . yet it cannot be that way with you" (Luke 22:25-26). In keeping with this directive, the doctrine concerning the papacy must be understood in ways that recognize the church's total subordination to Christ and the gospel and its obligation to respect the rights of all individuals, groups, and offices both within the church and beyond its limits. Monarchical absolutism in the church would violate the command of Christ. Generally speaking, Christians today are strongly conscious that the Holy Spirit works through all the ranks of the faithful and that a measure of interdependence exists among all who exercise ministry on different levels in the church. By setting the primacy of the pope within the broader context of a people-of-God ecclesiology, and by promoting a collegial understanding of authority in the church, Vatican Council II has called for modifications in the Roman Catholic understanding of papal leadership.

We share the concern of our Lutheran partners in dialogue that safeguards should be provided against violations of Christian rights and freedoms on the part of all ecclesiastical authority, papal included. Simultaneously, we are conscious of the need to proceed with caution. In particular, the effective exercise of the papal Ministry requires a large measure of power—and power, by its very nature, is capable of being abused. It is not yet clear what restrictions are compatible with the very nature of the Petrine function to be exercised by the pope—that is, his special unifying and ordering Ministry with reference to the church as a whole (see the Common Statement, par. 4). What limitations would leave room for the relative independence that the papacy must have in order to discharge its high mission? To impose juridical limits on papal power would presumably involve a transfer of some of that same power to other organs, which would likewise be capable of arbitrary and un-Christian conduct.

Our Lutheran partners in dialogue acknowledge that their independence from the papacy has not freed them from all abuses of ecclesiastical authority. They acknowledge that officers and assemblies on various levels in any church body are themselves capable of violating the rights and freedoms of the faithful and of resisting God's will for his church.

As Catholics we consider that, notwithstanding some human failings, the papacy has been a signal help in protecting the gospel and the church against particularistic distortions. It has served the faith and life of the church in ways too numerous to mention. While we look forward to changes in the style of papal leadership corresponding to the needs and opportunities of our times, we cannot foresee any set of circumstances that would make it desirable, even if it were possible, to abolish the papal office.

To our Lutheran brothers we wish to express our thanks for the wisdom and concern they have shared with us as we have in dialogue with them tried to formulate responsible views concerning the papacy. We have learned that they, as Lutherans, consider the faithful proclamation of the gospel in the Roman Catholic communion to be their concern as well as ours. We ask them to continue to support us by their understanding, counsel, and prayer.

In exploring the possible future relationships between the Lutheran churches and the papacy, as we have done in this consultation, we have been addressing central ecclesial issues raised by the Reformation. These issues have not been solved by the polemical approaches of the past four centuries, but we are bold enough to hope that the kind of collaboration we have experienced in this dialogue may be a prelude to a new relationship between our traditions. In terms of the Petrine function we believe that both Lutherans and Roman Catholics may no longer avoid the question: Could not the pope in our time become in some real way pastor and teacher of all the faithful, even those who cannot accept all the claims connected with his office? In the light of our experience in this dialogue we believe that the Roman Catholic church should take definite steps to face this question.

In view of their own particular spiritual patrimony and, not least, their own firm convictions concerning the papacy itself, Lutherans will presumably not be in a position to adopt the same relationship to the see of Rome that is currently held by Roman Catholics. But we suggest in our Common Statement (par. 33), that a distinct canonical status may be worked out by which Lutherans could be in official communion with the church of Rome. Scuh a restoration of communion, we believe, would be of great benefit to Roman Catholics, and to Lutherans, enabling them both to share in a broader Christian heritage. In such a wider communion of churches the papacy would be able to serve as a sign and instrument of unity, not simply for Roman Catholics, but for other who have never ceased to pray and labor for the manifest unity of the whole church of Christ.

Part IV

Procedures of the New Testament and Patristics Task Forces

In previous discussions and published volumes of the Lutheran—Roman Catholic Dialogue concerning creed, baptism, eucharist, and ministry, we have paid attention to, and have been strongly influenced by, both the scriptures and church history. But in the discussions on the papacy, the amount of biblical and historical data to be reviewed and analyzed was so enormous that it seemed impossible to have the data examined with scholarly precision by experts in each discipline at the bi-annual meetings of the dialogue or to print full treatment of the data in the current volume. Therefore a decision was taken in the dialogue meetings at Miami (February, 1971) and at Greenwich, Connecticut (September, 1971) to commission smaller task forces to study the background of the papacy during two particularly sensitive periods, namely New Testament and patristic times, and to digest the results of these studies for use in the dialogue.

In each instance two members from the National Dialogue, one Lutheran and one Roman Catholic, were appointed to chair these task forces in order to keep the National Dialogue abreast of the results. The New Testament co-chairmen were Raymond E. Brown and John Reumann; the patristics co-chairmen were James F. McCue and Arthur Carl Piepkorn. The New Testament task force met some fifteen times between October, 1971 and March, 1973. Since it was felt that a study of Peter's role in the New Testament as background for the papacy might serve many purposes, including the needs of other ecumenical dialogues, the membership of this task force was broadened to include Episcopal and Reformed scholars. The results of their inquiry were published in September, 1973 under the title, *Peter in the New Testament,* by a Lutheran (Augsburg) and a Roman Catholic (Paulist/Newman) publishing house.

The patristics task force originally envisaged a joint document analogous to *Peter in the New Testament.* After canvassing for suggestions it met in December, 1971. Arthur Piepkorn and James McCue then prepared drafts covering the pre- and post-Nicene periods respectively. These were discussed at a two-day meeting in December, 1972. After revision the two reports were presented to the dialogue group at San Antonio in February, 1973. Further revisions were then made. Because of the vastness and complexity of the material, it was out of the question for the entire task force to examine the primary and secondary documentation with the kind of detail possible for the New Testament. It was therefore decided that the papers would appear in this volume under the names of their principle co-authors rather than as joint reports.

Since the studies produced by the two task forces have their own integrity, readers of this volume are urged to examine them firsthand. However, the portions of our Common Statement which deal with the New Testament (par. 9-13) and with the patristic era (par. 15-18) have been written in light of the conclusions of the respective task forces. We present here a brief analysis of the thrust of these two task force studies.

Our discussions on the roles of Peter in the New Testament and on the relation of Peter's roles to the status of the bishops of Rome in the first five centuries must not be considered simply as informative background for this volume. Roman Catholicism has presented its claims for the papacy precisely in terms of a relationship of the bishop of Rome to Peter. It was the view of Vatican Council I that Christ constituted Peter chief of all the apostles and visible head of the whole church on earth, and that by Christ's institution Peter would always have successors in that office who are the bishops of Rome. Such a formulation expressed a point of Roman Catholic faith in historical language, and therefore raises at least two questions for contemporary scholars. First, how is the role of the bishop of Rome historically related to the roles of Peter as described in the New Testament? Second, to what degree are the pictures of Peter in the New Testament genuinely historical? To answer the first question requires information from both the patristic and New Testament fields; to answer the second question is a matter of New Testament research.

Since there is a strong element of history in the Roman Catholic claim, it was important that both task forces employ the methods in common use today for scientific historical study. At the same time it must not be assumed that historical criticism can answer with certainty the two questions asked. But such study sometimes changes the perspective of the discussion. In answering the first question, for instance, the Roman Catholic who is conscious of historical criticism will not expect to find Peter in the first century acting in the same manner as the pope in the fifth century. The Lutheran who is conscious of historical criticism will admit that if Peter did not act in the manner of a later pope, the relationship of the papacy to Peter is not necessarily disproved. Both of them must come to terms with the fact of historical development.

Awareness of this historical development on the part of the New Testament task force is illustrated in *Peter in the New Testament:*

. . . papacy in its developed form cannot be read back into the New Testament; and it will help neither papal opponents nor papal supporters to have the model of later papacy before their eyes when discussing the role of Peter. For that very reason we have tended to avoid "loaded" terminology in reference to Peter, e.g., primacy, jurisdiction. Too often in the past, arguments about whether or not Peter has a "universal primacy" have blinded scholars to a more practical agreement about such things as the widely accepted importance of Peter in the New Testament and his diversified image (pp. 8-9).

Similarly, the reports on the patristic period note that, as institutions are affected by the challenges and needs of the times, the papacy can be no exception. As a clearly identifiable institution the Roman primacy emerged gradually. Some of the elements that would later be combined to constitute the Roman primacy were already in existence before Nicaea. Yet it was in the post-Nicene period that a claim was clearly made by a number of Roman bishops that they succeeded Peter in his responsibility for all the churches. In neither the East nor the West were the responses to this claim without fluctuation and ambiguity.

These biblical and patristic studies have examined the roles of Peter and of the Roman pontiffs in the context of the first five centuries. As a result, they do not directly answer the later questions which the National Dialogue has faced. For instance, Paragraph 13 of the Common Statement portrays Peter as having various roles in New Testament times; attention is drawn in particular to his roles as the great fisherman (missionary), the shepherd (pastor) of the sheep, the martyr, the receiver of special revelation, the confessor of the true faith, the guardian of faith against false teaching. The line of development of such images is obviously reconcilable with, and indeed favorable to, the claims of the Roman Catholic church for the papacy. The same may be said of some images of Peter which appeared in early patristic times. Yet important questions remain: To what extent is the trajectory of these images, as traced by recent scholars, influenced by the events of later history? How do images not so favorable to papal claims, e.g., that of Peter as a weak and sinful man, affect the general picture? One may also ask the further theological question: How should these developments be interpreted in the light of God's providence?

Thus, the studies of the two task forces clear aside some of the obstacles faced in the past. They do not, however, relieve us of the difficult task of evaluating the historical developments of the Petrine image and of the papacy. But a discernment of the hand of God in history is not a matter of historical criticism; it is rather a question for theological reflection. In its work, therefore, the National Dialogue has had to go beyond the results of historical study as presented by the two task forces.

We are aware of the fact that the biblical and patristic reports do not reflect total agreement among scholars. Even within one church, researchers may disagree over the meaning of a text or document. No attempt has been made to gloss over the instances where no unanimous results could be arrived at. Diversity of scholarly opinion, especially in relation to the New Testament, may be misunderstood by those who believe that the interpretation of the Bible should not be subject to the vagaries of human scholarship and should reach divine certainty. Such a simplistic view has sometimes been fostered among Protestants by the assertion that the Bible, being the sole rule of faith, should be immediately clear to all Christian readers. Among Roman Catholics, this simplistic view has sometimes found support in the contention that since church authority is the infallible interpreter of scripture, its meaning has been decided once for all. However, while the members of this National Dialogue clearly accept their respective traditions on the interpretation of scripture, they recognize that scholarly analysis of the documents often blunts the edge of some affirmations found in these traditions. For instance, such a technical question as the exact historical description of Peter's role during his lifetime cannot be answered simply by citing scriptural texts or authoritative teachings of the magisterium.

The recognition of difficulties and the presentation of a tolerable diversity of opinions about the meaning of the sources studied constitute a challenge to the churches to reexamine some past assumptions. Do the positions that seemed clear in the Reformation and the nineteenth century remain equally clear today? Might not new possibilities of agreement be opened by a reconsideration of the relation of the papacy to Peter in the light of modern historical method? The only alternatives to the type of historical criticism that allow for diversity of interpretation are the opposing theses which either affirm or deny that the papacy is found in the New Testament or the patristic documentation. Such theses entail the corollary that those who do not find the clear doctrine, whatever it might be, must be either uninformed or in bad faith. This inference has, over the last four centuries, produced little progress in bringing Christians together. By contrast, the members of the National Dialogue have judged that historical criticism, though by no means the supreme arbiter, must be used as a gift from God in the contemporary discussions among Christians.

2

THE ROMAN PRIMACY IN THE PATRISTIC ERA

Introduction

The manner in which the two papers dealing with the Roman primacy in the patristic era were written is of some importance for their understanding and evaluation. Consequently, an account of their *Redaktionsgeschichte* is presented here by way of introduction. Originally, it had been planned that a task force would survey the materials relevant to the development of the Roman primacy during the patristic era, with the expectation that there was sufficient consensus in the interpretation of these materials to make possible a single paper that would appear over the signatures of all the members of the task force. Accordingly, the co-chairman of the task force, James F. McCue and Arthur Carl Piepkorn, were asked to prepare preliminary drafts of papers covering the pre- and post-Nicene periods, respectively.

These papers were then submitted to the task force, and their criticisms and suggestions were incorporated into successive revisions of the papers. What resulted, however, still bore so marked an impress of the original co-authors, that the members of the task force and of the Lutheran-Catholic Dialogue judged that it would be more appropriate if the two papers appeared separately, each over the signature of its principal author. The materials were simply too complex, the problems of time and geography too great, to enable the entire task force to work through all the issues that would have needed resolution if a single common paper was to result.

In each paper the author has attempted to give expression to what he understands to be a widely shared interpretation of the materials. Indeed, at some points the very wording reflects the work of other members of the task force. But though a very large measure of agreement existed within the task force, it cannot be assumed at every point that everyone consulted would agree with the position taken or emphasis given.

I. The Beginnings Through Nicaea

James F. McCue

In order to write a history of the Roman primacy prior to Nicaea one must make certain procedural decisions, for in this period of time one is dealing in the main with pre-history. One has to focus on those strands of early church life that are later worked together into the office exercised or claimed by the bishops of Rome. Obviously there is room for disagreement in singling out a set of factors in pre-Nicene Christianity as *the* antecedent conditions.

To provide focus for the pre-Nicene section of this paper, we propose the following as a rough definition of the papal office as it emerges in the claims of late fourth and early fifth century popes. It is exercised by the bishop of Rome, on the basis of his claim to be the successor to Peter; and it is a claim to genuine spiritual authority over all other bishops, with a view to the unity and universality of the church and the integrity of its faith.

The following appear to be the principal problems or elements in the pre-Nicene development of this office, and accordingly they provide the principal focuses for this section of the paper.

1) The problem of unity and universality in the early church. To what extent and in what ways were the churches united in the pre-Nicene period? What were the various means (assuming that there were more than one) used to secure this unity? Was it a matter of pressing concern? What expression do we find of a sense of being part of the single *world-wide* church?

2) The emergence of monepiscopacy as *the* form of

ministry in the church by the end of the second century.

3) The connection of monepiscopacy with the apostolic succession of bishops; a) the bishops of the apostolic churches as successors to specific apostles, or b) the bishops as a group successors to the apostles as a group.

4) The Peter tradition in the early church; its relationship to other traditions: Paul, James, John, Thomas.

5) The role (roles) played by Rome vis-a-vis other churches and the church universal through the time of Nicaea.

1. The Problem of Unity and Universality in the Early Church.[1]

The work of Walter Bauer presents the most basic challenge to any account of the unity and universality of the early church.[2] His argument is that Christianity was at the start a congeries of different and often mutually exclusive sects, all laying claim to the name "Christian." Through the end of the second century the majority of these were what we would call gnostic or heretical, and in many places this type of Christianity was for a long time the only one known. What we call orthodoxy predominated at first only in Rome, and elsewhere subsequently principally under Roman influence. Only in the third century did orthodoxy come to dominate generally and to appear as the main stream. The orthodox view of history which Bauer opposes is simply, in his view, a history written by the victors, and reflects theological conviction rather than historical reality.

We cannot satisfactorily adjudicate the matter here, nor is there a body of literature to which we can refer for a judicious sifting of the strengths and weaknesses of Bauer's argument. Here we can make but two comments. 1) Relative to Valentinianism, the principal form of heresy for Irenaeus and Clement of Alexandria, Bauer can be shown to be clearly in the wrong and Irenaeus or Eusebius closer to the historical truth.[3] And 2) granting that certain forms of second century Christianity, most notably Jewish Christianity,[4] are not derived from an originally unified main body, it is still possible and legitimate to trace in the main body of the second century the pre-history of main-stream developments of later times.

The written sources on which we must base our understanding of second century Christianity are very few, and for the most part these deal with very particular matters and were not written with an eye to the broad questions of later historians. We have a piece from Rome from the end of the first century, a few letters from Antioch from a bit later, a scattering of documents written we are not altogether sure where, why, or when.

We know, moreover, that often even in a single place the church was divided into a number of different and in some instances mutually exclusive groups. Justin, for example, reports (*Dial.* 47) that there are Jewish Christians who continue in their traditional observances but do *not* demand these of gentile Christians, other Jewish Christians who continue with their traditional observances and *do* demand these of all Christians; and reciprocally some non-Jewish Christians who refuse all *koinōnia* with either group, while others (Justin among them) join and associate with the first group but not the second. In addition Justin distinguishes (*Dial.* 80) those Christians who are altogether faithful to the Lord's teaching, the millenarians, and those who, though not counted among the heretics, have nonetheless been infected by the heretics' teachings, the anti-millenarians. This differentiation is compounded if we suppose that at this same time there were at Rome Christians from Asia who celebrated Easter at a different time than did those who celebrated eucharist under the presidency of Anicetus, and thus presumably constituted a distinct though not schismatic eucharistic fellowship. And all these complications exist quite apart from the vexed problem of the relationship of the heresies to this set of groups which we call the orthodox. Justin acknowledges that the Marcionites are called Christians (1 *Apol* 26), and we can with some confidence establish from Irenaeus that it was part of the Valentinian exoteric propaganda to claim to be part of the main body of Christians (*A.H.* 3.15.2).

Yet for all this differentiation and even fragmentation we meet again and again the assertion of the unity of the church, one body, one *koinōnia*. This oneness is sensed and asserted both at the universal or world-wide level, and with reference to the local community; and at both levels it is obviously not primarily an organizational matter, but rather a strong sense of belonging to the community of the one Lord. Ephesians 4:2-6 is paradigmatic: the unity of the church is a unity of the Spirit, depending on the one hope to which we are called, the one Lord, the one faith, the one baptism, the "one God and Father of us all, who is above all and through all and in all." *1 Clement* 46:5-7 develops the same idea, apparently in dependence on Ephesians. "Why are there strife and passion and divisions and schisms and war among you? Or have we not one God, and one Christ, and one Spirit of grace poured out upon us? And is there not one calling in Christ? Why do we divide and tear asunder the members of Christ, and raise up strife against our own body, and reach such a pitch of madness as to forget that we are members one of another?"

In both *Ephesians* and *1 Clement,* however, and in most of what Ignatius of Antioch has to say about the unity of the church, it is the harmony and unity among Christians in a single place that is the issue. Characteristic of Ignatius is the view that this unity takes place in the eucharistic celebration. His concern for the episcopal office is rooted in his concern for the unity of the *agape.* The sense of the world-wide unity of the many different communities is expressed by both *1 Clement* and Ignatius in their assertion that the church had already been spread throughout the world.[5] We see this in *1 Clement* 5:7; 42:4; 59:2. And in Ignatius we read: "Jesus Christ, the life which cannot be taken away from us, is the wisdom (*gnōmē;* "will" might be better) of the Father; so also, the bishops who have been appointed throughout the world, are in the wisdom (or "will") of Jesus Christ" (Eph. 3:2). What is specially to be noted here is the easily assumed reality of the church as a world-wide reality, unified in the one Lord, Jesus Christ.

This last idea is expressed even more strikingly in Ignatius, *Smyrnaeans* 8:2: "Whenever the bishop appears let the congregation be present; just as wherever Jesus Christ is, there is the catholic church." The reality of the universal church is strongly felt here; and it is the presence of the one Lord that is the unifying reality. Without wishing to magnify this one sentence into a treatise on Ignatius' ecclesiology, we might paraphrase: Just as it is Jesus Christ who unifies the church catholic, so it is the one bishop who draws together the local community in the eucharistic celebration.

The expression "the catholic church" appears in the pre-Irenaean literature only this one time in Ignatius and three or four times in the *Martyrdom of Polycarp.*[6] Its uses in this latter work are quite striking. The introduction runs as follows: "The church of God dwelling in Smyrna to the church of God dwelling in Philomelium, and to all the dwellings of the holy and catholic church in every place, mercy, peace, etc." The catholic church is the one reality existing throughout the world and dwelling at Smyrna, Philomelium, and wherever else a community of Christians has been gathered.

The second occurrence is of special interest: "And when he (Polycarp) had finished praying, having remembered all whom he had ever met, both small and great, high and low, and all the catholic church throughout the world" (8:1). Whether the account is historically exact or an idealized portrayal, it gives evidence of a keen sense of the reality of the one church throughout the world and of a prayerful concern for that catholic church.

The third textually certain occurrence is 19:2: ". . . our Lord, Jesus Christ . . . the shepherd of the catholic church throughout the world." This suggests Ignatius, *Smyrnaeans* 8:2, in that it assigns to Jesus Christ the task of caring for the church catholic.

This sense of the uniqueness and world-wide oneness of the church could be traced through writers over the next century and a half, and would show that before the development of structures and canonically defined techniques for guarding or preserving this unity and catholicity it was a felt reality in the Christian communities. And this is reflected not only in highly "ecclesiastical" writers like Irenaeus; one finds it as well in as "esoteric" a writer as Clement of Alexandria: "O mystic marvel! The universal Father is one, and one the universal Word; and the Holy Spirit is one and the same everywhere, and one is the only virgin mother. I love to call her the Church." (*Pedagogue*, 1:6—42:1; tr ANF, 2, p. 220 cf. *Strom*. 7:17).

In Irenaeus the unity of the church is already significantly institutionalized, in that the apostolic churches and their bishops provide a rallying center and norm for the church as a whole. In Clement the unity of the church is related to the oneness of the Father, the Word, and the Holy Spirit. With the Irenaean structures he does not concern himself.

2. The Emergency of Monepiscopacy.

Monepiscopacy, the church order in which a single person stands at the center of the eucharistic celebration and exercises supervision over doctrine, becomes in the course of the second century the principal form of church order. The bishop becomes the person around whom the local church is unified, and the bishops as a fraternity become the agents through which the church universal is unified. And in the emergence of the claim of the Roman bishop to be the first among the world's bishops this development of monepiscopacy is presupposed as something definitive and irreversible. Hence its importance in any consideration of the emergence of the papal office.

It is only gradually, and at different times in different places, that monepiscopacy emerges as *the* form of church organization. Though there may be some disagreement over matters of detail, disagreement that is unavoidable owing to the paucity and obscurity of our documents, there is general consensus as to the overall picture.

Most of the writings of the New Testament are not directly concerned with problems of church order and office, and we can therefore at best only conjecture about the structure of most New Testament communities. We know more about the church at Corinth than about any other early Christian community; and whatever else we may be able to say about the Corinthian church, there is no clear evidence that it was monepiscopal in the 50s and in all likelihood was still not in the 90s. 3 John *might* be interpreted as implying a monepiscopacy; the Pastorals probably should not be interpreted in the same way. Only the Pastorals use the term "bishop"—*episkopos*—in the singular. Acts and Phillipians speak of "bishops"—*episkopoi*. Philippians links the term with *diakonoi*. Singular or plural, the term is already becoming a quasitechnical one, and there is a frequent linking of *episkopoi* and *diakonoi* (cf. Phil 1:1; *Didache* 15:1; *1 Clem.* 42:4f.).

The earliest materials in which we *clearly* see monepiscopacy are the letters of Ignatius of Antioch. Though some (e.g. Walter Bauer) have denied the reliability of these letters as sources of information about the churches to which they are addressed, this is a scepticism *ex machina*. The churches to which Ignatius writes are certainly, in most instances, wracked by dissension, and obviously there are some in these churches who do assemble apart from the bishops and presbyters addressed by Ignatius; but that there is in each of the Asia Minor communities to which he writes a three-fold ministry of bishop, presbyters, and deacons which can at least be proposed as *the* center around which the entire church should coalesce, is clearly the case. The Asia Minor letters all arise out of direct contact with the bishops of these churches, and for all their similarity the letters address themselves to different problems—the challenge of Judaism (*Philad.* 8), of Judaizing Christians (*Magn.* 8-10), of docetism. (*Trall.* and *Smyrn*). It may well be that in his analysis of the role of the bishop, Ignatius provides an understanding many elements of which are his own and not otherwise current in the churches addressed; but while he recognizes that objections have been raised to the youth or to the taciturnity of a particular bishop, he nowhere indicates that the episcopal role itself is being resisted as a usurpation. Thus it seems reasonable to infer that an episcopally-headed three-fold ministry is functioning, not without problems and tensions and not without some who stand apart from the followers of the bishop in Ephesus, Magnesia, Tralles, Philadelphia, and Smyrna, as well as in Antioch, during the first quarter of the second century. Moreover, it is Ignatius' opinion that such ministry is or should be universal.[7]

That certain other churches had not taken on monepiscopal structure by about the end of the first quarter of the second century also seems to be the case. *The Shepherd* can with some confidence be assigned to Rome.[8] That *Vis.* 1-4 was not originally connected with *Vis. 5-Sim.* 8 can likewise be assumed here, and we can also assume a date for *Vis.* 1-4 not too distant one way or the other from A.D. 120. *Vis.* 2 (8:3) speaks of the presbyters (plural) who stand at the head of the local church. At this date then the church organization at Rome would seem not to have developed a monepiscopal form. At approximately the same time,[9] Polycarp of Smyrna, the bishop addressed most fully by Ignatius, in writing to Philippi addresses the presbyters and deacons and makes no mention of a bishop (5:3).

Just when monepiscopacy became so nearly universal that any other form of church order was felt to be anachronistic we cannot say. Certainly by the time that Hegesippus goes about securing the succession lists for various churches this would seem to be the case, but with Hegesippus we have come all the way down to the time of Eleutherus at Rome, i.e. to the 180s (Eusebius, *H.E.* 4.22.1-3). Eusebius' account of the paschal controversy describes Anicetus in what is clearly a monepiscopal role shortly before the death of Polycarp, so presumably at Rome the transition was made during the generation between 120 and 155. It was perhaps at about this same time that the transition was made in most of the other churches that earlier had a plural leadership, but certitude is not possible. By the time that Irenaeus writes, the 190s, monepiscopacy has become so self-evident that Irenaeus could make use of it for polemical purposes.[10]

It might seem that the entire question could be handled quite simply by reference to the early succession lists. Irenaeus, after all, gives us the names of the bishops at Rome from the beginning, and Eusebius adds the names of the bishops of Antioch, Jerusalem, and Alexandria. But there is no reference to these lists prior to Hegesippus and Irenaeus, that is, prior to the time when monepiscopacy had become the only known form of church order; and at least the Roman list identifies as bishops men (e.g. Clement) who it would seem were not bishops in the monepiscopal sense. Thus the question of the point at which the individuals named begin to be bishops in the later sense, as contrasted simply with eminent leaders, cannot be determined on the basis of the lists themselves.

Of the bishops of Rome whom Eusebius lists prior to Anicetus, he knows more than the name and date only of Clement and Telesphorus. Clement he knows as the author of the letter of the church at Rome to the church at Corinth. The other piece of information, that Telesphorus died a martyr, he could have gotten from Irenaeus. Thus apart from what we can infer from *1 Clement*, and the few scraps of information that we can puzzle out of Hermas, we come all the way down to the time of Anicetus before we begin to get some detailed knowledge of events in which the Roman bishop is involved. The precise dating of Anicetus is probably beyond reach. There is enough confusion in the early bishop-lists to place the beginning of his episcopacy anywhere in the latter half of the 150s. He was, however, according to Irenaeus, bishop at Rome at a time when Polycarp visited there. If one accepts 156 as the date of Polycarp's death,[11] one must push Anicetus up to 155 and perhaps a bit earlier.

Anicetus is introduced retrospectively within the context of the paschal controversy that erupted under Victor (189-?). We shall subsequently have more to say about this controversy. Here we wish to consider only what it tells us about the emergence of monepiscopacy at Rome. Since the material from Eusebius is of considerable importance we cite it here despite its length.

XXIII. At that time no small controversy arose because all the dioceses of Asia thought it right, as though by more ancient tradition, to observe for the feast of the Savior's passover the fourteenth day of the moon, on which the Jews had been commanded to kill the lamb. Thus it was necessary to finish the fast on that day, whatever day of the week it might be. Yet it was not the custom to celebrate in this manner in the churches throughout the rest of the world, for from apostolic tradition they kept the custom which still exists that it is not right to finish the fast on any day save that of the resurrection of our Savior. Many meetings and conferences with bishops were held on this point, and all unanimously formulated in their letters the doctrine of the church for those in every country that the mystery of the Lord's resurrection from the dead could be celebrated on no day save Sunday, and that on that day alone we should celebrate the end of the paschal fast. There is still extant a writing of those who were convened in Palestine, over whom presided Theophilus, bishop of the diocese of Caesarea, and Narcissus, bishop of Jerusalem; and there is similarly another from those in Rome on the same controversy, which gives Victor as bishop; and there is one of the bishops of Pontus over whom Palmas presided as the oldest; and of the dioceses of Gaul, of which Irenaeus was bishop; and yet others of those in Osrhoene and the cities there; and particularly of Bacchyllus, the bishop of the church of Corinth; and of very many more who expressed one and the same opinion and judgment, and gave the same vote.

XXIV. These issued the single definition which was given above; but the bishops in Asia were led by Polycrates in persisting that it was necessary to keep the custom which had been handed down to them of old. Polycrates himself in a document which he addressed to Victor and to the church of Rome, expounds the tradition which had come to him as follows. "Therefore we keep the day undeviatingly, . . . for in Asia great luminaries sleep, and they will rise on the day of the coming of the Lord, . . . Such were Philip of the twelve apostles, and two of his daughters who grew old as virgins, who sleep in Hierapolis, and another daughter of his, who lived in the Holy Spirit, rests at Ephesus. Moreover, there is also John, who lay on the Lord's breast, . . . He sleeps at Ephesus. And there is also Polycarp at Smyrna, both bishop and martyr, and Thraseas, . . . All these kept the fourteenth day of the passover according to the gospel, never swerving, but following according to the rule of the faith. And I also, Polycrates, the least of you all, live according to the tradition of my kinsmen, and some of them have I followed. For seven of my family were bishops and I am the eighth, and my kinsmen ever kept the day when the people put away the leaven. Therefore, brethren, I who have lived sixty-five years in the Lord and conversed with brethren from every country, and have studied all holy Scripture, am not afraid of threats, for they have said who were greater than I, 'It is better to obey God rather than men.'"

He continues about the bishops who when he wrote were with him and shared his opinion, and says thus: "And I could mention the bishops who are present whom you required me to summon, and I did so. If I should write their names they would be many multitudes; and they knowing my feeble humanity, agreed with the letter, knowing that not in vain is my head grey, but that I have ever lived in Christ Jesus."

Upon this Victor, who presided at Rome, immediately tried to cut off from the common unity the dioceses of all Asia, together with the adjacent churches, on the ground of heterodoxy, and he indited letters announcing that all the Christians there were absolutely excommunicated. But by no means all were pleased by this, so they issued counter-requests to him to consider the cause of peace and unity and love towards his neighbours. Their words are extant, sharply rebuking Victor. Among them too Irenaeus, writing in the name of the Christians whose leader he was in Gaul, though he recommends that the mystery of the Lord's resurrection be observed only on the Lord's day, yet nevertheless exhorts Victor suitably and at length not to excommunicate whole churches of God for following a tradition of ancient custom, and continues as follows: "For the controversy is not only about the day, but also about the actual character of the fast; for some think that they ought to fast one day, others two, others even more, some count their day as forty hours, day and night. And such variation of observance did not begin in our own time, but much earlier, in the days of our predecessors who, it would appear, disregarding strictness maintained a practice which is simple and yet allows for personal preference, establishing it for the future, and none the less all these lived in peace, and we also lived in peace with one another and the disagreement in the fast confirms our agreement in the faith."

He adds to this a narrative which I may suitably quote, running as follows: "Among these too were the presbyters before Soter, who presided over the church of which you are now the leader, I mean Anicetus and Pius and Telesphorus and Xystus. They did not themselves observe it, nor did they enjoin it on those who followed them, and though they did not keep it they were none the less at peace with those from the dioceses in which it was observed when they came to them, although to observe it was more objectionable to those who did not do so. And no one was ever rejected for this reason, but the presbyters before you who did not observe it sent the Eucharist to those from other dioceses who did; and when the blessed Polycarp was staying in Rome in the

time of Anicetus, though they disagreed a little about some
other things as well, they immediately made peace, having
no wish for strife between them on this matter. For neither
was Anicetus able to persuade Polycarp not to observe it,
inasmuch as he had always done so in company with John
the disciple of our Lord and the other apostles with whom
he had associated; nor did Polycarp persuade Anicetus to
observe it, for he said that he ought to keep the custom of
those who were presbyters before him. And under these
circumstances they communicated with each other, and in the
church Anicetus yielded the celebration of the Eucharist to
Polycarp, obviously out of respect, and they parted from
each other in peace, for the peace of the whole church was
kept both by those who observed and by those who did not.

The following appears to be the most satisfactory interpretation.[12] Eusebius has combined two separate problems or
two distinct aspects of a single problem. The Polycrates letter is concerned to withstand efforts being made to pressure
the churches of Asia to adopt a practice different from
their traditional one. The Irenaeus letter addresses itself
both to this larger problem and to a problem within the
church at Rome. Only the local problem is relevant to our
present concern, the growth of monepiscopacy; the larger
problem we shall consider subsequently.

The problem at Rome grew out of the cosmopolitan character of the church there.[13] Groups of people came to Rome
from throughout the Mediterranean world in large numbers
during the first centuries of the Christian era. Among them
were Christians who brought to Rome the traditional practices of their places of origin. Christians who came to Rome
from Asia Minor brought with them the practice of celebrating the crucifixion on the 14th day of Nisan, no matter
what day of the week that was, in contrast to the Roman
practice of celebrating the crucifixion on Friday and the
resurrection on Sunday. According to Irenaeus, the Roman
bishops from Sixtus through Soter (and presumably
Eleutherus) had lived in peace with Christians coming to
Rome from other areas. They were allowed to follow their
customary ways, and the bishops before Victor maintained
peace with them by sending the eucharist to them.

It would appear that Victor was trying to bring about a
tighter unity within the Roman church. If the Asiatic communities celebrated according to a different calendar, they
were to some extent celebrating apart, and we know from
the anti-heretical polemic of writers like Ignatius and

Irenaeus that celebrating apart was widely looked upon with considerable suspicion. Victor would seem to have been attempting to break down something of the semi-autonomous character of these ethnic communities, so that the bishop of Rome (and not the likes of Polycarp of Smyrna) would really be their bishop. From the fact that Irenaeus had occasion to write a letter to Blastus "On Schism" (*H.E.* 5.20), that this Blastus was expelled from the Roman presbytery, and that Ps-Tertullian ascribes to Blastus the position combatted by Victor (*Adv. omnes haereses,* 8), it would appear that this unification was not without cost, but it seems to have resulted in a more centralized church at Rome and a more significant role for its bishop.

The growth of monepiscopacy at Rome is, therefore a fairly complicated matter. Contrary to the assertions of some (e.g. G.F. Snyder, *Apostolic Fathers,* vol. 6: *The Shepherd of Hermas,* pp. 19-20), "The church of Rome" is not merely a fiction created by later scholarship. As early as *1 Clement* we see evidenced a strong sense of the unity of that church; and in the time of Anicetus, though ethnic diversity would appear to have been great enough to have given rise to separate liturgical traditions, yet one man is still and somehow regarded as the head or leader of the Roman church, the one to whom Polycarp is to address himself. This is at approximately the same time that Justin is describing the varieties of Christians to which we referred above. In the course of the next generation the community is pulled more tightly together; certain groups are newly excluded. Victor significantly diminishes the ethnic autonomy. Irenaeus seems unaware that there are significant variations among Jewish Christians and considers them all heretics.

There are many gaps in our knowledge of the history of the church at Rome in the second century, yet we know more about Rome than about any other church. Those churches of which we know anything had, by the time of Victor, taken on an episcopal organization; and there is no evidence that a non-episcopal church order was at all common or widely known by that time.[14]

3. The Bishops as Successors to the Apostles.[15]

Monepiscopacy is not at every point and necessarily linked with the idea of apostolic succession. Ignatius' letters, the first clear witness to the monepiscopal ideal, do not relate this to succession ideas; and the first clear witness to the idea of apostolic succession, *1 Clement,* says nothing of monepiscopacy. Yet by the end of the second century the two ideas are being commonly conjoined by Western writers and their conjunction provides the necessary setting for the *Roman* understanding of Roman primacy that emerges perhaps in the third, certainly by the latter part of the fourth century. How and when did this conjunction come about?

In *1 Clement* 42 and 44 we clearly have a linking of the authority of those presently governing the church with the apostles. Within the framework created by *1 Clement* no great transition is involved when one passes from plural to single leadership. The idea of apostolic succession does not appear again in the extant documents until quite late in the second century. Then we find apostolic succession ideas used one way or another by Ptolemaeus the Valentinian, by Hegesippus, and most clearly and fully by Irenaeus, all at approximately the same time.

Ptolemaeus' work seems to be the earliest of the three. Irenaeus in *Adv. Haer.* writes principally against Ptolemaeus' disciples, and is thus presumably though not certainly working a generation after him. The Roman succession list which Irenaeus gives us ends with Eleutherus. Thus, assuming that the entire work is written at one time, we can date it somewhere between 177 and 189; and since Eusebius preserves for us a text (*H.E.* 5.4.2) in which Irenaeus while still a presbyter is introduced to Eleutherus, it seems likely that *Adv. Haer.* was not written until some time well into Eleutherus' episcopate.

Hegesippus is reported by Eusebius (*H.E.* 4.11.7) to have come to Rome during the time of Anicetus (ca. 155-ca. 168) and to have stayed there until the time of Eleutherus (177-189). Eusebius subsequently quotes Hegesippus as follows:

> And the church of the Corinthians remained in the true doctrine until Primus was bishop of Corinth, and I conversed with them on my voyage to Rome, and spent some days with the Corinthians during which we were refreshed by the true word. When I was in Rome I recovered the list of the succession until Anicetus, whose deacon was Eleutherus; Soter succeeded Anicetus, and after him came Eleutherus. In each list and in each city things are as the law, the prophets, and the Lord preached. (4.22.2-3)

Clearly Hegesippus is writing at about the same time as Irenaeus—i.e. while Eleutherus is bishop of Rome. But he describes his activity of a decade or two earlier in such a way as to suggest that episcopal-apostolic succession ideas were already in the air. Indeed, Hegesippus seems to use *diadochē* as a synonym for church: *en hekastē de diadochē kai en hekaste polei houtōs echei hōs ho nomos kēryssei kai hoi prophētai kai ho kyrios.*

Thus in all likelihood Ptolemaeus' *Letter to Flora* is the earliest extant work after *1 Clement* to make significant use of apostolic succession ideas, and it is the earliest (except perhaps for the Pastorals) to connect apostolic succession with the handing on of teaching. The relevant text runs as follows: "For, if God permit, you will later learn about their origin and generation, when you are judged worthy of the apostolic tradition which we too have received by succession."

Lest this too easily be taken to show that apostolic succession in teaching is a gnostic creation that was subsequently taken over by the orthodoxy and turned against those who had created it, it should be noted that the *kai hēmeis*—"we too"—indicates that Ptolemaeus is countering an already advanced orthodox claim that the orthodox doctrine goes back through succession to the apostles. Thus wherever the idea originated, it presumably existed in orthodox writers or bishops prior to Ptolemaeus.

Eusebius does not provide us with a systematic account of how Hegesippus used the succession lists which he made, but he does provide us with a sufficient basis for conjecture. In the brief passages which Eusebius cities, Hegesippus discusses three churches, Rome, Corinth, and Jerusalem. In each of these he finds that where bishop follows bishop in due order there is soundness of doctrine. Heresy is introduced in Jerusalem only by someone who has been frustrated in his desire to become bishop. Though nowhere do we see Hegesippus connect the bishops with the apostles, it is probably significant that in Hegesippus' day Rome, Corinth, and Jerusalem were looked upon as churches of apostolic foundation. It would thus *appear* that Hegesippus is pointing out that those churches which have persevered in good order since the time of the apostles are in agreement concerning the faith.

With Irenaeus we need no longer conjecture. Matters are much clearer and more fully worked out. Basically the argument is that in the churches of apostolic foundation there is a public succession of teachers, the bishops, going back to the apostles themselves, the public character of their succession and their ministry serving to assure the identity of the gospel as preached now with what was preached by the apostles. These churches thus can function as touchstones of orthodoxy: in them and in their communion Christ is present. To disagree significantly with them would be to cut oneself off from the authentic gospel. The unity of the church is maintained by the common source of the teaching of the apostles, the teaching of Jesus, mediated through the apostles first and then through those who succeed them. It is by communion with the united apostolic churches that the more derivative churches are maintained within the unity of apostolic teaching. The apostolic and episcopal offices are different, but the bishops preside over the churches as successors to the apostles.

Similar ideas are picked up and developed by Tertullian and Hippolytus, both Western writers it should be noted, but the specific features of their ideas need not detain us here.[16] We may note, however, that somewhat later, in Cyprian, we have the apostles spoken of as bishops, all the bishops spoken of as successors of the apostles, and thus the distinction between apostolic and non-apostolic churches and between their bishops is eliminated. Cyprian's particular views on the bishop of Rome we shall consider below.

4. The Peter Tradition in the Early Church.

When Rome finally came to make clear claim to a unique role for itself in the church universal, it based that claim on its relationship to the apostle Peter. Therefore to understand the emergence of Rome's primatial claim we must know something of the traditions concerning Peter that circulated in the early church; and these we should see against the background of the traditions circulating about the other apostles.

The twelve apostles became a fixed element in the Christian recollection of its past at an early date, certainly prior to the writing of Luke-Acts.[17] In quite divergent and even antithetical forms of Christianity across the second century one finds them, variously interpreted but present nonetheless. For Marcion they are the Judaizing corrupters of the gospel, so completely misunderstanding the teaching of Jesus that a new revelation, to Paul, is required. In the *Epistula Apostolorum* they are the vehicle of the gospel, to whom Paul is subordinated, on whom he is dependent.[18]

But much more energy and sheer creativity is invested in the stories of the individual apostles than in the group as a whole. Some of this embellishment has clear polemical intent.

Some would seem to arise out of a popular fascination with the marvelous. In either case it is difficult to sift out very much that one can reasonably regard as fact, particularly from the later material.

The apostle who is the subject of the most extensive extant literature is Peter. Among at least some Jewish Christians Peter is cast in a most important role. In the *Epistula Petri,* which stands as the introduction to the *Pseudo-Clementine Homilies,* Peter casts himself in the role of the new Moses, giving instruction to James, "the lord and bishop of the holy church" (1:1), as to the proper way of passing on the books of Peter's preachings. These are to be kept away from "any one of the gentiles" (1:2), and are to be transmitted "to any one of our own tribe" (1:2) only after a lengthy probation. The purpose of all this is to preserve the truth from corruption by him who, according to Peter, advocates "the dissolution of the law" (2:4), a danger which Peter foresees will increase after Peter's death. What I would note here is that Peter is cast in the role of one who stands as it were above the church. James is the lord and bishop of the church, yet Peter clearly stands on an altogether higher level.[19]

We may also note, before turning to more "mainstream" materials, that Clement of Alexandria informs us that Basilides, the gnostic, claimed "for his master Glaucias, the interpreter of Peter" (*Strom.* 7.17). And in the strange, hard to date, gnostic-sounding, textually uncertain *Questions of Bartholomew,*[20] Peter is addressed by Bartholomew as his leader and teacher (*koryphaios kai emos didaskalos*), and by Mary the mother of Jesus as the great pillar (*koryphaie kai style megiste.*)

Of the mainstream materials we may first note the two canonical letters of Peter. On the supposition that the first of these was written toward the end of the first century, perhaps in the time of Domitian,[21] and that the second was written even later, these documents testify to the fact that Peter was one of several among the twelve whose authority was invoked through pseudepigraphy. In the course of the second century a large body of writing came to be associated with Peter. The Gospel of Mark is ascribed to Peter as its apostolic source by Papias (Eusebius, *H.E.* 3.39.15), who himself ascribes this ascription to "the presbyter." This would take us back to approximately the beginning of the second century, and perhaps even a bit earlier. There is, moreover, a *Gospel of Peter,* an *Apocalypse of Peter,* a *Kerygma Petrou* (not to be confused with the Jewish Christian *Kerygmata Petrou*), and an *Acts of Peter.* All of these are attributed by their Hennecke-Schneemelcher editors to the second century, several of them to the first half of that century.

That Peter worked, or even ended his career in martyrdom, at Rome is widely attested in the late first, the second, and on into the third century. Though it eventually becomes part of an argument for Roman ecclesiastical primacy, the earliest witnesses to the tradition do not seem to have used it polemically. 1 Peter 5:13 can be interpreted as presupposing a Peter-in-Rome tradition. *1 Clement* 5:3-6:1 speak of Peter and Paul as having endured tortures among us—*en hēmin.*

Ignatius of Antioch writes (*Rom.* 4:3): "I do not order you as did Peter and Paul," which seems to suppose that Peter played some role in the church at Rome.

Dinonysius of Corinth, writing to the Romans, says: (*H.E.* 2.25.8) "By so great an admonition you bound together the foundations of the Romans and Corinthians by Peter and Paul, for both of them taught together in our Corinth and were our founders, and together also taught in Italy in the same place and were martyred at the same time." Caius, a Roman writing at the beginning of the third century, was more detailed: "But I can point out the trophies of the Apostles, for if you will go to the Vatican or to the Ostian Way you will find the trophies of those who founded this Church" (*H.E.* 2.25.7).

We have, of course, in Irenaeus (*Adv. Haer.* 3.3.2) the view that the church at Rome was founded and organized by Peter and Paul—*fundata et constituta.* Futher: "The blessed apostles, then, having founded and built up the church, committed into the hands of Linus the office of episcopate—" Note here that it is both Peter and Paul who establish the Roman episcopacy, not just Peter alone.

In Clement of Alexandria (*Quis dives salvetur,* 21) we read of "the blessed Peter, the chosen, the pre-eminent, the first of the disciples." This is attached to Matthew 17:27. The same text suggests to Origen no such thoughts about Peter. Indeed, when Origen is commenting directly on Matthew 16:18f. he carefully puts aside any interpretation of the passage that would make of Peter anything other than what every Christian is to be.

. . . And if we too have said like Peter, "Thou art the Christ, the Son of the living God", not as if flesh and blood had revealed it to us, but because light from the Father in heaven had shone in our hearts, we become a Peter, and to us also he who was the Word might say, "Thou art Peter and upon this rock I will build my Church". For every imitator of Christ is a rock, of Christ, that is, who is the spiritual rock that followed them that drank of him. And upon every such rock is built every word of the Church, and the whole order of life based thereon; for whosoever is perfect, having the sum of words and deeds and thoughts which fill up the state of blessedness, in him is the Church that God is building.

But if you suppose that God builds the entire Church upon Peter and on him alone, what would you say about John, the son of thunder, or any particular apostle? In other words, are we to be so bold as to say that it is against Peter in particular that the gates of Hades shall not prevail, but that they shall prevail against the other apostles and the perfect? Does not the above saying "The gates of Hades shall not prevail against it" hold in regard to all, and in the case of each of them? And likewise with regard to the words "Upon this rock I will build my Church"? Are the keys of the kingdom of heaven given by the Lord to Peter only, and will no other of the blessed receive them? But if this promise, "I will give unto thee the keys of the kingdom of heaven", applies likewise to the others, how shall not all the things previously mentioned, and also the following sayings spoken to Peter, apply likewise to them? For in the passage before us, the words "Whatsoever thou shalt bind on earth shall be bound in heaven" and what follows do appear to be addressed to Peter individually; but in the Gospel of John, the Saviour, having given the Holy Spirit to the disciples by breathing on them, says "Receive ye the Holy Ghost" and what follows. For all the imitators of Christ are surnamed "rocks" from him, the spiritual rock which follows those who are being saved; . . . but from the very fact that they are members of Christ, they are called Christians by a name derived from him. And those called after the rock are called Peter. (*In Matt.* 12:10-11; ANF translation, extensively revised by E. Giles, *Documents Illustrating Papal Authority*, 1952, pp. 45-46).

This is the earliest extant detailed commentary on Matthew 16:18f. and interestingly sees the event described as a lesson about the life to be lived by every Christian, and not information about office or hierarchy or authority in the church.

Curiously, though Origen does not suggest any unique Petrine prerogatives when directly commenting on Matthew 16:18, in a subsequent passage in his Matthew commentary (Bk 13.14), apropos Matthew 17:27, he states that Peter was honored above the other apostles; and this leads him to a highly fanciful reexegesis of Matthew 16:18 (Peter given the keys not of one heaven but of all the heavens) in which Peter is seen as superior to the rest. Origen never puts these two interpretations together.

Tertullian, writing a few decades earlier, passes on a fair amount of Peter-tradition. He speaks of "the church of Rome, which makes Clement to have been ordained in like manner by Peter" (*Praesc.* 32), though he is aware of the tradition that Paul as well as Peter died there, and indeed that John was plunged into boiling oil there but emerged unhurt (*Ibid.*, 36). In the later, already Montanist, *Adversus Marcionem*, it is Peter and Paul who have bequeathed the gospel to the church at Rome.

Though Tertullian seems to know nothing of a Roman primacy, some kind of Petrine primacy is familiar. In *Scorpiace* 10 he says: "For though you think heaven still shut, remember that the Lord left here to Peter, and through him to the church, the keys of it." Indeed the Montanist Tertullian makes clear that the gift of the keys was made personally to Peter and derivately to the church of the Spirit, i.e. not to the church of the bishops. (*De pud.* 21). Here he would seem to be combatting a claim that the bishops (and not only or even primarily the bishop of Rome) had succeeded to the power of the keys originally conferred upon Peter.

A generation later Cyprian argues that Christ builds the church on one man, Peter. According to Cyprian, Christ established by his own authority a source for that oneness having its origin in one man alone" (*De unitate*, 4, ACW translation of the text of the CSEL edition). Elsewhere (Ep. 33:1) Cyprian interprets Matthew 16:18 to apply to all bishops. He speaks as though the church and the church's unity have existed in three distinct phases.

How much of this originates with Cyprian, how much of it has gradually grown up as part of the tradition at Carthage, we cannot say; but by his time there exists at Carthage a tradition which saw Peter as the foundation of the church in a certain sense, which related episcopacy to Peter, yet which did so in such a way that all bishops were equally sharers in and preservers of what had first been bestowed upon Peter.[22]

As noted previously, traditions developed around other

apostles as well. As with Peter, other apostles had ascribed to them works which were included in the church's canon, but which today are widely held to be pseudepigraphal. Paul, James, John, and Jude are all claimed as authors (though except for Paul they are not called "apostles") by the writings themselves, and from an early time the church ascribed a gospel to Matthew. Thomas, identified in some quarters as Jesus' twin brother, is claimed as the recorder of the sayings of Jesus known as *The Gospel of Thomas.* Paul, Andrew, and John are the subjects of late second and early third century Acts.[23]

Attempts have been made to localize various apostolic traditions. However, the materials are so few, and establishing their place of origin is so open to question, that such efforts must be viewed with considerable reserve. What does seem clear, however, is that there was not a single unified tradition, maintained by the church as a whole, relative to all the apostles. Rather there developed a variety of traditions, most of them perhaps localized at the start, some of which eventually came to be accepted as *the* tradition by the Christian mainstream. Even if we suppose that the tradition of Peter's leadership among the twelve derives from the *res gestae* of the pre-resurrection period, and that the various witnesses to this need not all derive from a single space-time point in the life of the early church; still we must allow for the possibility that this was not a *datum* in the tradition of Christians everywhere. After all, Peter is mentioned by name (as Peter or Cephas) only in *1 Clement, 2 Clement,* and Ignatius of Antioch among the apostolic fathers, and only in Justin's *Dialogue with Trypho* (twice) in the entire *corpus apologeticum.* That is to say, Peter was only occasionally referred to in what we know of orthodox Christianity in the early and middle second century; in much of it he does not appear at all.

5. The role played by Rome from 1 Clement *to Nicaea.*

All churches in the first several centuries did not play identical or equal roles. From the earliest days Jerusalem played a special role, and very early Antioch seems to have become something of a radiating center for the Gentile mission. Ephesus and Smyrna soon come to be centers, as do Rome and somewhat later, Alexandria and Carthage. The list here is not exhaustive. Given the informal nature of the centralizing process and the ill-defined nature of the prominence of these churches, an exhaustive list is in principle impossible. Across the Mediterranean world, leading cities were becoming leading churches; and Rome of course was the leading city of the world. Thus the emergence of Rome into a leadership position is not an isolated phenomenon. Rome was, in the pre-Nicene period, one of a number of churches that exercised leadership, and whose leadership was recognized by others. Thus it should be noted that it is clearer earlier that Rome is *a* leading church, and even that it is *the* leading church of the West, than that Rome lays claim to and has recognized an ecumenical primacy. Similarly, not every second or third century act of Roman leadership or authority should automatically be interpreted as exemplifying the claims made centuries later by Damasus or Leo. There are possibilities of leadership within more limited frames of reference which must be considered.[24]

In considering the role of Rome which is evidenced in *1 Clement* we must bear in mind what was said above. Rome at this time seems not to have had a monepiscopal church order. The letter is the first direct expression of "the church of God residing in Rome"; and perhaps significantly it is an effort to bring back into order "the church of God dwelling in Corinth."

It is not necessary to rehearse the details of this much commented upon letter. It has often in the past been interpreted by Catholic writers (Seppelt, Quasten, Karrer) as evidence for a significant Roman primacy. This tendency has been reinforced by those Protestant writers (E. Schweizer, E. Brunner) whose general theoretical prepossessions lead them to create the widest possible chasm between the New Testament and any other early Christian writings, and who thus tend to see in *Frühkatholizismus* the embryonic form of all the objectionable features of the later growth.

This primatial interpretation seems to be based on the following factors:

1) The letter explains why Rome has not written sooner, thus implying that it was under some obligation to do so (1:1).

2) The letter states that "if some be disobedient to the words which have been spoken by him through us . . ." they will be guilty of sin (59:1).

But neither of these two considerations requires or supports the view that Rome is acting in a unique or "proto-primatial" way. The responsibility of one church for another, especially if there is a sense of particular closeness as appears to have been the case between Corinth and Rome, (both are churches of Peter and Paul) is enough to account for the sense of responsibility expressed. As for the obligation of obedience under which those who are addressed stand (59:1), it would seem to derive from what has been said rather than from the status of the church saying it. We read (56:2), "Let us, beloved, accept correction, which no one must take in bad part. A reproof which we administer to one another is honorable and extremely helpful, for it unites us to the will of God." There is no reason to suppose that Rome considers that such admonition is a one-way affair. Presumably the "to one another"—*pros allēlous*—means that in other circumstances Corinth might be correcting Rome and that Rome would be obliged to take it in good part, and by means of such admonition be united to the will of God. Irenaeus' characterization of the letter says neither too much nor too little: "In the time of this Clement, no small dissension having occurred among the brethren at Corinth, the Church in Rome dispatched a most powerful letter to the Corinthians, exhorting them to peace, renewing their faith, and declaring the tradition which it had lately received from the apostles" (*Adv. Haer.* 3.3.3).

In the course of the second century, Rome became the principal Christian center of activity. Perhaps it was already this before the end of the first century, but the situation becomes clearer in the second. It cannot easily or confidently be stated how or why this happened, nor can we with precision define the extent of Roman influence. Yet we can show something of the growing eminence of Rome.

Ignatius of Antioch's address to Rome as *prokathēmenē tēs agathēs*—"pre-eminent in love"—coupled with his identification of Rome as *hētis . . . prokathētai en topō chōriou Rōmaiōn* indicates that Rome already enjoys a reputation for *some* kind of eminence or leadership. Ignatius here goes well beyond the conventional praise that one finds in most early Christian correspondence.

First we may call attention to the often noted fact that in the course of the second century confrontation between orthodoxy and heresy a remarkable number of heresiarchs and heretics made their way to Rome. That Marcion spent a considerable period of time in Rome is widely attested and seems beyond doubt. Valentinus also spent much of his life there, as did Cerdo and Marcellina. None of these was native to Rome, but each seems to have come there to learn or to teach. Similarly, orthodox and anti-gnostic writers also came to Rome as to some kind of center, Justin and Hegessippus from Palestine, Irenaeus and Polycarp from Asia Minor.

But this should not be interpreted as indicating an implicit view of the primacy of Rome and its bishop on the part of either the heretics or the orthodox. Similar clustering of heretics can also be noted at Alexandria. And just as the orthodox Justin comes to Rome, so the more or less orthodox Clement finds his way to Alexandria. Rome and Alexandria were in fact the two principal centers for religious-intellectual teaching in the Mediterranean world; and it is not altogether superfluous to note that the career of the greatest non-Christian philosopher of late antiquity, Plotinus, was spent almost entirely in just these two cities.

Throughout the course of the third century we continue to see leaders of heretical movements coming to Rome (cf. Hippolytus, *Ref.* 9.8), yet it remains a question whether this should be interpreted as a recognition of Roman primacy. The eminence of Rome as capital and largest city of the world, its position as an intellectual center, the influence exerted by the church at Rome as far away as Asia Minor, North Africa, and Gaul, the identification of Rome as the church of Peter and Paul, the apostles *par excellence,* are presumably all factors in this Rome-ward tendency.

Alongside this "testimony of the heretics" we see a growing and spreading activity on the part of the Roman church. Dionysius of Corinth, writing to Rome when Soter was bishop (presumably ca. 170), states: "This has been your custom from the beginning, to do good in manifold ways to all Christians, and to send contributions to the many churches in every city, in some places relieving the poverty of the needy, and ministering to the Christians in the mines, by the contribution which you have sent from the beginning, preserving the ancestral custom of the Romans, true Romans as you are. Your blessed bishop Soter has not only carried on this habit but has even increased it, by administering the bounty distributed to the saints and by exhorting with his blessed words the brethren who come to Rome, as a loving father would his children" (*H.E.* 4.23.10-11). How widespread was this practice of sending contributions to other churches we cannot say, but it does indicate that the church at Rome played a role of some size in the lives of a good many other churches.

Not long after the time of Soter and Dionysius we come to Victor and the paschal controversy. We have already seen the Eusebian text which is the source of our information, and I have indicated why some of these materials seem to point to an intradiocesan dispute. The other materials, however, and in particular the letter from Polycrates, point to a dispute between Rome and the churches of Asia Minor. Victor has apparently asked (*aksioō*, it is difficult to pin down the tone of this) Polycrates to convene the Asian bishops in order to determine their custom in the matter of celebrating Easter. From the defensive and at points defiant tone of Polycrates' response, it is reasonable to infer that he is aware of a certain pressure to conform to the Roman custom. One may question whether Victor actually severed relations with the Asian churches because of Polycrates' letter as Eusebius reports, or whether perhaps Eusebius erroneously drew this inference by taking Irenaeus' letter to refer to such interdiocesan action. But whatever choice one makes in this matter, we clearly have to do, in the Roman request-demand for an account of the Asian custom, with a noteworthy instance of far-reaching Roman activity. Though Eusebius gives us no additional texts, and is perhaps reporting at third- or fourth-hand, he tells us that in addition to the bishops of Asia, bishops met in Palestine under the bishops of Jerusalem and Caesarea, in Pontus under Palmas, under Irenaeus in Gaul, under Bacchyllus at Corinth, in Osrhoene "and the cities there,"[25] and perhaps a bit extravagantly: "and of very many more who expressed one and the same opinion and judgment."

Rome thus seems to have taken the initiative in soliciting from churches in various areas information on their Easter practice, with perhaps the intent of bringing about uniformity of practice in conformity with the Roman custom. Whatever the pressure put on the Asian churches to conform, it was evidently insufficient and they decided "to obey God rather than men"—i.e. to follow the practice of *their* apostles and luminaries rather than someone else's. Only gradually did the Asian practice change. Firmilian of Caesarea in Cappadocia, in his letter to Cyprian (Cyprian, *Ep*. 75:6), points to a different (and non-apostolic) Roman practice concerning the celebration of Easter, which suggests that the uniformity which had been sought by Victor sixty years earlier had not yet been achieved, and that it was still somewhat bitterly resisted. The Synod of Arles (314) decreed that the bishop of Rome was to establish the time for Easter for the entire world, and the Council of Nicaea excommunicated the remaining quartodecimans, but by that time the churches of Asia Minor had ceased as a group to constitute a variant tradition and had fallen into step with the rest. Though it would appear that eventually things went the way Victor wanted them to go, it does not appear that his action had any immediate positive effect, and the only response which we have to his action identifies it as a command of man and not of God.

At about this same time we get the first extant appeals to the Roman tradition as an especially suitable norm for orthodoxy. In the two earliest uses of the apostolic succession argument it is Rome—in one case (Irenaeus) along with Smyrna and Ephesus in subordinate positions, in the other (Tertullian, *Praesc.* 32, 36) with first Smyrna, then Corinth, Philippi, Thessalonica, and Ephesus adjoined—that is featured most prominently. For these Western but non-Roman writers Rome functions not in a primatial way precisely,[26] but as the most obvious and impressive bearer of the apostolic tradition. (Curiously, the Roman writer who develops a similar anti-heretical argument, Hippolytus, makes no special reference to Rome, or indeed to any particular church.) Though no unique theoretical claim is being advanced, Rome's prominence is again underscored.[27]

It is not until we come down to the time of Cyprian that we get an explicit discussion of the status of Rome among the world's churches. Unfortunately, a voice that we do not hear directly at this time is that of the Roman bishop.

According to Cyprian's interpretation of Matthew 16:18, Jesus first conferred upon Peter the authority with which he subsequently endowed all the apostles. This, according to Cyprian, was to make clear the unity of the power that was being conferred and of the church that was being established. Cyprian frequently speaks of Peter as the foundation of the church, and his meaning seems to be that it was in Peter that Jesus first established all the church-building powers and responsibilities that would subsequently also be given to the other apostles and to the bishops.

The significance of this for the role or status of the Roman church and the Roman bishop is not altogether clear. In a letter written to Cornelius (A.D. 252) before serious conflict arose between Rome and Carthage, Cyprian speaks of Rome as ". . . the throne of Peter . . . the chief church whence priestly unity has arisen"—*ad Petri cathedram adque ad ecclesiam principalem unde unitas sacerdotalis exorta est* (*Ep.* 59:14). Here the Petrine role seems to be transferred to the church of Rome. Whereas most frequently Cyprian speaks of Peter as the source of the church's oneness,[28] here he speaks of an *ecclesia principalis* as the source of the episcopal unity. The difficulty in making any coherent sense out of this transfer from Peter to the *cathedra Petri* is that Peter is the source of the church's unity only in an exemplary or symbolic way. That is, Peter does not create or strengthen the church's unity by what he does (or at least it is not Cyprian's point that he does), but rather Jesus makes clear the oneness of the church by originally creating the church or the plenitude of the apostolic-episcopal powers in one man. It would seem that the only church that could in some way parallel Peter in this regard would be Jerusalem. In principle this role of being chronologically first cannot be inherited. It would seem therefore, that this parallel has not been worked through very systematically by Cyprian. We may tentatively reconstruct his thought as follows: Rome is the *cathedra Petri*. Though in *De unitate*, 4, this expression does not refer to Rome in *Ep.* 59 it clearly does. Even Firmilian in his harshly critical letter of 256 (*Ep.* 75) does not criticize Stephen's claim to have the *cathedram Petri per successionem*. Cyprian is therefore following along with a rather common tradition in so identifying Rome. And because of the Petrine basis of the Roman church, and in light of the widespread influence of the Roman church already in evidence by 252, Rome can be considered as the church that in a special way has present responsibility for the unity of the bishops and the churches. But this responsibility is not really supported by any authority. Peter himself seems, in Cyprian's thought, to have had no *authority* over the other apostles, and consequently the church of Peter cannot reasonably claim to have any authority over the other churches. Consequently, when this view of Rome's *principalitas* collides with those ecclesiological views which are at the heart of Cyprian's thought, the result is predictable. The Roman "primatial" view simply disappears, and from Cyprian's point of view the issue must be settled on the basis of his "episcopal" theory of church order.[29]

Cyprian is sometimes accused of having changed his primatial views when they threatened to undermine his position at Carthage. This is not incorrect, but it can be misleading if we do not bear in mind that his primatial views were never more than marginal, that precise consequences and inner coherence had never been worked out, and that the collision that destroyed them was not merely with Cyprian's self-interest but with the deeply held and frequently articulated convictions that had all along been the very substance of his ecclesiology.

Dionysius of Alexandria (*H.E.* 7.5.4) reports that Stephen broke off communion with those whose practice in the matter of heretical baptism differed from his; Firmilian (*Ep.* 75:24f.) says the same. Yet at least from Firmilian it is difficult to establish that this was done on the basis of a primatial claim. Firmilian indicates that Stephen has placed great emphasis on the fact that it is Peter's succession that he holds: "*qui sic de episcopatus sui loco gloriatur et se successionem Petri tenere contendit . . . Stephanus qui per successionem cathedram Petri habere se praedicat*" (*Ep.* 75: 17). But it is not clear that Stephen was claiming that *qua* successor to Peter's chair he held authority over other bishops. It is quite possible here that the reference to Peter, upon whom the church was founded, was simply a way of advancing the impressively apostolic credentials of the Roman church. There is nothing in the Cyprianic correspondence relative to the dispute with Rome that shows that Stephen's reference to Peter was not of basically the same character as Polycrates' reference to the apostolic luminaries of whose tradition he was the latter-day defender. From the fact that neither Cyprian nor Firmilian attacks a more ambitiously primatial use of the Petrine claims, which they surely would have found outrageous, it would seem likely that no such use was there to be attacked. This is an argument from silence, but if Stephen were claiming that because of the Petrine origin of his see all bishops were subject to his authority, silence on Cyprian's and Firmilian's part would be inexplicable.

Since the letters are silent on this point, we ought to be cautious about interpreting the differences in the two texts of *De unitate*, 4, as representing Cyprian's response to Roman primatial claims. Even if one accepts the Bevenot analysis of the text history and supposes that both versions are by Cyprian, but that one is a revision made subsequent to the dispute with Stephen, it should still be noted that the presumedly earlier text would be embarrassing for Cyprian even if Rome were making no primatial claims. In that earlier text Cyprian had written that if one "deserts the Chair of Peter upon whom the Church was built, has he still confidence that he is in the Church?" The reference then had not been to Rome. However, it might be interpreted that way, and now Cyprian, indeed the whole of North Africa and many of the churches in the East, are no longer in communion with Rome. The modification was made (again, supposing that Bevenot is correct in his textual judgment) in order to preclude the interpretation that unity with Rome was essential to being "in the church"; but the correspondence gives no support to the view that Rome was actually making that claim at that time.

And yet, this is not the entire story. Both Stephen here and Victor earlier somehow assume that the Roman tradition is normative for other, quite distant churches. The bishops who oppose them seem to be concerned only to maintain their own traditions and not to impose them on Rome. The relationship of Rome to the other churches is significantly asymmetrical.

The history of the church at Rome between the death of Cyprian and Stephen and the Council of Nicaea is difficult to write. No one who occupied the chair of Peter during the time has left any marked impression. Dionysius (259-268) would be the nearest to an exception. Fragments of his correspondence do survive, and he was involved in mutual clarification of theological opinion with Dionysius of Alexandria; but from what remains one would have to say that the Alexandrian Dionysius played a more active role in the life of the church catholic than did his Roman namesake. The Alexandrian wrote a number of letters to various people, Roman and non-Roman, arguing that those who follow in the African tradition on the question of the baptism of heretics should be allowed to do so; thus in apparently milder fashion joining his voice to Cyprian's and Firmilian's, even though his own practice was closer to Rome's (*H.E.* 7.4-9). It was this more conciliatory position which seems to have prevailed in the West, at least to judge by the position taken by the thirty-four Western bishops who assembled at the Synod of Arles (314) and communicated to "the dearly beloved Pope Sylvester."

At Arles those who rebaptize heretics are still identified as the Africans. A decade later at Nicaea there is no reference to a peculiarly African practice; and the practice required of all calls simply for a laying on of hands for those coming to the church from Novatianism, while followers of Paul of Samosata are to be rebaptized.

At the Council of Nicaea Rome played no very significant role, and in the canons of the council is referred to but once. There (can. 6) the situation at Rome (presumably vis-a-vis unspecified Western ecclesiastical districts) is cited as a justifying parallel for the authority of the bishop of Alexandria in Egypt, Libya, and the Pentapolis.

We may briefly summarize. Throughout the period under consideration the following developments took place:

1) Rome alone among the Western churches vigorously claimed apostolic origin, and its apostolic origins went back to the two apostles *par excellence,* Peter and Paul.

2) Rome played a leading role in the Western development of Christianity.

3) Rome claimed to be the Petrine see, and this claim was widely heard and accepted even by those who resisted Roman leadership or influence (Cyprian, Firmilian).

4) On at least two occasions (under Victor and under Stephen) Rome apparently broke off communion with churches following a practice different from its own, apparently considering its own tradition normative for far-distant churches. In both cases the Roman practice came largely to prevail; but in neither case can it be shown that Rome was acting out a theory of its own primacy, and in both cases the evidence indicates that the others involved did not suppose that Rome had authority over other bishops and churches.

5) Nicaea presupposes a regional leadership of Rome, but indicates nothing more.

Thus one concludes that down through the Council of Nicaea, a Roman universal primacy of jurisdiction exists neither as a theoretical construction nor as a de facto practice awaiting theoretical interpretation. We must, therefore, look with special care at the events and ideas that separate Nicaea from the Council of Sardica and from the series of Roman bishops, beginning perhaps with Damasus (366-384), in whom the claim to a universal Roman primacy of jurisdiction on the basis of the Petrine succession is clearly and repeatedly made. In the pre-Nicene period we have some of the raw materials and some of the pressures.

II. From Nicaea to Leo the Great[1]

Arthur Carl Piepkorn

The factors making for stability in the historical matrix of this period derive in large part from the highly effective, even though repressive, solutions to the problems of the Roman Empire that Diocletian and Constantine had devised.

Among the factors making for change was the initial legitimation of Christianity a dozen years before the beginning of the period and the gradual "establishment" of the church beginning with the reign of Constantine (306-337). The permanence of this arrangement successfully met the challenge of pagan resistance and the brief return to power of the old religion under the imperial patronage of Julian in 362/363. Gratian removed the altar of Victory from the Senate in 382. Theodosius I (379-395) enacted stringent antipagan laws. In 408 Honorius denied pagan religious associations the right to hold property. Constantine seems to have seen himself as possessed of the same power in the church that he had had in the state and as a kind of unbaptized and unordained "bishop of those outside."[2] His successors, in varying degrees, saw themselves in parallel roles.

Prior to its legitimation, Christianity had been a religion of a relatively poor and rather small group of predominantly lower-class and middle-class people. It now became attractive to the upper classes and grew rapidly not only in numbers but also in power. In spite of the way that churchmen at times abused their influence, the impact of Christianity upon both the Eastern and Western empires was incalculably great. So was the impact of the empire on Christianity.

A second major agency of change was the invasion of the empire by the barbarians. The effect of this was heightened in parts of the empire by the restlessness of the *coloni* who used the barbarian invasions as a pretext or an opportunity for revolt or for flight into barbarian-held territories. Jovian bought peace for the eastern frontier by his costly concessions of 363. Europe continually felt the impact of the barbarian incursions from 376 on, when the Visigoths, displaced by the invading Huns, crossed the Danube and achieved federated status as the guardians of the frontier. Their subsequent wanderings carried them to Italy and to the practical control of the south of France. The second wave of barbarians—Vandals, Suebi, and Alani—moved in over a thirty-year period beginning in 406 and marched across Gaul, Spain, and North Africa. In 439 they took Carthage and established the first independent German kingdom on former Roman territory in the Mediterranean area. At the end of the period the disintegration of the empire of the Huns sent the Ostrogoths and others across the imperial boundaries in search of food and land.

Thanks to Ulfilas (311?-383), the imperial authorities often tended to regard all the Germanic invaders as Arians, even when it was not the case. This was an additional reason why Valentinian made intermarriage between barbarians and Romans a crime punishable by death. The religious difference unquestionably contributed to the tension that existed in some degree between the groups throughout the empire. The Vandal persecution of the Catholic church helped to heighten the authority of the church of Rome, which became a source of strength and support for the victims of Vandal harassment.

The decline of the political significance of Rome, far from minimizing, actually enhanced the city's spiritual importance. In a sense it presaged the necessity that compelled Pelagius II (579-590) and Gregory the Great (590-604) to assume political authority over the city. The transfer of the imperial capital to Constantinople conferred on the bishops of Rome a measure of freedom that they would not have had if the seat of empire had remained on the Tiber. Their independence was increased by the de facto establishment of the court of the Western emperor at Milan in the days of Maximian (285-305) and by the formal relegation of the western court first to Milan in 384 and then, twenty years later, to Ravenna. In the late fourth century, the see of Milan was in practice the equal of Rome in authority and it exercised its power throughout northern Italy and southern Gaul. In part, of course, this development reflects the great prestige of Ambrose (339?-397), who could dare to excommunicate even the emperor and compel his repentance.

Within the church the crises of heresy were only imperfectly overcome. Arianism persisted in a variety of forms. Donatism divided the church in the West. Cyril of Alexandria triumphed over his Byzantine archrival at Ephesus in

431, but Nestorianism had its revenge in its conquest of much of the non-Roman East. Pelagianism received formal condemnation, but the theological victory of Augustine (354-430) was not without its ambiguities; the issue was not really adjudicated until the sixth century. Dioscorus of Alexandria tasted defeat at Chalcedon in 451, but that council's solution to the christological problem was at best formal; the "Three Chapters" controversy and the Monothelite controversy still lay ahead.

During this period the Christian East and the Christian West developed in increasing independence of one another, both structurally and theologically. Periodic efforts at restoring the ancient unity or at least creating persuasive symbols of unity failed and were punctuated by actual schism. A case in point is the schism between Rome on the one side and Constantinople, Antioch, and Alexandria on the other during the episcopate of Innocent I (402-417) as a result of his intervention on behalf of John Chrysostom (347?-407) in the controversy between the latter and Theophilus of Alexandria (died 412).

Each of the great sees had its own ambitions and its own jealousies. With the establishment of Constantinople as the major seat of government, the bishops of Old Rome began consistently to resist the elevation of New Rome to the dignity of the second see in the church. Their support of the claims of Alexandria to be the second see was based not only on the sixth canon of Nicaea I but also on the long linkage between the two sees and a joint desire to keep Constantinople down.

The rivalry between Rome and Alexandria was long latent; it finally broke out at the end of our period. In spite of Antioch's demonstrable link with Peter and its very considerable size as late as the beginning of the fifth century, its influence had begun to decline as early as Nicaea I, and while Jerusalem gained in prestige throughout the period, it remained a suffragan see of Caesarea and became one of the great sees only in the mid-fifth century.

All thirteen bishops of Rome from Sylvester (314-335) to Leo the Great (440-461) have been elevated to the honors of the altar in the West. Their sanctity is thus a matter of official determination. But they were not eminent theologians for the most part. Leo is the great exception of course, although Damasus (366-384), Innocent, and Celestine (422-432) played significant roles in the controversies that agitated the church during their episcopates. The contribution of the bishops of Rome during this period to the history of Christian thought consists chiefly in securing acceptance of solutions advanced by other theologians. But their success added significantly to the prestige of the church of Rome and its bishops.

Similar benefit accrued from their sponsorship of the proponents of the views that triumphed as orthodox—the open door that Athanasius (296?-373) found at Rome and the moral support that bishops of Rome gave to Cyril of Alexandria (died 444), to Flavian of Constantinople (died 449), and to Augustine and his anti-Pelagian allies. Where the bishops of Rome made mistakes, as in the case of the support that Julius (337-352) gave to Marcellus of Ancyra (died 374?), whose heretical eschatology led to the insertion of the words "and his kingdom will have no end" in the Creed of the 150 Fathers, or the concurrence (under duress) of the exiled Liberius (352-366) in the deposition of Athanasius, or in initial acquittal of Celestius (fl. 410-431), the associate of Pelagius (fl. 405-418) by Zosimus (417-418), their actions were, happily for them, without serious adverse consequences.

A significant datum is the quality of theological leadership exercised outside of Old Rome by Athanasius, Gregory of Nazianzus (329-389), Basil of Caesarea (330?-379), Gregory of Nyssa (330?-395?), John Chrysostom, Ambrose, Augustine, and (while he was in the East) Jerome (342-420). Most of these theologians were either allied with Rome or—as in the case of the great Cappadocians, for example—they posed no threat to Roman prestige precisely because they were not located in a rival great see.

The change in the status of the church was reflected in the episcopal style of the bishops of Rome (and of the prelates of the other great sees). While the thrust of the ante-Nicene period was predominantly pastoral, in the post-Nicene era the political and administrative concerns of prelates who were becoming more and more aware of their responsibilities for the church throughout an entire region almost inevitably came to the fore in an increasing measure. From another standpoint, one can think of the see of Rome in the period before Nicaea as "pre-curial"; in the post-Nicene era, particularly from the episcopate of Damasus on, it is increasingly "curial," again like the other great sees.

Sylvester (314-335) and Mark (336)

Sylvester was in a sense the victim of the triumph of Christianity and of Constantine's subsequent aggressive intervention in the affairs of the church. This interference left Sylvester little scope, whatever his personal capacities and inclinations may have been. In fact he did not take any very memorable part in either the Donatist or the Arian controversies, although the Council of Arles regretted that his absence made its condemnation of Donatism less severe than it would have been had he been present. He is less remembered for any historical accomplishments than for the part assigned to him in the Sylvester-Constantine legend (first written down, it appears, in the late eighth century). This legend tells how Sylvester baptized Constantine and thereby healed him of leprosy. In return, the emperor invested Sylvester and his successors with the Lateran palace, the city of Rome, and all the provinces and territories of Italy and the regions of the West—the forgery known as the Donation of Constantine. The historical nucleus of the legend is the apparently authentic gift of the Lateran to Sylvester by the emperor.

Nicaea I, which took place during Sylvester's episcopate, is of interest here because of canon 6. It invoked ancient customs in assigning Egypt, Libya, and the Pentapolis to the bishop of Alexandria, affirming the customary jurisdiction of the bishop of Rome, and asserting the traditional authority of the bishop of Antioch and of the provincial metropolitans (Mirbt-Aland, no. 263). The canon does not fix the boundaries of Roman regional power. But the expansion of the canon in Rufinus (345?-410) seems to limit Rome's authority to the suburbicarian sees. This may reflect the actual jurisdictional situation at the end of the fourth century.

Mark's episcopate—which lasted less than three months—is without significance for the issue to which this paper addresses itself.

Julius (337-352)

The year after Julius became bishop of Rome, the Eusebians declared that Athanasius was no longer the rightful bishop of Alexandria. They wrote to Julius and asked him to call a synod to settle the issue and invited him to be the judge if he so desired (MPG, 25, 280). Julius called a synod to meet in Rome and sent two presbyters to Alexandria to invite the Eusebian bishops to be represented. He also up-braided the Eusebians for their wrong judgment of Athanasius and Marcellus, for disturbing the church's peace, and for abandoning the Nicene position. According to Sozomen, the Eusebian bishops conceded that the Roman church was en-titled to the honor of all, but they had no hesitation in call-ing Julius to account for what they regarded as an insult to their synod (MPG, 67, 1052).

The Eusebians rejected the invitation of Julius to attend the Roman synod, which met in 340 and at which over fifty Italian bishops acquitted Athansius and Marcellus of the Eusebian charges and admitted them to communion. Julius communicated the acquittal of Athanasius and of Marcellus to the Eusebians at Antioch. In this letter he declares: "Judgment ought to have taken place according to the law of the church and not as it did! You should have written to all of us, so that what is right could have been determined by all." He asks: "Don't you know that it is the custom to have written to us first and then the things that are right to have been determined from here?" He also asserts that what he had pointed out to them is "what we have received from blessed Peter the apostle" (Mirbt-Aland, no. 271). Whether or not the canons attributed to the Dedication Council of Antioch in 341 are a reply to the letter of Julius is debated.[3]

In 343/344 (or, according to others, 342) the synod of Sardica (Serdica), the modern Sofia, met under the presi-dency of Hosius of Cordova (257?-357). More Greek-speak-ing bishops were present than Latin-speaking prelates; this was natural in view of the location of Sardica only a short distance west of the boundary between the areas for which Rome and Constantinople were respectively responsible. Nevertheless, it was primarily a synod of the area that Rome controlled. The chief exceptions were the Eastern bishops whose depositions were being reviewed (notably Athanasius, Marcellus, and Asclepas of Gaza), the bishops of Rhodope, and the two bishops from Palestine and Arabia who had defected from the predominantly Eusebian Eastern delega-tion.

Three canons of this synod, numbered 3, 4, and 5 in the Greek text, are of special relevance to the present inquiry.

Canon 3, moved by Hosius, provided that "if a bishop has been judged in some action and holds he has a good cause for the judgment to be reviewed, let us, if you agree (*si vobis placet; et dokei*), honor the memory of the most holy apostle Peter: Let either those who examined him [the Latin version adds: or the bishops living in the nearest province] write letters to the bishop of Rome. If he decides that the sentence must be reviewed let it be reviewed, and let him designate the judges. But if he regards the case as of such a kind that it is inexpedient to reopen the issues as decided, his decisions shall be confirmed."

Canon 4, moved by Gaudentius of Nissa, provided that when such an appeal had been made to Rome, "let no other bishop on any account be ordained in his place in the same see, unless the case shall have been determined by the judgment of the bishop of Rome."

Canon 5, also moved by Hosius, provided that when an appeal had been made directly to the bishop of Rome and the latter had agreed to a reopening of the case, "let him deign to write to the bishops in the adjacent [the Latin adds: and neighboring] province that they diligently investigate everything and render a decision that accords with the truth." Whether or not the bishop of Rome would send presbyters to whom he had delegated authority to pronounce judgment in his stead or whether he would leave the matter to the bishops of the neighboring province, acting as his appointed judges, would be a matter for him to determine (Mirbt-Aland, no. 272).[4]

Properly to evaluate the canons of Sardica, we need to understand that a unique situation had developed in the church during the half generation after Nicaea. The Roman see had become the acknowledged citadel of Nicene orthodoxy, and Julius stood committed to the preservation of Nicene doctrine with all the means at his disposal. When he called upon Athanasius to come to Rome at the time of the latter's deprivation of his Alexandrian See, he took a step beyond anything that had happened before, although precedents of at least a regional sort existed. The Spanish bishops Basilides and Martial for instance, had appealed their deposition to Stephen (254-257) and the Novatian bishop Fortunatus had sought recognition from Rome as the rightful bishop of Carthage. Under these circumstances, it is intelligible that Sardica should have taken the position that it did.[5]

These bold canons of Sardica were shortly to receive added theoretical force at Rome by being attributed to the Council of Nicaea. Otherwise they had little practical effect;

this was so not only in the East but also in the West, especially in Africa.

In the aftermath of Sardica, the Eusebians, writing from Philippopolis to Gregory of Alexandria, Amphion of Nicomedia, Donatus of Carthage (fl. 315-347), and other addressees, report that "the entire synod," that is, the Eusebian caucus, "according to the most ancient law, condemned Julius of the city of Rome," whom they describe as "the chief and the leader of the wicked," and his fellow-bishops (Mirbt-Aland, no. 275).

Liberius (352-366)

The case of Liberius, the successor of Julius, deserves special attention. To his great credit he was at least initially willing to accept exile to Berea in Thrace rather than to accede to the demand of Constantius (337-361) that Liberius recognize the Arian bishops of the east as in communion with him. After Liberius' departure from Rome in 355, the presbyter Felix (died 365)—although bound by an oath to recognize no other bishop of Rome than Liberius during the latter's lifetime—was elected as Liberius' successor and received consecration at the hands of three Arianizing bishops. The Roman clergy generally accepted Felix, but the people remained loyal to Liberius. To end the schism, Liberius finally concurred in the deposition of Athanasius and subscribed to an ambiguous statement of faith,[6] to which he added a codicil that anathematized anyone who denied that the Son is "like the Father in being and in everything." After entering into communion with the Arianizing Eastern bishops,[7] Liberius was allowed to return to Rome in 358 (Mirbt-Aland, nos. 278-281). Once back at Rome, however, Liberius was one of the few bishops who dared to reject the version of the "Dated Creed" of Sirmium (359) which affirmed only that "the Son is like the Father, as the sacred scriptures say."

The restoration of Liberius in 358 evoked new disorders of such dimensions that no representatives of the Roman church attended the synod of Ariminum in 359.[8]

The case of Liberius, whom the Middle Ages regarded as a heretic, is probably more significant for the question of infallibility than for the question of primacy.

Damasus (366-384)

Damasus, the Spaniard who succeeded Liberius, and the synod of Rome of 371 argued that the deviations from orthodoxy of the 400 Western bishops at the synod of Ariminum did not actually express the faith of the church, since "neither the bishop of the Romans, whose opinion ought to have been waited for before all the others, nor Vincentius [of Capua] who had kept his episcopate untainted so many years, nor the rest gave their approval to such doctrine" (MPG, 82, 1053).[9]

In 378 Damasus and the synod of Rome of that year found it convenient to appeal to the emperors Gratian (367-383) and Valentinian II (364-375) to support the processes of ecclesiastical discipline with the imperial power (Mirbt-Aland, no. 301). It also asked that the bishop of Rome be finally tried only by the imperial council (Mirbt-Aland, no. 303). The emperors complied with the former request. The judgment of Damasus is to be confirmed by at least five other bishops. In cases arising in more distant areas, the emperors also allow for local episcopal judgment as an alternative to prosecution at Rome. In such instances those who see themselves at a disadvantage because of the bias or prejudice of a superior, specifically a metropolitan, are—as the Roman synod had requested—privileged to appeal to the bishop of Rome or to a council of fifteen bishops of the neighborhood (Mirbt-Aland, no. 305). The emperors made no reply to the second request.

Gratian's cession of Dacia, Macedonia, and Achaia to the Eastern empire in 379 gave Damasus the occasion for taking the first steps toward what ultimately became the Western vicariate of Thessalonica (which continued until 732).[10] The intention of Damasus was obviously to forestall having the political realignment result in a parallel ecclesiastical realignment that would diminish the jurisdiction of Rome as the great see of the West. This action must be seen as a "patriarchal" rather than a "papal" action, since according to the Roman view the Christians of the prefecture of Eastern Illyricum would still have been no less under the ultimate jurisdiction of the bishop of Rome, even though they were under the regional authority of Constantinople. The action of Damasus provided his successors Siricus (384-399), Anastasius (399-402?), and Innocent with a precedent.

It is significant that the edict *Cunctos populos* (February 27, 380) of Gratian, Valentinian II, and Theodosius (379-395) affirms the trinitarian faith "which the holy apostle Peter delivered to the Romans," as both Damasus of Rome and Peter II of Alexandria (373-380) confess it (Mirbt-Aland, no. 310).

The third canon of the First Council of Constantinople (381), an all-Eastern council in terms of its composition, decreed that the bishop of Constantinople, until then a suffragan bishop of the metropolitanate of Heraklea in Thrace, as the bishop of New Rome, was to have precedence of honor immediately after the bishop of Old Rome, to whom it continued to accord first place (Mirbt-Aland, no. 312). Although this canon was thus not directed against Rome, it did arouse Roman suspicions. As a consequence the synod of Rome of 382, without mentioning the canon of Constantinople, asserted that "the holy Roman Church has not been set before the rest by any conciliar decision but has obtained primacy by the word of the Lord our Savior in the gospel: 'You are Peter'." Furthermore, it has been consecrated to Christ the Lord by "the most blessed apostle Paul, a 'chosen vessel,' " who died for the faith on the same day that Peter did. "The first see of the apostle Peter is therefore the Roman church, 'without spot or wrinkle or any such thing.' But the second see was consecrated at Alexandria, in the name of blessed Peter, by Mark, his disciple, the evangelist. He was directed into Egypt by the apostle Peter. . . . The third see of the most blessed apostle Peter is at Antioch, which is held in honor because he initially lived there before he came to Rome and because there the name of the new race of Christians first arose."

The Meletian schism from 362 to 391 is a special and complex case. The argument from the third and fourth epistles of Damasus to Paulinus (MPL, 13, 356-357; 358-364), from Basil's Epistle 92 to Damasus (MPG, 32, 477-484), Epistle 214 to Count Terence (MPG, 32, 785-789), Epistle 242 to Damasus (MPG, 32, 900-901), Epistle 259 to Epiphanius (ibid., 948-953), and Epistle 263 to Damasus (MPG, 32, 976-981), from Theodoret's *Church History* (MPG, 82, 1197-1201), from Socrates' *Church History* (MPG, 67, 569-572), from the letter of the synod of Aquileia of 381 to the emperors (MPL, 16, 987-990), and from Epistle 13 of Ambrose and the Italian bishops to Theodosius I (MPL 16, 990-993) is an involved one. There is at least no explicit evidence that Meletius (died 381) was reconciled to the Roman see before his death. But Meletius presided over the Council of Constantinople in 381. Although it was convoked as an all-Eastern regional assembly without any Western bishops present, the bishops of Rome from the sixth century on recognized it as ecumenical. In the view of some, however, the primacy of the bishop of Rome is called into question if it is possible to preside over a council like Constantinople I and not be in fellowship with the Roman see. It cannot be shown that this situation meant then what it would mean to Roman Catholics today.

Siricius (384-399) and Anastasius 399-402?)

In 385 Siricius published what is in fact the first surviving Roman decretal, addressed to Himerius of Tarragona in Spain and written in the brusque and imperative style of the documents emanating from the imperial chancery. Siricius concludes the letter with the admonition to bring these *decretalia constituta* to the attention of the bishops of the neighboring provinces. He attributes to them the same binding force as the canons of synods. This document for the first time incorporates a formula that subsequently became a standard affirmation in documents emerging from Rome: "We—or rather, the blessed apostle Peter in us, who, as we trust, protects and keeps us in everything as the heirs of his government—bear the burdens of all those that are burdened." This is apparently the first time that the idea finds expression that Peter continues to live in the person of the bishop of Rome for the time being.[11] Siricius comments on all the cases that Himerius has referred "to the Roman church, as to the head of your body." He declares that "no priest of the Lord is free to be ignorant of the statutes of the apostolic see or of the venerable decisions of the canons" (Mirbt-Aland, nos. 343, 351).

In the episcopate of Siricius a Roman synod of 390 condemned Jovinian (died 405?) and eight of his companions "by the divine sentence and our judgment" (MPL, 13, 1171). A synod held at Milan in the next year declared that "the accused whom your holiness has condemned, have also been condemned by us, in accordance with your judgment" (MPL, 16, 1124).[12]

The three-year episcopate of Anastasius contributed nothing to the development of the primacy of the bishop of Rome.

Innocent (402?-417)

Innocent continued the new "decretal" style. In 404 he demanded that the bishop of Rouen (and the bishops of other sees) conform church discipline in their dioceses to the Roman pattern in line with the prescriptions of Nicaea (actually Sardica) and refer all major cases (*causae majores*) to Rome for decision. (Mirbt-Aland, no. 393).

"All must preserve that which Peter the prince of the apostles delivered to the church at Rome and which it has watched over until now, and nothing may be added or introduced that lacks this authority or that derives its pattern from somewhere else," Innocent wrote to Decentius of Gubbio in 416. With a disregard (or ignorance) of the data of history he declared that it is "obvious that in all Italy, the Gauls, the Spains, Africa, and Sicily, and the islands that lie between them, no one has founded churches except those whom the venerable apostle Peter or his successors had set up as priests. Let people examine the record and see if any other apostle is found or is recorded as having taught in these lands. But if such an apostolic ministry is not recorded, because it is not found anywhere, then they must follow that which the Roman church—from which they without doubt have their origin—has preserved" (Mirbt-Aland, no. 400). This is, again, a "patriarchal" rather than a "papal" pronouncement, since the entire area referred to is within the region traditionally presided over by Rome.

Not that Innocent did not try to intervene in the affairs of the other parts of the church. In the case of his strong advocacy of the cause of John Chrysostom, who had been exiled from his see in Constantinople in 404 and who had appealed to the bishops of Rome, Milan, and Aquileia for support, the result was a schism between Rome on the one hand and Constantinople, Antioch, and Alexandria on the other. The schism did not fully end until 417. One of the schismatic primates was Theophilus of Alexandria. Although he died out of communion with Rome and the West in 412, even Leo could refer to him as a "bishop of holy memory."

The destructive sack of Rome by Alaric (370?-410) during Innocent's episcopate created a political vacuum in the West which enhanced the political significance of the see of Rome.

The church of Africa—where the Donatist schism persisted—suffered a new invasion of heresy when Pelagius and Celestius personally brought their doctrine about the ability of human beings to keep the law of God even without divine grace around 410. A Carthaginian synod held in 411 labeled their views as unorthodox. Pelagius went on to Palestine. Here two bishops from Gaul, Heros of Arles and Lazarus of Aix-en-Provence—subsequently charged with having obtained their posts through unworthy means (MPL, 20, 651)—submitted written accusations against Pelagius, but failed to appear at the investigation that followed. Pelagius had accordingly been declared innocent in December 415. This development was reported to Carthage. The Carthaginian synod of 416 reviewed the case against Pelagius and repeated its condemnation of Pelagius and Celestius. The 69 bishops of the synod transmitted their resolutions to Rome to secure for them the added force of confirmation by the Roman see (Mirbt-Aland, no. 401).

About the same time a synod meeting at Mileve also asked Innocent to condemn Pelagius and Celestius, since they will "more easily yield to the authority of your holiness, taken from the authority of the sacred scripture" (MPL, 33, 763).[13] A letter from five African bishops to Innocent, also in 416, asked for his approval of their synod's action that by his reply they "might be consoled from their participation [with Innocent] in one grace" (Mirbt-Aland, no. 402).

Innocent, replying the next year, praised the Carthaginian synod for following "the examples of ancient tradition" and for not despising what the fathers had "decreed not by a human but by a divine sentence, that whatever is done, even in distant and remote provinces, should not be brought to an end unless it comes to the knowledge of [the Roman] see" (Mirbt-Aland, no. 403).

Innocent commended the synod of Mileve because it "had consulted diligently and duly the secrets (*arcana*) of the apostolic office," the office which has "the care of all the churches," a reference to 2 Corinthians 11:28 which Innocent took over from his predecessor Siricius (MPL, 13, 1132). Innocent judged that his brothers and fellow-bishops ought to refer issues of faith "exclusively to Peter, that is, to the author of their name and office" (Mirbt-Aland, no. 404).

It was this reply, in which Innocent excommunicated Pelagius and Celestius, that Augustine referred to in the famous words, spoken in a sermon that he delivered in the same year: "In this matter [the decisions] of two councils were sent to the apostolic see and from it the rescripts have come back. The matter is finished! If only the error also were some time to come to an end!" (Mirbt-Aland, no. 372).[14]

Zosimus (417-418)

Innocent's successor, Zosimus—possibly in part because he was a Greek and had difficulty in thinking himself into the Roman situation—displayed less than superior judgment in connection with a number of administrative actions. This was particularly true of his dealings with Celestius and Pelagius. In 417 Celestius offered to Zosimus a confession of faith "for the approval of your apostleship" so that if it contained any error, "it may be corrected by your decision" (MPL, 45, 1718). After a public examination of Celestius in the Basilica of St. Clement, Zosimus acquitted the defendant (Mirbt-Aland, no. 410).

Next Zosimus reviewed the declaration of faith that Celestius had sent to Innocent, but that had arrived in Rome only after the addressee's death. In this too Celestius had asked the now deceased bishop of Rome, "who holds both Peter's faith and his see," to correct his profession; if "our confession is approved by the judgment of your apostleship," anyone who would further blacken Celestius would prove that he is inexperienced, malicious, or un-Catholic (Mirbt-Aland, no. 411). Again Zosimus wrote to Aurelius of Carthage (died 430?) and the African bishops that he found nothing wrong with Celestius' doctrine (Mirbt-Aland, no. 412).[15]

In spite of Zosimus' endorsement, the 214 bishops attending the synod of Carthage of 417 informed the bishop of Rome: "We have decreed that the sentence against Pelagius and Celestius, issued by the venerable bishop Innocent from the see of the most blessed apostle Peter, shall remain in force, until in a most open confession they will say that the grace of God through Jesus Christ our Lord helps us not only to know, but also to do justice, in every single act; so that, without it, we could not have, think, say, or do anything that pertains to true and holy religion" (Mirbt-Aland, no. 413).

Zosimus replied the next year with an agitated letter that almost defies translation. The tradition of the fathers accords to his see such great authority, he wrote, that "no one would dare to debate its judgment." "Canonical antiquity in the opinion of all has willed such power" to Peter "through Christ's promise to loose what is bound and to bind what is loosed." This power "is equally given to those who have deserved with his approval the inheritance of his see." Peter "has the care of all churches, most of all of this church where he had his seat, and he does not permit any of its privileges or possessions to totter." He "established its foundations firm and unshakable by any movements, that is, his own name. No one shall rashly attack [these foundations] except at his own peril." The Roman church is "established by all the laws and disciplines, human as well as divine." Peter's "place we rule, and it is not concealed from you either that we possess the power of his name. You know this, dearest brothers, and as priests you ought to know it. Since we have such great authority . . . no one can take anything away from our sentence." At the same time Zosimus protests that he "had not given credence to Celestius in everything" and had not "given assent as it were to every syllable without discussing his words" (Mirbt-Aland, no. 415).

Shortly after this, Zosimus reversed himself completely and in his famed *Epistola tractoria* he condemned Pelagius and Celestius (MPL, 45, 1687.1689).[16] It has been debated whether he did this before or after the emperor banished Celestius and Pelagius from Rome on the grounds of criminal heresy (Mirbt-Aland, no. 414). Possidius of Calama (370?-440?) says that the bishop of Rome acted first (MPL, 32, 48-49).[17] Many scholars have read the limited evidence as pointing in the opposite direction.

For refusing to go along with the altered view of Zosimus, Julian of Eclanum (386?-454) and eighteen other Italian bishops were deposed, excommunicated, and banished. Julian announced that he was appealing to a plenary council. Augustine declared: "Your cause is in any case finished by a competent decision of bishops in common" (MPL, 44, 704).

The contemporary case of the North African presbyter Apiarius (fl. 417-423) is likewise highly complex. A canon attributed to the synod of Carthage of 407 read: "[Any cleric who,] after having been excommunicated (*non communicans*) in Africa, creeps into communion overseas, shall be cast out of the clergy" (MPL, 67, 216). Late in 417 or early in 418, the Numidian bishop Urban of Sicca excommunicated one of his presbyters, Apiarius (fl. 417-423). The latter appealed in person to Zosimus, who directed the restoration of Apiarius. On May 4, 418, the synod of Carthage established a system of appeals for the lower clergy within Africa and forbade appeals "beyond the sea" (*ad trans-marina*); violation of this prohibition was punishable with excommunication (Mirbt-Aland, no. 418). Zosimus sent three delegates to Africa. In following his instructions they appealed at the Carthaginian synod of 419 to a canon of "the council of Nicaea," authorizing appeals to Rome (Mirbt-Aland, no. 419). The Africans responded that they knew of no such canon, but that they would observe it until authentic copies of the Nicene canons could be secured from the East. After half a year the copies of the Nicene canons that the Africans had asked for from Alexandria and Constantinople arrived. The Africans forwarded them to Rome in November 419, vindicated.

Boniface (418-422)

Writing to Rufus of Thessalonica, his vicar in Eastern Illyricum, Boniface declared in 419 that "the most blessed apostle Peter watches with his eyes in what manner you use the office of the supreme rector. He who was appointed perpetual shepherd of the Lord's sheep must be very close to you; he cannot but watch over any church, wherever located, in which we have laid a foundationstone of the universal church" (MPL, 20, 762).

In 421, Atticus of Constantinople (406-426) persuaded Theodosius II (408-450) to transfer the vicariate of Thessaly to the spiritual jurisdiction of the Byzantine patriarch. The emperor explicitly based the propriety of his action on the ecclesiastical precedence that Constantinople had as the imperial residence. Boniface reacted on March 11, 422, by instructing Rufus that "it has never been licit to consider anew what has once been determined by the apostolic see" (MPL, 20, 776). On the same day he wrote to Rufus and the bishops of Thessaly that it was from Peter "as source that ecclesiastical discipline spread through all the churches." Nicaea did not venture to make a decree concerning the bishop of Rome, Boniface declared, since it recognized that nothing could be added to his merit. "It is certain," he declared, "that this church is to the churches dispersed throughout the whole world as the head is to the members. Whoever separates himself from [this church] becomes an exile from the Christian religion, since he cannot begin to be part of its structure" (Mirbt-Aland, no. 422). Again on the same day, he wrote to Rufus and the bishops of Macedonia that "none has ever been so rash as to oppose the apostolic summit (*culmini*), a decision of which may not be considered anew. No one rebels against it, unless he wants to be self-condemned" (MPL, 20, 782).

The western emperor Honorius (395-423) seconded the position of the bishop of Rome, and Theodosius relented and rescinded his edict.[18]

The case of Anthony of Fussala also raises some questions. A mere reader and an emergency replacement candidate for the episcopal vacancy at Fussala, Anthony turned out to be a tyrant and dishonest to boot. A synod of nearby bishops deprived him of his jurisdiction but not of his rank. His primate, who had consecrated him on Augustine's misguided recommendation, exculpated Anthony. Thereupon the latter made contact with Boniface either personally or by letter. The bishop of Rome also acquitted him, "if he has faithfully indicated the state of things to us" (MPL, 33, 955). Rumor had it in Fussala that the civil power would now reinstate Anthony, whereupon the reluctant Fussalians protested to Celestine, who had succeeded Boniface. Augustine, who had recommended Anthony for consecration in the first place, also wrote to Celestine, asking the bishop of Rome to reverse the action of the African primate. Augustine's letter is interesting because it refers to three cases where, it seems, the bishop of Rome had intervened in the affairs of the African church (ibid.).[19] But they are described as recent, that is, they could have taken place in the interim when the church in Africa was awaiting confirmation of the fact that the [Sardican] canons that Zosimus had cited were really Nicene. The attitude of the North African church toward Rome is complex in this period. The cases that Augustine cites may illustrate some of this ambivalence.

At all events, in 424 the synod of Carthage had had once more to take up the case of Apiarius. Certain now that they had Nicaea on their side, the bishops of Africa upbraided the bishop of Rome for sheltering clergy from other jurisdictions, since Nicaea had put the clergy of all grades—including bishops—under the discipline of their own metropolitans. (Actually canon 5 of Nicaea did not expressly refer to bishops.) The fathers of Nicaea, the Africans averred, did not foresee that "the grace of the Holy Spirit through which the right course would be apparent would be lacking in any province for the priests of Christ to hold to it wisely and consistently." The Africans express doubt that anyone could believe "that our God can inspire any single individual with justice and deny it to numberless priests gathered in a synod." With a politeness that did not wholly conceal their anger, they told the bishop of Rome not to send "your clerical executors" to Africa and expressed their confidence that the church there would be spared having further to endure Faustinus, the chief legate of the bishop of Rome (Mirbt-Aland, no. 425).

Celestine (422-432)

Celestine's intervention in the controversy between Cyril of Alexandria and the Antioch-trained Nestorius (died 451?) seems at this distance from the events to have been premature.

In evaluating this controversy, due weight must be given to the traditional rivalry between the great sees of Alexandria and Antioch and its personal embodiment in the two main protagonists. Nevertheless, many historians see in this episode an illustration of a persistent theme in the relations of the churches of the East with the bishop of Rome. The Easterners are willing to accord a kind of primacy, to the see of Rome on a political-historical basis. Thus when the Roman see enunciates its claims to universal primacy, the Eastern churches listen and politely refrain from explicitly rejecting these claims, in part at least out of a genuine respect for the see of Peter. The bishops of Rome in turn seem at least at times to have interpreted this Eastern silence as concurrence in the Roman position.

In April 430 Cyril appealed to Celestine for support in his campaign against Nestorius (MPG, 77, 80-89). The bishop of Rome promptly complied; at a Roman synod in August of 430 Celestine justified the designation of the Blessed Virgin Mary as *theotokos* by appealing to utterances of Ambrose, Damasus, and Hilary of Poitiers (315?-368?) (MPL, 50, 457).

Celestine communicated the verdict of the Roman synod to Cyril of Alexandria and instructed him: "Taking to yourself the authority of our see and acting in our place, you shall carry out this sentence with resolute vigor: That either [Nestorius] shall within ten days . . . condemn by means of a written profession his wicked assertions, and shall affirm that with reference to the birth of Christ our God he will hold the faith which the Roman church, the church of your holiness, and the Catholic religion holds." If he fails to do so, let him know that "he is in every way removed from our body." The judgment of the bishop of Rome about Nestorius is "the divine sentence of our Christ" (Mirbt-Aland, no. 427).[20]

The letter of Celestine demanding that Nestorius recant within ten days reached the latter's hands on December 7, 430. The sentence would have then have taken effect on December 17, since Nestorius did not recant. Nevertheless he was haled before the Council of Ephesus in 431.

At the council the Roman legate Philip asserted: "No one doubts, and indeed it has been known in all ages, that the holy and most blessed Peter, the prince and head of the apostles, the pillar of the faith, the foundation of the Catholic Church . . . even to the present and always lives and judges in his successors. Our holy and most blessed Pope Celestine the bishop is therefore assuredly in due order his successor and lieutenant" (ACO, I/I, iii, 60).[21]

To Celestine the council wrote an account of its transactions which begins by praising his zeal for piety, his admirable solicitude for orthodoxy, and his customary testing of every major issue and "making [his] own all the concerns of the churches." Having learned of his deposition of the proponents of Pelagianism, the members of the council "rule that the matters which [his] reverence has determined are to remain valid and firm," (MPL, 50, 512-513.521).

To the emperors the council wrote: "The men who came disclosed the opinion of an entire synod of the West through a letter to this our synod and they showed that they agreed with us in faith and religion. . . . Your pieties may rest assured that the judgment which lately went out from us is the one common sentence of the whole world" (ACO, I/I, iii, 64).

Sixtus III (432-440)

Sixtus III was able early in his episcopate to rejoice at the restoration of intercommunion between the great sees of Antioch and Alexandria in 433, although their supporters on both sides were less than happy with the formula of reunion. He also found it necessary to resist new efforts of Proclus of Constantinople (died 446/447) to interfere in the vicariate of Thessalonica.

In the compilation, "Authoritative Utterances of Past Bishops of the Apostolic See on the Grace of God" (*Quia nulli;* "Syllabus on Grace") (435), variously attributed to Prosper of Aquitaine (390?-463?) and to Leo while he was still archdeacon at Rome, the author noted that the Semi-Augustinians "profess to follow and approve only what the most sacred see of the blessed Apostle Peter has approved and taught through the ministry of its presidents." He stated that "the apostolic prelates made [certain decisions of the African synods] their own when they approved them." The synod of Carthage of 418 "embraced the position of the apostolic see." The "sanctions of the most blessed and apostolic see" are "inviolable." "For the establishment of the grace of God . . . we believe it to be quite enough to believe whatever . . . the writings of the apostolic see have taught us" (MPL, 45, 1756-1760).

Leo the Great (440-461)

The episcopate of Leo, whose experience as a deacon extended back to the period of Celestine, saw the claims of the bishop of Rome reach their zenith during this period. "Blessed Peter . . . has not given up the helm of the church which he received. . . . Therefore if anything is rightly done and rightly decreed by us, if anything is obtained from God's mercy by daily petitions, it is due to his works and merits whose power lives in his see and whose authority prevails there." In the successors of Peter he is being honored "in whom the concern that all shepherds have for the care of the sheep entrusted to them continues and whose dignity sustains no loss even in the case of an unworthy heir."[22] Peter is "not only the president of this see, but also the primate of all the bishops. Therefore . . . believe that he is speaking to you in whose stead we act" (MPL, 54, 146-147).

"The most blessed Peter . . . does not cease to preside over his see and obtains an abiding partnership with the eternal Priest." The stability that Peter received from Christ "he conveyed also to his successors." "All parts of the church are ruled by his care and enriched by his help" (MPL, 54, 153).[23]

In exercising his spiritual authority Leo availed himself of the enforcement power of the imperial government, to which he attributed a concern for the true religion equal to his own. (To the "princes of our time" he concedes a "priestly teaching role" [*sacerdotalem doctrinam*] and "priestly holiness" [MPL, 54, 1036.1038]). For example, he appealed to the emperor for political assistance against the obstinate Manichaeans of Old Rome and Valentinian III (424-454) obligingly banished them; an imperial edict of 445 further punished them by depriving them of their civil rights.

Within the patriarchate of the West, Hilary of Arles (403-449), the metropolitan of Vienne, ambitiously envisioned a kind of regional authority for himself that would cover all of southern Gaul, that is, the territory that still remained within the empire. When Hilary tried in 445 to depose two bishops, one of them in another province, Leo intervened to restore them. By acting as Hilary had done, Leo said, the bishop had quit the path that the fathers had handed down (MPL, 54, 629). Leo deprived Hilary of his rank and privileges as a metropolitan and restricted him to "the priesthood of his own city alone," that is, to his own diocese of Arles, which was reduced from a metropolitical see to a mere bishopric (MPL, 54, 635).[24] The imperial decree that Leo obtained to enforce his sentence bases the primacy of the Roman see on the "merit of St. Peter, who is chief of the episcopal circle, the rank of the city of Rome, and the authority of the sacred synod." It also observes that "this same sentence would have been valid throughout the Gauls without imperial sanction, for what"—the emperors ask rhetorically—"is not allowed in the churches to the authority of so great a pontiff?" (Mirbt-Aland, no. 455). This meant that the civil authority of the Western empire recognized without restriction the power of the bishop of Rome within what has come to be called the Roman patriarchate.

Leo's *Tomos* of 449 to Flavian may well be the most important theological document framed by any bishop of Rome up to then. But when Leo's legates attempted to read it at the Council of Ephesus that same year, Dioscorus of Alexandria (died 454) prevented them from doing so. The council affirmed—against the claims of Constantinople but in line with the traditional position of Rome—the primacy of the see of Alexandria in the East. It also endorsed the monophysite doctrine of Eutyches—against both Flavian and Leo's *Tomos*. Thus reduced to dire straits, Flavian appealed to the supreme juridical authority of the Roman see. Leo responded with a letter in which he gave the council of Ephesus the name by which it has become generally known, the Latrocinium, and declared its decisions null and void.

Dioscorus excommunicated the bishop of Rome (Mansi, 6, 1048).

Theodoret of Cyrrhus (393?-458?), whom the Council of Ephesus of 449 also deposed, like Flavian appealed to the "right and just tribunal" of the bishop of Rome and agreed to respect whatever verdict Leo would hand down (MPL, 54, 852).[25] In a supporting letter to Renatus the presbyter, Theodoret assigns "many reasons" for the hegemony of Rome, chiefly the fact that "it has remained free from all heretical stench" and that "no one holding false opinions has ever sat upon its [episcopal] throne, but it has kept the grace of the apostles undefiled" (MPL, 83, 1324-1325).[26]

In the letter in which Leo protested to Theodosius II against the actions of the Council of Ephesus of 449, he, like Zosimus before him, appealed to the canons of Sardica as Nicene, even though the error of Zosimus had been exposed to both Boniface and Celestine (MPL, 54, 831).

Theodosius' horse conveniently reared and threw his imperial rider, who died from his injuries. Marcian (450-457), the late emperor's brother-in-law and successor, called another council at Chalcedon in 451.

In the events of 449 through 451 one can see traces of a kind of bipolar thrust that intermittently characterizes imperial policy in this period. Whenever strife in the church over a given issue begins to reach an intolerable level, the emperor seeks to unite the church around some orthodoxy. Depending on his own orientation (or that of his more influential advisers), it may be about the regnant orthodoxy of the New Rome or it may be the traditional orthodoxy for which Old Rome stands.

For his part, Leo saw his *Tomos* to Flavian as finally decisive, and insisted that the council accept it without debate. When it was read at the second session, the bishops acclaimed it: "This is the faith of the fathers; this is the faith of the apostles; this is the faith of all of us; Peter has spoken through Leo" (ACO, II/I, ii, 81 [277]).

On the principle that the Roman see has the authority to endorse or reverse all synods, even ecumenical councils, one of the charges that Lucentius, a Roman representative at Chalcedon, leveled against Dioscorus was that he had presumed in unlawful fashion to hold a synod without the consent of the Roman see (ACO, II/I, i, 65).

Leo's legates to the council at Chalcedon affirmed that the

bishop of Rome is "the bishop of all the churches" and the "bishop of the universal church" (ACO, II/I, i, 65; ii, 93.141). In the letters of accusation against Dioscorus from his own see, Leo is called "ecumenical archbishop and patriarch of Great Rome" (ACO, II/I, ii, 15[211].20 [216]). The Roman legates announce the condemnation of Dioscorus in this way: "The most holy and blessed Leo, archbishop of the great and elder Rome, through us and through this present most holy council, together with the thrice blessed and all glorious Peter the apostle, who is the rock and support of the Catholic Church and the foundation of the orthodox faith, has stripped him of the episcopal rank and removed from him all priestly dignity" (ACO, II/I, ii, 29 [225]).

The creed of Chalcedon gives clear evidence of its debt to the *Tomos.*

Leo's authority was not able to achieve the enforcement of the council's decrees, particularly in Syria and Egypt. More was involved than a rejection of Rome's right to determine the dogma of the church. Local pride, political rivalries, and the rising tide of antiimperialist feeling were also contributing factors. In Alexandria the monophysite Timothy Aelurus (died 477) succeeded in displacing the new orthodox patriarch Proterius (452-457), whom the populace finally murdered in his own church.[27] The chaotic conditions of the church in the East provided Leo in 453 with the occasion for appointing a permanent vicar, Julian (fl. 448-457), at the imperial court; his duties were to discharge the concern of the bishop of Rome for orthodoxy in the Eastern empire, to counsel the imperial court, and to report to Rome on a continuing basis about events that took place in the Eastern church. Julian was in a sense the precursor of the later papal *apocrisiarii* in Constantinople.

Even with these limitations, Chalcedon was not an unmixed victory for Leo. In the absence of his legates, the council passed its 28th canon, which expanded the third canon of Constantinople I to accord to the patriarchate of Constantinople a primacy of authority and honor above that of the other Eastern patriarchates (Mirbt-Aland, no. 456). When the Roman legates returned to the council the next day, they tried to reopen the question, asserting that those who had signed the canon had done so under duress. The signatories rejected the charge. The legates cited the sixth canon of Nicaea from what seems to be a late fourth century Latin version: "The Roman Church always had the primacy. Let Egypt therefore so hold itself that the bishop of Alexandria have authority over all, for this is also the custom of the Roman bishop. So he too who is established at Antioch. And in the other provinces let the privileges of the churches be preserved" (ACO, II/I, iii, 95[454]). To the final protest of the Roman legates, the judges responded: "The whole council has approved what we proposed" (ACO, II/I, iii, 99[458]).

The council, the emperor, and Anatolius of Constantinople (died 458) all sought Leo's approval of canon 28 (Mirbt-Aland, no. 457; MPL, 54, 974; 980-984). Anatolius suggested that Leo's delegates had not understood his mind. Leo proved him wrong by himself condemning the canon: "We dismiss as invalid, and by the authority of the blessed apostle Peter we totally disannul by a general decree in all ecclesiastical cases" all "resolutions of bishops that are in conflict with the rules of the holy canons set up at Nicaea" (MPL, 54, 1000). But Leo's renewed assertion of the authority of his office could not halt the development that was making the bishop of New Rome the leader of the entire Eastern church.[28]

The Thessalonian vicariate, administered at the time by Anastasius, exhibited difficulties of its own during Leo's episcopate. The unwise interventions of Anastasius in the affairs of his metropolitans compelled Leo to remind his vicegerent that the latter had been called to participate in the concern of the bishop of Rome for the vicariate, but not to exercise the fulness of the Roman authority. In a letter to Anastasius Leo sets forth his conception of the proper organization of the church. All bishops have a common dignity, but not the same jurisdictions. The bishops of a province are under the one who has the "first opinion," that is, the metropolitan. The metropolitans of a patriarchate are under one who has an even "ampler concern," that is, the patriarch. "Through [the last-named] the care of the entire church flows together to the single see of Peter." (Mirbt-Aland, no. 444)

Leo's courageous confrontation of the invading Vandal king Gaiseric (Genseric) (428-477) in 455 saved the city of Rome from fire, although not from a fortnight of looting and pillage that left its people alive but reduced to the lowest poverty (Mirbt-Aland, no. 454). This second sack of Rome to all intents and purposes marked the end of imperial power in the ancient capital and established the bishops of the city as the real advocates, protectors, and governors of its people.

In Africa the Vandal invasion had created chaos in the Catholic church of that province. As a result some of the surviving sees had been filled in ways that violated the pertinent canons. Other abuses had likewise crept in. Leo's interventions[29] met no resistance from the African Catholics in this ambiguous situation.

In death Leo received an honor not accorded to any of his predecessors. They buried him in the Basilica of St. Peter that Constantine had built over the traditional site of Peter's grave. Considering Leo's conviction that he was in a mystical sense Peter himself and considering Leo's role in the story of the evolution of the claims to powers of the bishop of Rome, there is an undeniable propriety about his interment.

To summarize from all of this material:

(1) The bishops of Rome by the time of Leo have developed a self-image which represents them as the heirs and successors and, in a sense, the continuing embodiments of Peter. They feel endowed over against the universal church with all of the authority that their exegesis of the Petrine passages of the New Testament gave to the prince of the apostles.

(2) This view is generally accepted in the patriarchate of the West. The exception is Africa, which did not totally reject the authority of Rome but which resisted the uninvited interventions of the bishop of Rome into the second quarter of the fifth century.

(3) This view is tolerated in the Christian East when it is in the interest of the East to do so; otherwise it tends to be rejected in practice. (There are at the same time some strands of Eastern thinking that recognize a Roman primacy of considerable dimensions.)

(4) The bishops of Rome frequently think, write, and act in a "patriarchal" (or regional) fashion rather than in a "papal" fashion.

(5) The bishops of Rome lack the power to enforce their decisions outside the patriarchate of the West and even there they often must and do solicit the assistance of the civil authorities.

3

THE PAPACY IN THE MIDDLE AGES

George H. Tavard

Since it is not possible to cover everything between St. Gregory the Great and the Reformation, I will select some high points of the development of the papal idea.

The Eighth Century

The eighth century is a transition period—during which three doctrines on the Primacy may be discerned.

The *oriental doctrine* predominates at Byzantium, in the other Eastern Patriarchates and at the iconodulic councils (Nicaea, 787). In keeping with the 6th canon of Nicaea and the 28th of Chalcedon, the pope of Rome is the first bishop, chiefly on account of the traditional imperial standing of the city of Rome. The primacy is a "presidency in love"; it entails duties more than rights: the chief duty is that of assistance and support to the bishops everywhere for the guardianship of the faith, which is the joint responsibility of all.

The *doctrine of the Franks*, manifested in the policy of Charlemagne, in the theological statements of the Frankish councils and the *Libri Carolini* (c. 793) and in the practise of the bishops of the Empire of the Franks. The bishop of Rome is the first bishop chiefly because he has succeeded Peter, through whom the power of the keys was conferred on all the bishops. Like all episcopal authority, the primacy is to be exercised according to the rules laid down by the Holy Spirit through the holy councils and canons. Strict boundaries are set to the exercise of power on the part of the pope: he must respect the consensus of the churches, as reflected in the canons, and the authority of bishops and metropolitans as defined by the canons. A right of supervision is recognized, so that, in cases of conflict between bishops, appeal to the pope is proper. In matters of doctrine, however, the Frankish bishops function independently of Rome. Although election of bishops and archbishops is done locally, the practise of asking the pope to grant the *pallium* as a sign of archepiscopal authority is growing; this practise was imposed by Charlemagne in his territories. Interpreted by Nicholas I and John VIII, this meant that the metropolitan receives his jurisdiction from the pope through the grant of the *pallium*.

The *Roman doctrine*. The title "universal pope," used by some of the Greek and Syrian popes of the sixth and seventh centuries, but rejected by Gregory the Great, is not used in official Roman titles. The title originally corresponded to similar oriental titles used by the pope of Alexandria or the *catholicos* of the Menophysites: it connoted supreme authority within a certain territory. However, Roman theology associated it with the theory of Peter's universal primacy, so that it came to connote the universal authority of the bishop of Rome as Peter's successor. During this period, the letters of Gregory II (715-731) and Gregory III (731-741) relative to the mission of St. Boniface in Germany, and the dealings of Zacharias (741-752) with the Frankish bishops under Peppin and especially his strict orders to Boniface not to introduce Gallican customs to Germany show that, in Rome, the chief standard of doctrinal and disciplinary orthodoxy is agreement with the Roman see rather than fidelity to the canons inherited from the past. The principle, formulated in the Symmachan forgeries (c. 500), but already implied in the writings of Pope Gelasius (492-496), that *prima sedes a nemine judicatur*, is frequently appealed to.

The Ninth Century

Several events of the ninth century should be noted.

The appearance of the *False Decretals* (*Collectio Isidori Mercatoris, Capitula Angilramni, Capitula* of *Benedictus Levita, Collectio Hispana-Gallica Augustudonensis*). Composed between 847 (reference is made in them to the death of Otgard of Mainz, d. 847) and 852 (when Hincmar of Reims quotes them), the Isidorian Collection appears in Gaul, probably among Hincmar's numerous opponents. Used by

Rothad of Soissons and Hincmar of Laon, it is introduced to Rome by Rothad in October 864. The other collections are attributed to the same source. Their original purpose was to strengthen episcopal power against the king and the metropolitan. However, by reserving to the pope the right to judge bishops (hitherto held by Metropolitans), they re-inforced papal authority. Used by Hincmar's adversaries and occasionally by Hincmar himself (who, however, doubted their authenticity), they were not used extensively by the popes before Gregory VII.

The disagreements between Hincmar of Reims and several popes (Nicholas I, 858-867; Hadrian II, 867-872; John VIII, 872-882) on the rights and authority of metropolitans highlight the conflict between the Frankish and the Roman conceptions of the primacy. For Hincmar, the primacy derives from the gift of the keys to Peter and is regulated by the canons (especially the canons of Sardica, 343). Yet the authority of metropolitans and bishops derives from the same source, for the power of the keys was given, through Peter, to all the bishops. Its exercise is also regulated by the canons (Sardica, and also the "African Canons" of The Council of Carthage of 418). Accordingly, the diverse seats of authority should work together in the consensus of the whole church, respecting each other's tasks, functions and rights. The primacy is regulated by the canonical tradition.

The Roman pontiffs, however, especially Nicholas and John, hold that the power of the keys allows them to introduce new regulations and canons, that may depart from the older rules. Bishops and metropolitans must operate within the limits assigned to them by the holy see, where Peter's authority perdures.

There is a serious conflict between Rome (Nicholas II, Hadrian II, John VIII) and Byzantium over the election of Photius to the patriarchate, over the mission of Cyril and Methodius in Moravia and over the Bulgarian mission. The attitude of the popes seems dominated by the determination to make Moravia a Germano-Latin rather than a Slavonic-Byzantine church, to deny King Boris of Bulgaria the right to give the Bulgarian church a Byzantine orientation and, in general, to restrict the authority of the patriarch of Byzantium by withdrawing from his jurisdiction some of the lands over which he exercises a de facto primacy.

In some conflicts with kings, especially with Lothair II (825-869) over the question of Lothair's divorce from Queen

Tewtberga, the popes, especially Nicholas I, speak as though they could judge the legitimacy of the king's authority: they proceed on the assumption that the king's legitimacy depends on his Christian behavior.

The Tenth Century

These positions are maintained through the papal decadence at the end of the ninth century and during the tenth century. However, the posthumous anathematisms against Pope Formosus (891-896) by his successors, the depositions (by popular pressure, royal power and politics, or synodal action) of John XII (955-964) in May 963, of Benedict V (964-966) in June 964, the refusal of the bishops of "Italy, Germany, France and Gaul" to recognize the election of John XVI in 996, the successive depositions of Benedict IX (1032-1044) in 1044, 1045, and 1047, that of Gregory VI (1045-1046) at the synod of Sutri (1046), show that the principle, *prima sedes a nemine judicatur*, is not applied, although it is theoretically maintained by the popes. At the end of the tenth century, the quarrel between Gerbert d'Aurillac and Arnulf, both claiming the see of Reims, brought into the open the principle adopted by Gerbert and his supporters, especially Arnulf of Orleans: the privilege of the see of Rome depends upon the wisdom, virtue and legality of the exercise of authority by the pope. The venality of the popes of the time made it impossible to accept their judgment. In 999, thanks to the intervention of Otto III, Gerbert was elected Pope as Sylvester II (999-1003). He ended his conflict with Arnulf, whom he had previously called "a heathen and a publican," by confirming him as archbishop of Reims. He did not repudiate his previous qualifications of papal authority.

Gregory VI

A new papal order begins with the election of Gregory VI (1045-1046), the first reforming pope of the period. Through some remarkable personalities (especially Leo IX, 1049-1054), the reform movement culminated with the pontificate of Gregory VII (1073-1085). The energies of the reforming popes were directed equally against simony in the clergy (the "re-ordinations") and against the effective power which, since the end of the ninth century, the princes exercised over the higher clergy by controlling the elections of bishops (the "Investiture" question). Thus they reasserted, or asserted in a new way, the papal doctrine of authority. Gregory VII gave it its sharpest formulation in the *Dictatus Papae* (March 1075), a series of 27 propositions, which assert the primacy of the Roman pontiff, his legislative authority and his power over councils, his jurisdiction over local churches, especially over bishops, his judiciary authority, and the universal right of appeal to Rome, his immunity from judgment, his right to depose emperors. The theological foundation for all this is contained in Proposition I: *Quod Romana Ecclesia a solo Domino sit fundata.* In his own legislation, Gregory VII makes ample use of the *False Decretals* of the nineth century.

During this period, two distinct conceptions of papal authority are found in Rome itself. With Leo IX and his chief advisor, Humbert de Moyenmoutiers, the seat of the highest authority is not the pope alone, but the Roman church. Although this term remains somewhat vague, it implies at least that the pope governs the church together with the cardinals, who share his authority and responsibility. With Gregory VII, against some of the cardinals who accuse him of tyranny, the pope alone has supreme power: all authority in the church comes from him.

The reform is made possible largely by the influence of the Order of Cluny, itself exempt from episcopal jurisdiction and centralized in its government. It is embodied in a new way of electing the pope (decree of Nicholas II, 1059) and in new canonical collections, centered on papal authority.

The ecclesiology of Leo IX–Humbert, however, clashes headlong with that of the patriarchs of Byzantium. In 1954, Humbert excommunicates Patriarch Cerularius. The Orient, meanwhile, develops no new ecclesiology. It remains on its former positions, until, in the twelfth century, the idea of the pentarchy (especially with Balsomon) becomes the orthodox equivalent of the Latin monarchy: the pope is the first of the five patriarchs, with no authority over them.

Scholasticism

Several elements of the theory of papal authority during the great perod of Scholasticism are worth mentioning.

Among the canonists, the church is described as the *corpus christianorum,* patterned on the political conceptions of the times concerning the organization of society and the source of authority. With Huguccio (canonist at Bologna, teacher of Innocent III) and Hostiensis (d. 1271), the church is a corporation, where power is shared by all. This will be one of the sources of the conciliarist theories of papal authority that will be put forward during the Western schism. On the basis of the Roman Law principle, *par in parem non habet imperium,* the decretists generally hold that no pope is bound by his predecessors's decrees. This does not endanger the continuity of faith. For, on the one hand, they also generally believe, with the theologians of the period, that all Christian doctrine *de fide et moribus* is already in scripture. On the other, the Roman Law principle can only apply to what the church has the power to change, namely, disciplinary decisions. It has no relevance for dogmatic definitions of the revelation. In matters of faith, the popes are themselves bound by the revelation, when encapsulated in the dogmatic decisions of their predecessors.

The personal infallibility of the pope as *successor Petri* or *vicarius Christi* is therefore not a canonical thesis. Yet the great scholastics, Bonaventure, Thomas Aquinas, John Duns Scot, favor some form of this conception.

The bull *Unam sanctam* (1302) of Boniface VIII (1294-1303) comes at the end of a long evolution of canonical thought. In the *Decree* of Gratian (c. 1140) spiritual and temporal authorities are independent, although the prince is subject to the spiritual power (bishops, pope) for what is spiritual. The image of the "two swords" has been used for a long time with diverse interpretations, some of which do not refer to authority. By and large, it designates the association of temporal power (the prince) and spiritual power (bishops, pope) in the oneness of Christian society. The decretals of Innocent III (1198-1216) continue to recognize the distinction between the two powers; but Innocent III subordinates the temporal to the spiritual even in its own order by virtue of his interpretation of the papal *plenitudo potestatis.* The Roman pontiff, who alone has received *plenitudo potestatis,* calls others to *pars sollicitudinis.* The creation of the Latin patriarchate of Constantinople after the conquest of this city by the crusaders (Fourth Crusade, 1202) shows that Innocent placed the traditional patriarchs on no higher level than primates and metropolitans, whose status simply corresponds to a greater share of *pars sollicitudinis.* This line of thought is embodied in the bull *Unam sanctam:* submission to the Roman pontiff is necessary to salvation.

4. In the conflict between John XXII (1313-1334) and

the Franciscans over the poverty of Christ, Michael of Cesena (d. 1342) and William of Ockham (c. 1285-1349) see a dogma of faith in the bull *Exiit qui seminat* (1279), by which Nicholas III has approved the Franciscan way of life. John XXII, however, revokes *Exiit* in his own bull *Cum inter nonnullos* (1323). In the course of the conflict, both sides elaborate detailed doctrines of papal infallibility, William of Ockham to prove that John XXII is a heretic and therefore no true pope, Guido Terreni (d. 1342) to show the continuity of teaching between John XXII and his predecessors. This monarchic conception of papal power, however, is contradicted, in the fourteenth century itself, by other theologies. The Dominicans, John of Paris (d. 1302) and Petrus Paludanus (d. 1342), Dante Allighieri (1265-1321), Marsilius of Padua (1290-1343) defend other theories of papal authority.

The Western Schism

The Western schism (1378-1417) had the effect of drawing attention away from the pope as traditional symbol and guardian of the church's unity, toward other constituents of the church and their function in relation to unity. The conciliarist movement resulted from the current failure of the papacy. It was partly fed by revival of pre-monarchic conceptions of the papacy, like that of Hincmar. In keeping with the replacement of feudal by corporative relationships in society, it also saw the rise of a populist conception of the church as the *congregatio fidelium* where power resides in the people: this could find support in the tradition of the decretists. It also was a fertile ground for the spread of anti-papalist ecclesiologies, from that of Ockham to the less orthodox views of Wycliffe (d. 1385) and John Huss (d. 1416).

Conciliarism triumphed at the fifth session of the Council of Constance (1414-1418), when the decree *Haec sancta* declared that all members of the church, the pope included, must obey the council in matters regarding the faith, the ending of the schism, and the general reform of the church *in capite et in membris*. However, once conciliarism had restored unity to the church, the attempt to insure a permanently conciliarist form of government (Council of Basle, 1431) failed. The acceptance of the decree *Haec sancta* by popes Martin V and Eugenius IV is a debated matter among historians. In any case, conciliarism did not last in Rome.

The influential *Summa de Ecclesia*, by John of Turrecremata (d. 1468), again embodied a papal, monarchic conception of the Roman primacy. Conciliarism continued to be taught in many universities, notably in Paris. It was actively supported by the kings of France and a number of French bishops and theologians (Pragmatic Sanction of Bourges, 1438; Council of Pisa, 1511).

The actions of the Renaissance popes were largely dominated by their efforts to reaffirm the papal monarchy in theory and to reinforce it in practise. Eugene IV condemned the Council of Basle after approving its convocation. The Decree of Union with the Greeks at the Council of Florence (1439-1445) included a definition of the universal primacy of the Roman pontiff. Aeneas Sylvius Piccolomini (d. 1461), who was a convinced conciliarist at Basle, became an ardent papalist after his election to the papacy as Pius II in 1458 (*Execrabilis*, 1460). Against Alexander VI, Savonarola (1452-1498) vainly urged the church at large and the princes and bishops to hold a council that would depose the pope. Julius II called the fifth Council of the Lateran against the French-conciliarist Council of Pisa: at its eleventh session, (1516), Pope Leo X promulgated the bull *Pastor aeternus*, where he re-affirmed that obedience to the Roman pontiff is necessary to salvation. This brings us to the time of the Protestant Reformation.

4

THE BULL *UNAM SANCTAM* OF BONIFACE VIII

George H. Tavard

The bull was issued on November 18, 1302 by Boniface VIII (1294-1303) against the demands of Philip the Fair of France (1285-1314). The king's claim to dominion over the temporalities of the church in France ran afoul of the bull *Clericis laicos* of 1296. Defending the more traditional practice of fiscal exemption of the clergy (and trying to cut off some of the sources from which the kings funded their wars), the pope confronted the fundamental problem of the relations between the two powers, temporal and spiritual. This problem had been at the core of the Gregorian reform since the beginning. *Unam sanctam* formulated Boniface's theoretical solution. It affirmed the total freedom of the church from interference by temporal powers, by asserting the subservience of the temporal to the spiritual power, which was identified with that of the pope.

The practical result was not exactly the one the pope expected. Boniface was arrested at Anagni by the king's chancellor, Guillaume de Nogaret, and released shortly before his death. In Paris, theologians and canonists from the king's side issued a protest against the bull, though the greatest theologian of the time, John Duns Scot, did not sign the protest. The move of the papacy to Avignon, under Boniface's second successor, Clement V, was an indirect result of *Unam sanctam*.

Text of the Bull

We are obliged by faith to believe and hold—and we do firmly believe and sincerely confess—that there is one Holy Catholic and Apostolic Church, and that outside this Church there is neither salvation nor remission of sins. . . . In which Church there is one Lord, one faith, one baptism. At the time of the flood there was one ark of Noah, symbolizing the one Church; this was completed in one cubit and had one, namely Noah, as helmsman and captain; outside which all things on earth, we read, were destroyed. . . . Of this one and only Church there is one body and one head—not two heads, like a monster—namely Christ, and Christ's vicar is Peter, and Peter's successor, for the Lord said to Peter himself, 'Feed My sheep.' 'My sheep' He said in general, not these or those sheep; wherefore He is understood to have committed them all to him. Therefore, if the Greeks or others say that they were not committed to Peter and his successors, they necessarily confess that they are not of Christ's sheep, for the Lord says in John, 'There is one fold and one shepherd.'

And we learn from the words of the Gospel that in this Church and in her power are two swords, the spiritual and the temporal. For when the apostles said, 'Behold, here' (that is, in the Church, since it was the apostles who spoke) 'are two swords'—the Lord did not reply, 'It is too much,' but 'It is enough.' Truly he who denies that the temporal sword is in the power of Peter, misunderstands the words of the Lord, 'Put up thy sword into the sheath.' Both are in the power of the Church, the spiritual sword and the material. But the latter is to be used for the Church, the former by her; the former by the priest, the latter by kings and captains but at the will and by the permission of the priest. The one sword, then, should be under the other, and temporal authority subject to spiritual. For when the apostle says 'there is no power but of God, and the powers that be are ordained of God,' they would not be so ordained were not one sword made subject to the other. . . .

Thus, concerning the Church and her power, is the prophecy of Jeremiah fulfilled, 'See, I have this day set thee over the nations and over the kingdoms,' etc. If, therefore, the earthly power err, it shall be judged by the spiritual power; and if a lesser power err, it shall be judged by a greater. But if the supreme power err, it can only be judged by God, not by man; for the testimony of the apostle is 'The spiritual man judgeth all things, yet he himself is judged of no man.' For this authority, although given to a man and exercised by a man, is not human, but rather divine, given at God's mouth to Peter and established on a rock for him and his successors in Him whom he confessed, the Lord saying to Peter himself, 'Whatsoever thou shalt bind,' etc. Whoever therefore resists this power thus ordained of God, resists the ordinance of God. . . . Furthermore we declare, state, define and pronounce that it is altogether necessary to salvation for every human creature to be subject to the Roman pontiff.[1]

Analysis of the Bull

The following ideas appear successively:
n. 870 (The numbers refer to DS):
- Statement of faith in the church, outside of which there is no salvation. According to an old tradition, the text

does not say: "to believe *in* the church," but "to believe the church" (*Ecclesiam credere . . .*).[2]

- The church "represents one mystical body", whose head is Christ.
- The Church is one (*una*), with unity of one Lord, one faith, one baptism.
- Analogy of Noah's ark, which had one governor, and outside of which there was no salvation.

n. 871

- The church is also unique (*unica*).
- Christ is the soul and the head of it.
- This soul corresponds to a single body, called the church. There is oneness of the spouse, the faith, the sacraments, the love.
- Analogy of the seamless tunic.

n. 872

- This one body of the one and single church is not a two-headed monster; it has one head.
- This head is Christ and his vicar, who is Peter and Peter's successor. Quotation from John 21:17. The word "my" (in "my sheep") identify the sheep as all the sheep of the Lord.
- Conclusion about those who claim that they have not been entrusted to Peter (Greeks and others): if so, they are not of the flock of Christ. Quotation from John 10:16: There is only one flock, one shepherd.

n. 873

- In this power, there are two swords, spiritual and temporal.
- The two swords are in the power of the church.
- The material sword is used *for* the church, the other *by* the church.
- The spiritual sword belongs to the *sacerdos,* the other is in the hands of kings and soldiers, but at the discretion of the *sacerdos.*
- Argumentation from the concept of hierarchy: the spiritual is higher than the temporal.
- The spiritual power can "institute" the earthly, and "judge if it is good".
- Therefore the earthly power is judged by the spiritual.
- The inferior spiritual power is judged by the higher.
- The highest spiritual power is judged only by God. Quotation from 1 Corinthians 2:15.

n. 874

- This power, although exercised through a man, is not human, but divine.
- It was given in Christ to Peter and his successors. The quotation (Matt. 16:19) refers to the power of the keys: *Quodcumque . . .*
- He who resists this power resists God.
- He who asserts two principles is a heretic (Manichee). Argument from Genesis, 1:1: *In principio coelum Deus creavit et terram.*

n. 875

- "We declare, state, define and pronounce that it is altogether necessary to salvation for every human creature to be subject to the Roman pontiff."

Theology of the Bull

Several theological lines converge and meet in *Unam sanctam:*[3]

The "mystical" conception of the celestial and ecclesiastical hierarchies, deriving from the writings of (Pseudo-) Denys the Areopagyte, and significantly altered in the Middle Ages. It was in favor with the Franciscan School, especially St. Bonaventure. As the orthodox Franciscans, reacting against the heterodoxy of the Spirituals, were staunch promoters of papal supremacy, the expression of this supremacy in terms of the hierarchy of creation came, as it were, naturally, although this implied, in fact, a gross distortion of what Denys had meant by hierarchy.[4]

In the same line, the exegesis of scriptural passages is highly spiritual, not to say allegorical. This was a common method of illustrating theological or canonical positions.

The theology of the *corpus christianorum*. It is significant that the bull does not say: "The church *is* the mystical body . . .", but, "The church represents one mystical body." The mystical body in question is not exactly what we would put under this expression today: it is Christendom, the sum total of all Christian believers in both their spiritual and their social interrelationships. The *corpus* (body, with the connotation of order) is visible; yet it has an invisible, mystical, dimension. These two aspects persist in the head of the body; and therefore, Christ, being now invisible, mystical, is visible in the pope, so that both constitute one head of the body on earth. To this head everything that is joined to it is subject: union, here, implies obedience.

The theology of the *plenitudo potestatis* of the pope. Originally used by St. Leo, who contrasted it with the *pars sollicitudinis* granted to his legates, it came to be applied to papal, as being intrinsically different from episcopal, authority: the pope alone has *plenitudo potestatis*, whereas the bishop has only *partem sollicitudinis*, that is, a participation in the pope's authority. This second sense of the expression had appeared for the first time in the *False Decretals* of Isidorus Mercator. Gregory VII had used both senses. The *Decree* of Gratian included it with its original meaning. But St. Bernard gave it, in the *De Consideratione*, the later sense. It is in use in the curial style in Rome since Celestine III (1191-1198). In this context, the expression is taken in three different senses:

- *Plenitudo potestatis* designates papal authority in its universality, extensively, but not essentially, different from episcopal authority (v. gr., Huguccio).

- It designates papal authority as essentially different from episcopal authority (Innocent III), but within the ecclesiastical order.

- It designates papal authority as supreme even outside of the ecclesiastical order, i.e., the pope's power over kings and emperors and his right to interfere in the temporal order (Innocent IV, 1243-1254, claiming the right to dispose of all benefices in France, a point which was not admitted by St. Louis IX, 1226-1270).[5]

- In its extreme form, *plenitudo potestatis* is identified by some canonists with God's own power over creation. It is limited only by the Christian faith, which the pope has no right to change (v. gr., Durand de Mende, Bernard of Parma, [d. 1266], Innocent IV).

The theology of the two powers, by which the Middle Ages tried to regulate the relations of pope and emperor: Since the ninth century (Hincmar of Reims, Nicholas I, 858-867, John VIII, 872-882), the bishops and popes, faced with the degradation of the Carolingian monarchy in France and Lotharingia, had upheld the principle that a king who turns bad loses thereby his legitimacy. As a necessary consequence, the spiritual authority was judge of the king's exercise of his function and, by extension, of the capacities of a claimant to the throne. The ceremonies of the coronation were widely interpreted in this sense. In the thirteenth century itself, the emperors reversed the meaning of the principle: in order to safeguard the harmony of the two powers, the emperor shares both; he is priest and king; he must judge the pope in case the pope turns bad. Whence the conflict between Frederic II and Innocent IV, both using the same theoretical conception, but putting the onus of preserving the harmony of the *corpus*, the former on the emperor, the latter on the pope. The mood of Philip the Fair was much more radical: rather than claim authority over the spiritual, he wanted to separate the two domains, thus breaking the unity of Christendom and, by the same token, opening the door to the modern world. The bull *Unam sanctam* attempted to stem the tide by reasserting a classical theology. Not unnaturally, it stated this theology in its extreme form: the temporal power must be exercised by the king, within the church, for the church, at the discretion of the *sacerdos*, that is, practically speaking, of the pope.[6]

Sources

Direct sources: The bull may have been written by Matthew d'Aquasparta, Franciscan, cardinal and friend of Boniface. (In his *Quodlibet* VI, p. 9, Matthew teaches that papal authority extends to infidels, Jews, pagans, and Moslems.) One of the other sources of the language of the bull is the canonist Gilles de Rome. (In his *De ecclesiastica potestate*, Gilles teaches that the pope represents Christ as head of the mystical body; all power on earth is exercised by Christ through the pope. Gilles even adopts the thesis that a man's right of ownership depends upon the pope's permission to own something.) The doctrine of Gilles de Rome throws light on the meaning of *"instituere"* as used by Boniface VIII: it means "to legitimize" authority. The pope's doctrine would then be that temporal authority becames lawful when authorized by the pope.[7]

Remote sources: Unam sanctam may be read as the culminating formulation of the principle of freedom of the church from secular power, which was one of the main points of the Gregorian reform since the eleventh century. The most important precedents of it are: the decree of Nicholas II (1059), which reserved papal election to cardinals, thus neutralizing the imperial or popular control of the papacy; the *Dictatus Papae* of Gregory VII (1075); the third Lateran Council (1179) under Alexander III (1159-1181), when for the first time the decrees of a general council were promulgated by the pope rather than by the council (*de consilio fratrum nostrorum et sacri approbatione Concilii*); the policy of Innocent III (1198-1216), who persuaded several kings to become legal vassals of the pope (Sicily, Anjou, Portugal, Hungary, England, Ireland); the action of Innocent IV in deposing Frederic II, his bull *Eger cui levia* of 1245, where the pope's universal authority over temporal government was said to be founded on the power of the keys, and his unusual claim that the pope governs "not by human policy, but by divine inspiration"; the Second Council of Lyons (1274), under Gregory X (1271-1276), where the Byzantine Emperor Michael VIII Paleologos signed a profession of faith containing the following passage:

> *Ipsa sancta romana Ecclesia summum et plenum primatum et principatum super universam Ecclesiam catholicam obtinet; quem se ab ipso Domino in beato Petro apostolorum principe sive vertice, cujus Romanus Pontifex est successor, cum potestatis plentitudine, recepisse veraciter et humiliter recognoscit* (DS, n. 861).

Binding value of *Unam sanctam*

The history of the two centuries that followed the publication of *Unam sanctam* shows clearly that this bull was not received by all theologians and canonists of the times as binding on the Christian faith. It goes without saying that in any case one cannot speak of "infallibility" at that period. The first use of the term "infallible" as applied to the pope appears in 1320 in the works of Agostino Trionfo (*Summa de potestate ecclesiastica*, LXIII, 1, ad 1). In the language of that period, one can speak of *plenitudo potestatis*. This, however, was not universally accepted in the sense of *Unam sanctam*, where it entails hierocracy and implies the pope's authority over princes. Admittedly, Boniface VIII had himself protested, at the consistory of June 24, 1302, in the presence of Philip's legates, that he had no intention of usurping the king's authority: the pope's authority extended over it only *ratione peccati*.[8] Even so, the theoretical dualism of powers practically disappeared within a hierocracy. The violent reaction of King Philip had political and mercenary more than theological motives. Yet the subsequent policy of the king, who managed to have a French pope, Clement V (1305-1314), elected in 1305 and to move his living quarters to Avignon, cannot be dismissed as purely political. It corresponded to another view of the relationship between the two powers. This was implicitly recognized by Clement V: on February 1, 1306, his brief *Meruit* considerably toned down Boniface's doctrine concerning the sub-ordination of temporal authority to the pope.

In his account, Congar depicts the theologians of the fourteenth century as divided along four lines.[9] (1) The hierocrats: besides Matthew d'Aquasparta and Egidius Romanus, Jacques de Viterbe (d. 1307) Barthélemy de Lucques (d. 1327), Agostino Trionfo (d. 1328; *De duplici potestate praelatorum et laicorum; De potestate collegii mortuo papa*), Alvaro Pelayo (d. 1349 or 1353; *De planctu ecclesiae*), Guido Terreni (d. 1342; *Questio de magisterio infallibili*), Henri Totting de Oyta (d. 1397; *In Sententiis*), the anonymous *Determinatio compendiosa* (1342). These, with minor differences, considered the pope to be the head of the mystical body, wielding authority over all men and all things.

(2) Others recognize the autonomy of the temporal order, in the line of the theology of Thomas Aquinas: Jean Quidort of Paris (d. 1302; *De potestate regia et papali*), Pierre de la Palu (d. 1342; *De potestate papae*). This Thomist position subordinates the temporal to the spiritual in the order of final causality, not, as for the hierocrats, in the order of efficient causality.

(3) Some assert the autonomy of the temporal order without qualification: the Ghibeline party in Italian politics, Dante (1265-1321; *De monarchia*), and, in a more extreme form, Marsiglio de Padua (d. 1342; *Defensor pacis*). Several statements from the *Defensor pacis* were condemned by John XXII on October 27, 1327 (DS, 941-946).

(4) William of Ockham (d. 1349), *Dialogus adversus haereticos,* in his conflict with John XXII over the Franciscan ideal of Christian perfection, defines papal authority as purely spiritual. He admits a primacy in the church, even a *plenitudo potestatis* over temporal matters, but only if temporal authority fails to function. He also admits that a General Council may be called without the pope when this is necessary for the good of the church.

This division of opinion on the questions which Boniface VIII tried to settle in his bull *Unam sanctam* became sharper with time. The conflict between conciliarists and papalists was yet to come; the fifth session of the Council of Constance (April 1415) was to "define" an ecclesiology at odds with that of Boniface VIII.

In these conditions, one must say that the doctrines of *Unam sanctam* were not received by the church as authoritative. Until the end of the Middle Ages, the church's formal doctrines were still determined by their reception by the body of the church. Although never clearly formulated in theology, this principle had been affirmed by Hincmar de Reims in the ninth century. It was accepted by the canonists who, like Huguccio or Hostiensis (Henri de Séguse, d. 1271), assimilated the church to a medieval corporation. It persisted into the fifteenth century with Cardinal Zarabella (d. 1417) and Panormitanus (Nicholas de Tudeschis, d. 1445) and was predominant among the theologians of the Council of Constance.

Congar[10] mentions two relatively recent authors who maintain the binding value of the bull *Unam sanctam* taken in its totality: Louis Veuillot in the nineteenth century and an author otherwise unknown to me, Fr. Segarra (*Iglesia y Estado*, Barcelona, 1956). One could certainly quote other nineteenth century names. The thesis of *Unam sanctam* fitted perfectly into the philosophy of the traditionalists (Louis Ambroise de Bonald: *Théorie du Pouvoir Politique et Religieux*, 1796; Joseph de Maistre: *Du Pape*, 1819).

Some theologians distinguish between the conclusion of the bull (DS, n. 875), to which they ascribe permanent value, and the preliminaries, which they regard as too time-conditioned to be authoritative. Thus Cardinal Journet[11] or the author of the remark in DS, p. 279: "The final sentence alone is the dogmatic definition". In line with this, the last section of *Unam sanctam* was the only one mentioned by the eleventh session of the Fifth Lateran Council (bull *Pastor aeternus*, condemning the Pragmatic Sanction of Bourges, 1438, a decree in 23 articles, with a conciliarist orientation, signed by the king of France, Charles VII, and accepted by the Sorbonne). The Lateran Council explicitly stated that it also stood by the declaration *Meruit* of Clement V. Congar, who mentions this distinction between the body of the text and its conclusion, does not endorse it clearly.[12]

Fr. Chenu identifies the "permanent value" of *Unam sanctam* as "the dogmatic teaching that all political action falls under the light and within the scope of grace". He adds: "No doubt, the arguments of this document are steeped in an unacceptable theocratism; but this resulted from a theology that is outmoded today, and it does not nullify the truth that was enunciated".[13] Such an interpretation severs the message from the medium, a procedure which, as will be explained below, I cannot accept. The bull then becomes an allegorical document expressing a truth in terms that are no longer acceptable (theocratism). Chenu effectively discerns the pope's motivation; this, however, does not adequately account for the formulation of his doctrine.

In any case, the bull *Unam sanctam* does not, in my opinion, meet the requirements of Vatican Council I on infallibility. Boniface VIII does not clearly present himself in it as "pastor and doctor of all Christians". (In particular, one may wonder if "we" in the last sentence is the same "we" as in the first sentence.) He does not openly invoke his "supreme apostolic authority". He does not formulate his doctrine as one that is "to be held by the universal church". It is debatable whether the doctrine in question is covered by what Vatican I understood as being *de fide vel moribus* (cf DS, n. 3074), or is only a point of time-bound political wisdom.

On September 7, 1955, speaking to the tenth International Congress of Historical Sciences, Pius XII said:

> . . . When our predecessor Boniface VIII, on April 30, 1303, said to the legates of the German king, Albert of Hapsburg: . . . *sicut luna nullum lumen habet nisi quod recipit a sole, sic nec aliqua terrena potestas aliquid habet nisi quod recipit ab ecclesiastrica potestate . . . Omnes potestates . . . sunt a Christo et a nobis tanquam a vicario Jesu Christi*,—this was perhaps the strongest formulation of the medieval idea concerning relations between the spiritual and the temporal powers. Men like Boniface drew the logical consequences of this idea. But, even for them, this concerned normally only the transmission of authority, not the selection of its holder, as Boniface himself declared at the consistory of June 24, 1302. This medieval conception was conditioned by its time. Those who are acquainted with its sources will probably admit that it would be still more surprising had it never seen the day.[14]

Admittedly, Pius XII did not mention *Unam sanctam*. His remarks, nonetheless, bear on the theology embodied in this bull, which Pius XII judged to have been a time-conditioned view of papal authority, not a permanent expression of Catholic doctrine. From the context of this address, it is clear that Pius XII did not share Boniface's view of the pope's authority over the temporal power; he said nothing, however, touching directly on the conclusion of *Unam sanctam*.

The problem raised by *Unam sanctam* is that of doctrinal formulation. Several remarks are called for.

First, I cannot see how one can, in a statement about doctrine, separate the conclusion from the preliminaries which introduce it and, by outlining its context, determine the features and the limit of its horizon.

Second, this relates to the question of theological method. *Either* the conclusion need not follow upon the premises. In this case it must be somehow protected from error by a sudden charism, but at the cost of the intelligibility of the discourse of which it is a part. It would then be theologically legitimate, although rationally absurd, to elaborate the arguments after reaching the conclusion, and these arguments need not be logically cogent as long as they are apologetically effective.

Or theological language must follow the rule of all language, i.e., effectively reflect the on-going effort of the mind searching for intelligibility. In this case the conclusion will flow from the premises and preliminaries as stated in the discourse.

Third, I would stress this point with the help of the structural analysis of language. Like all languages, the theological language (i.e., the language in which theological conceptions are communicated) is made of semantics (implying a taxonomy of units of meaning) and syntax (a system which allows the units of meaning to be related to each other in diverse combinations). A language is a model in which a given semantic system is used for communication through a syntatic system. For instance, "papal authority" is a unit of meaning. In order to fit in a total system of Christian thought, this unit of meaning must be related to other units, regarding which it needs to be located syntactically. The more elements it is related to, the better it fits. The ways in which these relationships are stated constitute the syntax of theological language. To isolate one, or even a few units of meaning from the total system of meaning which is their intelligible horizon makes them a functional, deprived of ultimate purpose. The meaning of the units in question fulfils a function only when they are actively involved in a theological syntax. To cut off the conclusion of a discourse from the discourse itself implies separating it from the sentences that delineate its horizon; and this amounts to voiding it of its total meaning. Thus, the statement: "We declare, state, define and pronounce that it is altogether necessary to salvation for every human creature to be subject to the Roman pontiff", needs a setting in order to be intelligible. Outside of this setting, *in se,* it has no functional meaning.

This may be shown in the following way.

The statement includes a certain number of units of meaning: (1) "we make a declaration, statement, definition"; (2) "necessary to salvation"; (3) "every human creature"; (4) "subjection to authority"; (5) "authority of the Roman pontiff". The relationship of these units of meaning is materially or verbally expressed in the sentence. But the formal or vital explanation is provided by the more complex syntax of the entire discourse in which the sentence fits. The syntax of the conclusion must be completed by that of the preceding discourse. This enables us to add the following precisions to the conclusion:

- "necessary to salvation" = yielding to God;
- "every human creature" = man as political animal;
- "subjection to authority" = readiness to be judged by the spiritual power, or *sacerdos;*
- "spiritual power, or *sacerdos*" = (at the highest level) the Roman pontiff.

By making the conclusion more precise and clear, the syntax of the discourse makes it intelligible. But, in the present case, this intelligibility makes it unconvincing and even, I would say, unacceptable as a statement of the Christian faith. For none of these identifications pertains with certainty to the Christian Revelation.

Fourth, one may express this in more familiar terms: Boniface did not state the conclusion of the bull by itself, but as explained in the context of the bull. In this context, the conclusion refers to the pope's authority over "every human creature" insofar as this human creature wields, or is subject to, temporal authority. The conclusion reflects the same theology as the complete bull. Its meaning is restricted and its validity qualified by the theology of temporal and spiritual power which the bull embodies.

Fifth, if it is advisable to speak in terms of infallibility, we should not say that infallibility protects one sentence from error, while the rest of the discourse may well be erroneous. Rather, the whole discourse conveys, or does not convey, a truth. A true discourse is one that the church acknowledges to be such. Infallibility, in this case, is identical with truth.

It is not a fruitful exercise to try to abstract a core of permanent truth from such a culturally dated and politically limited document as *Unam sanctam*. That such a core of permanent truth may be arrived at, I would not deny. But this core is not evident from what the text itself says. We may reach it by making educated guesses as to what can, may, or ought to have been at the back of Boniface VIII's mind. The result is so dependent on our knowledge of the historical, social, and psychological conditions in which Boniface VIII lived and worked, that, if it properly belongs within the field of scholarly investigation, it cannot be claimed as a norm for the faith of Catholics who are utterly remote from those conditions. Accordingly, *Unam sanctam* does not provide an adequate springboard for an approach to the question of development of doctrine. Only documents whose doctrine is recognized as expressing the Catholic faith are directly relevant to the problem of development. This is far from the case with *Unam sanctam*.

However, the question of theological language is closely related to that of doctrinal development, insofar as the semantics and the syntax of dogmatic statements (creeds, conciliar or pontifical definitions) are also subject to the laws of language. The distinction of John XXIII between the "substance" and the "formulation" of the faith raises a major question here.[15] For the substance of speech is never given without a formulation, and furthermore, in the analysis of language that I would accept, no two formulations ever cover exactly the same substance. If substance is the meaning, the formulation is itself a syntactic combination of themes without which no meaning is available. Accordingly, the suggested contrast between "substance" and "formulation" is misleading. It tends to raise a barrier between the substance or ideal content of doctrine, and its formulation, as though the substance of doctrine could stand by itself in a Platonic world of essences. The real contrast does not lie, to my mind, between substance and formulation; one cannot separate that which is said (substance) from that which says it (formulation). The contrast is between the person of Jesus Christ, together with the sacramental events in which the faithful experience him (let us call this: the gospel), and the discourse in which the church as a community and each believer for himself express their faith about Christ. The problem therefore resides in judging the adequacy of a given formulation of doctrine to the task of preserving and transmitting the gospel in the cultural circumstances which determine its language. Accordingly, a doctrinal formula is always relative, not only to the gospel as experienced, but also to the present as placing certain linguistic tools at the church's disposal to express the gospel. No doctrinal formulation, not even that of the New Testament, is absolute, though many enunciations, and those of the New Testament first of all, remain normative for our judgment of other eunciations of doctrine. Their normativity is proportional to the extent to which they protect and convey the gospel. Two consequences follow: first, a doctrinal enunciation remains normative only as long as its language is understood; after that, it becomes an interesting subject for archeological research.[16] Second, the unavoidable fluency of human language, including the technical languages of theology, which, at the end of a triumphal period, necessarily decays and eventually dies, after sometimes giving birth to new languages, makes re-enunciation and re-definition of the gospel one of the permanently urgent tasks of the church.

5

IUS DIVINUM AND *ADIAPHORON* IN RELATION TO STRUCTURAL PROBLEMS IN THE CHURCH: THE POSITION OF THE LUTHERAN SYMBOLICAL BOOKS

Arthur Carl Piepkorn

Divine Right

In their discussion of the papacy Roman Catholics and Lutherans are immediately confronted by the scope of divine right (*ius divinum*).

The canon that concludes the crucial second chapter of *Pastor aeternus* anathematizes everyone who would say "that it is not by the institution of Christ the Lord himself, or *by divine right* (*seu iure divino*), that blessed Peter has perpetual successors in his primacy over the entire church, or that the bishop of Rome is not the successor of blessed Peter in that same primacy" (DS 3058). In 1896, in the encyclical *Satis cognitum*, Leo XIII insisted that "just as oneness of faith is necessary for the oneness of the church inasmuch as it is an assembly of the faithful, so for its oneness inasmuch as it is a divinely established association oneness of direction (*unitas regiminis*), which effects a oneness of communion, is required *by divine right*" (DS 3306).

The Smalcald Articles, part of the symbolical books to which Lutherans stand committed, declare that "*by divine right* (*iure divino*) or out of the word of God (*aus Gottes Wort*)[1] the pope is not the head of all Christendom (because that is the peculiar privilege of one individual alone—he is called Jesus Christ), but only the bishop or rector of the church at Rome" (Part Two, 4, 1). The Treatise on the Authority and Primacy of the Pope proposes to demonstrate "from the Gospel that the bishop of Rome is not *by divine right* above other bishops or pastors" (10), and proceeds to cite Luke 22:24-27; Matthew 18:1-4; John 20:21; Galatians 2: 2, 6; 1 Corinthians 3:4-8,22; and 1 Peter 5:3 (7-11).

For Lutherans, legitimate institutions and practices exist in the church either "by divine right" or "by ecclesiastical right," that is, by a kind of human right. The right of any part of the empirical, institutional church as a public association to make prudent rules for its internal government and to insure the just application of these rules is not contested. But the source of this authority is not the divine institution that distinguishes the empirical Christian community from every other community and association, but the human necessity that confronts every human association of facilitating its operations by commonly accepted rules.

"Legitimate" in the first sentence of the preceding paragraph stands in opposition to abuses and evils. Differences may exist within the Lutheran community over the question if a particular and concrete institution or practice is actually a legitimate institution or an abuse or an evil. If it indeed unmasks itself as an evil, it must be eliminated. If it is an abuse, it must be corrected, although here too Lutherans endorse the principle: "An abuse does not take away but confirms the substance (*Abusus non tollit sed confirmat sub-*

stantiam)" (Large Catechism, Baptism, 59). Thus for Lutherans divine right and human, including ecclesiastical, right constitute a perfect dichotomy.

Although both Roman Catholics and Lutherans speak of divine right, certain still persisting differences of thrust in our respective doctrines of the church, along with differences in our definitions of *ius divinum*, suggest that we do not mean precisely the same thing by the term. As a result the scope of divine right is different in our respective communities. In these differences part of the resolution of our differences may lie.

In turning to *ius divinum* in the Lutheran symbolical books we may well note that the term occurs more frequently in discussions of structures within the church than in any other context.

The Lutheran symbolical books argue that monastic vows are not binding by divine right, because the bishop of Rome has dispensed religious from them, and human authority cannot dispense anyone from an obligation that exists absolutely by divine right (*quae simpliciter est iuris divini*) (Augsburg Confession, 27, 24). The same line of argument is invoked elsewhere. Bishops in the past have frequently altered so-called universal apostolic traditions, but if these were of divine right human authority could not alter them (Apology, 7, 40). A concrete case is the date of Easter, and the insistence of the Audians in the days of St. Epiphanius of Salamis on keeping the "Jewish" rather than the "church" date (ibid., 42-44). Again, the satisfactions and penalties imposed in the sacrament of penance can be remitted by human authority; such compensatory satisfactions are accordingly not necessary by divine right (*iure divino*), because the divine law (*ius divinum*) cannot be abrogated by human authority (Apology, 12, 175).

Bishops have secular authority and the power of the secular sword not by divine right (*nicht . . . aus gottlichen Rechten*), but by human right (Augsburg Confession, 28, 19).

By divine right (*nach gottlichen Rechten*) bishops are to preach the gospel, forgive sin, judge doctrine, reject doctrine that contradicts the gospel, and expel manifest sinners from the Christian community by God's word without coercion (*Ibid.*, 21). The Latin version of this text is illuminating. It uses *de iure divino* as a gloss on *secundum evangelium* ("according to the gospel") and thus gives the former concept a less totally juridical and a more soteriological thrust. It also states that the churches are bound by divine right on the basis of Luke 10:16 ("He who hears you hears me") to obey the bishops in such matters (*Ibid.*, 22).

The Lutheran symbolical books affirm that absolution is by divine right, although the obligatory enumeration of sins is not (Apology, 12, 12). They derive their conviction about absolution from the dominical commands to the apostles to remit sins. The Apology declares in Article 23 that the breaking up of clerical marriages contradicts divine law, natural law, and the canons (3, 6).

Part Two of the Smalcald Articles equates divine law with God's command: "I shall posit the situation that the pope were to waive his claim to be the highest officer (*der Oberst*) by divine right or out of God's command, and [were to argue] that one would have to have a head to which all the others would adhere in order that the oneness of Christendom might the better be preserved against sects and heresy" (4, 7).

The Treatise on the Authority and Primacy of the Pope asserts on the basis of Galatians 2:2,6, that the apostolic authority of Peter is not by divine right superior to that of Paul in the sense that the latter needed to acknowledge Peter as his superior and to seek confirmation of his apostolic office from Peter (10).[2]

It may be useful to recall some of the institutions and practices that exist by divine right according to the Lutheran symbolical books. The Treatise says that "the Levitical pontifex was by divine right the high priest," although this did not require obedience to impious high priests (38). The authority of all prelates that preside over churches, regardless of their title, is common by divine right (61). An ordination administered by a pastor in his own church to fit candidates is valid (*rata*) by divine right (61). The church is compelled by divine right to ordain pastors and ministers, using its own pastors as ordinators (72). The civil government (*magistratus mundani*) is obligated by divine right to provide courts for the adjudication of marriage cases (77).

Divine right or *ius divinum* is thus a juridical concept that describes certain aspects of the will of God. These may find expression in his creative activity (such as the obligation of authorities to rule justly, the obligation of their subordinates to obey, and lifelong monogamous marriage). Or they may find expression in his saving activity (such as the establishment of the church as an agency of salvation and the institution of the sacred ministry of the word of God and of the sacraments, of one water baptism for the forgiveness of sins, of the sacrament of the body and blood of Christ, and of absolution and reconciliation for the restoration of penitents). The creation aspects of the *ius divinum* are linked with the divine ordinance (*mandatum Dei*), the salvation aspects with the gospel (*juxta evangelium*).

Adiaphora

The Lutheran equivalent for the items that fall under the head of *ius ecclesiasticum* is the concept of adiaphoron ("a thing that makes no difference").

This category achieved considerable intra-Lutheran importance in connection with the so-called Adiaphoristic Controversy. This controversy occupied especially the first of the two decades that followed the efforts to introduce the "interims" of Augsburg and Leipzig (1548) into the Lutheran communities of the Holy Roman Empire. The issue in the controversy was confused and has frequently been misunderstood. At bottom it was this: Can a church, confronted by a hostile government, make concessions even in indifferent matters in order to escape persecution, when such concessions seem to involve theological capitulation?

The effort to resolve the controversy in Article 10 of the Formula of Concord was almost academic. The controversy had ceased largely to have practical relevance after the collapse of the Imperial policy signalized by the Convention of Passau in 1552 and confirmed by the Peace of Augsburg in 1555.

Genuine adiaphora—as distinguished from divinely instituted items on the one hand and abuses and evils on the other—were defined as potentially constructive and useful institutions and practices which the word of God explicitly neither commands nor forbids. (See Formula of Concord, Solid Declaration, 10, 5-9)

The symbolical books prudently offer no list of adiaphora. They speak in such general terms as those things that contribute to the good order, the Christian discipline, the evangelical weal of the churches, and their edification. The highly polemical books, pamphlets, and published university disputations that are the literary monuments of the controversy raised such issues as processions with banners, some of the more dramatic ceremonies of Holy Week, the restoration of the sacrament of confirmation, extreme unction, episcopal ordination to the priesthood, the use of Latin, the medieval rite of the mass, the observance of Corpus Christi, and the wearing of rochets (*Chorrock*), all of which the antiadiaphorist followers of Matthias Vlačić (Flacius) roundly denounced, but which others regarded as tolerable in varying degrees. Authentic adiaphora, even in the view of men like Flacius, included hymns, chants, the liturgical lessons, times and places of divine service, distinctive ecclesiastical garb, church-bells, private disciplines of fasting and abstinence "for the sake of prayer or other Christian discipline," set times for personal prayer, and (at least in the case of Flacius himself) the sex of candidates for ordination.

Bishops have the power to make liturgical enactments such as the fixing of Sunday, the feasts of the church year, and similar ritual matters, just as in his time St. Paul directed women to cover their heads as a piece of temporary apostolic liturgical legislation. The Christian community in turn, out of charity and for the sake of peace in the church, ought to obey such legislation, but the bishops must not demand compliance under pain of mortal sin (Augsburg Confession, 28, 53-60). Even the decrees of the Council of Jerusalem (Acts 15:20, 29)—which seemed good to the Holy Spirit as well as to the apostles and presbyters and the whole church at Jerusalem—were of this temporary order (Augsburg Confession, 28, 65-66).

How willing the leaders of the Church of the Augsburg Confession were to retain the inherited institutions and practices of the past is underlined by the conservative liturgical principle that they enunciated in Article 15 of the Augsburg Confession: "Of ecclesiastical ordinances instituted by human beings we teach that those that can be observed without sin and that serve the ends of peace and good order in the church, are to be kept" (1).

Even more illuminating is the list of the things that they actually retained in practice. The Lutheran symbolical books specifically refer to the periscopal system, sermons, the ordinary of the mass and other chants, Sunday, Easter, Pentecost, and the rest of the liturgical year, eucharistic and other vestments, candles, altar ornaments of gold, Latin, chanting of the Psalter, the sign of the holy cross made by the worshiper on himself, the customary ceremonial of the mass and of the baptismal rite, kneeling for prayer, folded hands, life in community, ejaculatory prayers, ascetic disciplines, prayers for the departed, and episcopacy. The list could easily be extended by canvassing the church orders of the sixteenth and seventeenth centuries.

Within the concept of adiaphoron one might theoretically differentiate various levels.

One would certainly be decisions made by the empirical church or a part of it after having invoked the assistance of the Holy Spirit. Some of these decisions may have been undertaken with a view to an acute crisis, requiring an immediate short term solution. Other decisions may have been taken with the intention of providing long-term solutions.

Another level would be decisions made by individual leaders in the church or on their counsel and urging through the exercise of managerial prudence in the interest of good order.

In an essentially conservative institution like the church past decisions—even those made with limited and short-term ends in view—have a tendency to perpetuate themselves and very rapidly to become revered traditions. In the process they sometimes outlive their usefulness. Again, solutions to new problems are likely to involve the economical adaptation of an existing tradition or the establishment of a new solution that is deliberately analogous to a traditional procedure. These solutions too sometimes outlive their usefulness.

The problem of course lies in distinguishing the clear guidance of the Holy Spirit from purely human prudence or possibly even from the intrusion of a demonic suggestion. We have no objective source from which to obtain an infallible answer.

The sacred scriptures do not provide an absolute guide to the rightness of a particular decision. Indeed, it is frequently their silence or the (at least apparent) ambiguity of the evidence that they do provide which necessitates a decision by the church or the church's leadership.

Again, the teaching office (*magisterium*) in the church—which both the Roman Catholics and the Lutherans recognize—does not provide an absolute guarantee that the decision of the church or the church's leadership will be wholly or permanently right. In part this is so because the invariable competence of the teaching office to decide matters like this is itself an assumption to be demonstrated. In part the teaching office can provide no absolute guarantee because the history of the church indicates that the witness of the teaching office has not been in fact entirely or universally consistent.

When all of Christendom is existing in mutual schism, no one part of the magisterium can confidently speak for all.

Again, historical developments are not absolutely decisive in determining the rightness of a decision that the church or the church's leadership has made. In part this is so because the historical evidence at crucial points is often fragmentary and opaque. In part it is so because a given historical development took place in response to a concrete situation that has altered or even disappeared subsequently. In part it is so because the historical development in question has not been identical in all parts of the church. In part it is so because not every historical development has vindicated its necessity or its validity in actual practice.

Summary

As Roman Catholics and as Lutherans we recognize that there are certain institutions and practices in the church that we both agree are divinely instituted and soteriologically significant.

It is also true that there are certain institutions and practices that we both see as existing by ecclesiastical right.

It is regrettably true that in each of our traditions there are developments that one of our two communities regards as of divine right by its definition of *ius divinum* and that the other regards as of merely human right.

Where either community sees an institution or practice as clearly of divine right, that community has no choice in conscience except to affirm the necessity of this institution or practice at least for itself.

Where either community sees an institution or practice as clearly of human right, it cannot make such an institution or practice binding in conscience on anyone, although it may very properly urge considerations of charity and the necessity of orderly procedure in seeking compliance.

Where one community sees an institution or practice as being of human right while the other community sees it as of divine right, each must seriously ask itself if it may not be in error and the other community may not be right. This calls for a willingness to hear and to learn and a readiness to consider and, if need be, to change.

If, and as long as, the difference remains irreconcilable,

each community must ask itself if its view stands so high in the hierarchy of truths and is so central to its understanding of the gospel that it must regard this difference as divisive to the point where a common participation in the sacrament of the altar is impossible.

6

A LUTHERAN UNDERSTANDING OF PAPAL PRIMACY

Fred Kramer

The title of this paper appears to call for more than the opinion of any individual Lutheran or group of Lutherans on the question posed in the title. To be a truly Lutheran understanding, the understanding must be based in the Lutheran Confessions, which all Lutherans acknowledge, although not all to the same extent or in precisely the same way.

Papal primacy belongs into the area of church government and polity, and a Lutheran understanding of what papal primacy might mean must proceed on the basis of the Lutheran understanding of church government and church polity. In the Roman Catholic Church papal primacy has been claimed and debated and enforced to the extent that this was possible since long before the Reformation. It was one of the burning issues during the Reformation. We find, however, that the clearest dogmatic formulation and definition of papal primacy comes out of Vatican I, in *Dogmatic Constitution on the Church of Christ,* often referred to as *Pastor aeternus.*

In this document Pius IX undertakes "to set forth the doctrine on the institution, perpetuity, and nature of the Sacred Apostolic Primacy, in which the strength and solidarity of the whole Church consist, to be believed and held by all the faithful . . . and to proscribe and condemn the contrary errors . . ."[1]

Two Canons, including anathemas, show clearly how the primacy of the pope is to be understood according to Pius IX and the First Vatican Council.

Canon 1:
If anyone then says that the blessed Apostle Peter was not established by the Lord Christ as the chief of all the Apostles, and the visible head of the whole militant church, or, that the same received great honor but did not receive from the same our Lord Jesus Christ directly and immediately the primacy in true and proper jurisdiction: let him be anathema.

Canon 2:
If anyone then says that it is not from the institution of Christ the Lord Himself, or by divine right that the blessed Peter has perpetual successors in the primacy over the universal church, or that the Roman Pontiff is not the successor of blessed Peter in the same primacy, let him be anathema.[2]

The document leaves no doubt that the anathemas mean that anyone who does not accept the Roman Pontiff's claims to primacy over all Christians is irrevocably lost.

Furthermore we teach and declare that the Roman Church, by the disposition of the Lord, holds the sovereignty of ordinary power over all others, and that this power of jurisdiction on the part of the Roman Pontiff, which is truly episcopal, is immediate; and with respect to this the pastors and the faithful of whatever rite and dignity, both as separate individuals and all together, are bound by the duty of hierarchical subordination and true obedience, not only in things which pertain to faith and morals, but also in those which pertain to the discipline and government of the Church (which is) spread over the whole world, so that the Church of Christ, protected not only by the Roman Pontiff, but by the unity of communion as well as of the profession of the same faith is one flock under the one highest shepherd. This is the doctrine of Catholic truth from which no one can deviate and keep his faith and salvation.[3]

There can be no doubt that this is an official Roman Catholic view of what the primacy of the pope means to Roman Catholics, although it must be freely admitted that this view was not accepted by all Roman Catholics at the time of Vatican I, and that there are today probably far more Roman Catholics who find themselves unable to accept this view of the primacy and the anathemas which attempted to enforce it on all Roman Catholics.

In contrast to the official Roman Catholic teaching with respect to papal primacy, the official Lutheran Confessions consider the particular form of church government and polity an adiaphoron. They stress the importance of the right teaching of the Gospel and the right administration of the sacraments as necessary for the very existence and unity of the church, and the importance of the public ministry. On the ministry itself the *Augsburg Confession* has these two short statements:

> To obtain such faith God instituted the office of the ministry, that is, provided the Gospel and the sacraments (Art. V).

> It is taught among us that nobody should publicly teach or preach or administer the sacraments in the church without a regular call (Art. XIV).

There is no attempt to define any kind of hierarchial structure.

In the *Apology* Melanchthon testifies that the Lutherans were by no means opposed to a hierarchical structure of the ministry per se:

> . . . we have given frequent testimony in the assembly to our deep desire to maintain the church polity and various ranks of the ecclesiastical hierarchy, although they were created by human authority. We know that the fathers had good and useful reasons for instituting ecclesiastical discipline in the manner prescribed by the ancient canons (Art. XIV).

The abolition of canonical government in the churches of the *Augsburg Confession* is blamed squarely on the bishops themselves, who sought to hinder the preaching of the gospel:

> . . . the bishops either force our priests to forsake and condemn the sort of doctrine we have confessed or else, in their unheard of cruelty, they kill the unfortunate and innocent men. This keeps our priests from acknowledging such bishops (*Apology*, Art. XIV).

Under these circumstances the reformers, who did not find that scripture prescribes any ideal form of church government and polity, proceeded in accord with the existential necessities of their day. According to Lutheran thinking all matters of external church polity must be decided according to prevailing conditions. The one thing on which Lutherans, according to their confessions, cannot yield in the matter of church polity and government, is that the two essential functions of the church be present and carried out, namely that the gospel is proclaimed and taught, and that the sacraments are administered according to Christ's command. To the extent that the historical structure of the Roman Catholic Church at the time of the Reformation served this purpose, the Lutherans were willing to retain it.

What has been said thus far concerned in particular the office of bishops. What have the Lutheran Confessions to say of the papacy, and of the possibility of retaining the papacy? The harsh judgments of the Lutheran Confessions on the pope and on the papacy are well known, ranging from "apostle of the devil" to "antichrist."[4] There are, however, passages in the Lutheran Confessions which, theoretically, at least, seem to leave open the possibility of a certain primacy of the bishop of Rome, though strictly *de iure humano*.

On the one hand the *Smalcald Articles* deny that the church needs a visible head.

> . . . it is manifest that the holy church was without a pope for more than five hundred years at least and that the churches of the Greeks and of many other nationalities have never been under the pope and are not at the present time. Manifestly (to repeat what has already been said often), the papacy is a human invention, and it is not commanded, it is unnecessary, and it is useless. The holy Christian church can exist very well without such a head, and it would have remained much better if such a head had not been raised up by the devil. The papacy is of no use to the church because it exercises no Christian office. Consequently the church must continue to exist without the pope (Art. IV).

It is evident from the quotation that Luther was judging the papacy as he and the church of his time had experienced and were experiencing it. But Luther is also willing to speculate on what other forms the papacy might take, in order to become acceptable to the church everywhere.

> Suppose that the pope would renounce the claim that he is the head of the church by divine right or by God's command; suppose that it were necessary to have a head, to whom all others should adhere, in order that the unity of Christendom might better be preserved against the attacks of sects and heresies; and suppose that such a head would then be elected

by men and it remained in their power and choice to change or depose this head. This is just the way in which the Council of Constance acted with reference to the popes when it deposed three and elected a fourth (Art. IV).

While Luther concedes all this in theory, he is convinced that the pope could never accept a position where he is the head of Christendom by human right only, subject to the will of the electors, to be elected or deposed as they deemed necessary.

If, I say, the pope and the see of Rome were to concede and accept this (which is impossible), he would have to suffer the overthrow and destruction of his whole rule and estate, together with all his rights and pretensions. In short, he cannot do it. Even if he could, Christendom would not be helped in any way. There would be even more sects than before, because, inasmuch as submission to such a head would depend on the good pleasure of men rather than on a divine command, he would very easily and quickly be despised and would ultimately be without any adherents at all. He would not always have to have his residence in Rome or some other fixed place, but it could be anywhere and in whatever church God would raise up a man fitted for such an office. What a complicated and confused state of affairs that would be!

Consequently the church cannot be better governed and maintained than by having all of us live under one head, Christ, and by having all the bishops equal in office (however they may differ in gifts) and diligently joined together in unity of doctrine, faith, sacraments, prayer, works of love, etc (Art. IV).

The last quote from the *Smalcald Articles* shows that Luther had given thought to the matter of retaining a pope, shorn of the pretension that he holds his position *de iure divino*. Whether his judgment about what would happen if this were tried is correct is certainly debatable. With his experience of the popes of his time his pessimism is understandable.

Important for our discussion of the possibility of conceding to the pope a certain primacy in the church is Philip Melanchthon's subscription to the *Smalcald Articles*. While other pastors merely subscribed the Articles with name and position in the church, Melanchthon wrote:

I, Philip Melanchthon, regard the above articles as right and Christian. However, concerning the pope I hold that, if he would allow the Gospel, we, too, may concede to him that superiority over the bishops which he possesses by human right, making this concession for the. sake of peace and general unity among the Chritians who are now under him and who may be in the future.[5]

A comparison of the statements of Luther in the *Smalcald Articles* with Melanchthon's subscription indicates that both granted that the primacy might be granted to the bishop of Rome *de iure humano,* if he would serve the God-given purpose and task of the church. Luther, however, felt sure that the pope could not, and would not, do this. Melanchthon is willing to grant that it is conceivable that he would. Luther could see no good coming from the attempt. Melanchthon could see some benefit for the peace and general unity among Christians.

With this background from the Lutheran Confessions it should be possible to risk a statement on what *a Lutheran understanding of papal primacy in the church might mean.*

1. It would be a primacy strictly *de iure humano;*
2. It would be a primacy over the bishops, making the pope a *primus inter pares;*
3. The individual pope's position would depend on the good will of those who elected him, and who could also depose him;
4. Such a pope would therefore be responsible to those who elevated him to his position;
5. Such a pope should serve the cause of peace and unity in Christendom.

This is all spoken theoretically. It would hold provided the pope accepted such a condition, and provided the church accepted the pope under these conditions.

Luther was of the opinion that the pope never could or would accept such conditions. Certainly, the popes in his day would not have accepted them. There is grave doubt that a present-day pope could or would accept them, or that a major part of the Roman Catholic Church could make such a shift, at any rate at the present time.

There is every reason to doubt also that any major part of the rest of Christendom would accept a pope at present even under these conditions. Most Protestant churches are definitely allergic to the idea of a pope.

Finally, granted for the sake of argument that both the pope and all the churches were agreed to accept a pope on the terms as outlined above, where could a man be found, or rather, a perpetual succession of men, who would be sufficient for these things?

Papal primacy, it would appear, continues to be a problem for the Roman Catholic Church, rather than for all Christendom. As the Roman Catholic Church wrestles with the problem it might do well to consider the points brought out above from the confessional writings of Luther and Melanchthon.

7

THE TEACHING MINISTRY OF THE CHURCH IN LUTHERAN PERSPECTIVE

Warren A. Quanbeck

1. The Lutheran Confessions assert repeatedly and in a variety of ways that Christ alone is Lord of the church.

"The church is not merely an association of outward ties and rites like other civic governments, . . . but it is mainly an association of faith and of the Holy Spirit in men's hearts. . . . This church alone is called the body of Christ, which Christ renews, consecrates and governs by his Spirit, as Paul testifies (Eph. 1:22, 23). (Book of Concord 169:5).

"The church cannot be better governed and maintained than by having all of us live under one head, Christ" (300:9).

"Christ is our mediator, redeemer, king, high priest, head, shepherd" (600:47).

Christ "is present with his church and community on earth as mediator, head, king and high priest" (607:78).

"I believe that there is on earth a little holy flock or community of pure saints under one head Christ. It is called together by the Holy Spirit in one faith, mind and understanding" (417:51. Cf. 298:1, 299:7, 577:44).

2. Christ rules the church through his Holy Spirit. "I

believe that by my own reason or strength I cannot believe in Jesus Christ, my Lord, or come to him. But the Holy Spirit has called me through the Gospel, enlightened me with his gifts, and sanctified and preserved me in true faith, just as he calls, gathers, enlightens and sanctifies the whole Christian church on earth, and preserves it in union with Jesus Christ in the one true faith" (345:6).

"Neither your nor I could ever know anything of Christ, or believe in him and take him as our Lord unless these were first offered to us and bestowed on our hearts through the preaching of the Gospel by the Holy Spirit. . . . God has caused the Word to be published and proclaimed, in which he has given the Holy Spirit to offer and apply to us this treasure of salvation (415:38).

"To obtain such faith God instituted the office of the ministry, that is, provided the Gospel and the sacraments. Through these, as through means, he gives the Holy Spirit, who works faith, when and where he pleases, in those who hear the gospel" (31:1, 2).

"God gives no one his Spirit or grace except through or with the external Word which comes before" (312:3, cf. 82:8, 9. Concerning the giving of the Holy Spirit through the sacraments, cf. 105:35, 441:41).

3. The Gospel in word and sacrament is the means by which the Holy Spirit exercises his sovereignty in the church. Where the gospel is proclaimed and the sacraments administered in accordance with Christ's will, there the Holy Spirit is present to call men to Christ, to unite them to him in his body the church, to build them up in faith and in love, and to produce the gifts of the Spirit (Gal. 5:22, 23).

"The Gospel offers counsel and help against sin in more than one way, for God is surpassingly rich in his grace: First, through the spoken word, by which the forgiveness of sin (the peculiar function of the Gospel) is preached to the whole world; second, through Baptism; third, through the holy Sacrament of the Altar; fourth, through the power of the keys; and finally, through the mutual conversation and consolation of the brethren" (310, IV).

4. The Holy Scriptures are the bearers of the Word of God, and therefore the source from which the church's teaching is to be drawn, and the standard by which it is to be judged.

"We believe, teach, and confess that the prophetic and apostolic writings of the Old and New Testaments are the only rule and norm according to which all doctrines and teachers alike must be appraised and judged" (464:1).

"Other writings of ancient and modern teachers, whatever their names, should not be put on a par with Holy Scripture" (464:2 cf. 503:3ff.). "The Word of God shall establish articles of faith and no one else, not even an angel" (295:15).

5. The Reformers were aware that the interpretation of Scripture raises many problems, and that the exegetical perspective of Jesus and the apostles differs from that of the rabbis or philosophers.

"All Scripture should be divided into these two chief doctrines, the law and the promises. In some places it presents the law. In others it presents the promise of Christ: this it does either when it promises that the Messiah will come and promises forgiveness of sins, justification, and eternal life for his sake, or when, in the New Testament, the Christ who came promises forgiveness of sins, justification, and eternal life. By 'law' in this discussion we mean the commandments of the Decalogue, wherever they appear in the Scriptures (108:5, 6).

6. The Lutheran church accepts the three ecumenical creeds as aids in the understanding of the Scriptures and in the presentation of the doctrine of the church.

"Immediately after the time of the apostles—in fact, already during their lifetime—false teachers and heretics invaded the church. Against these the ancient church formulated symbols (that is, brief and explicit confessions) which were accepted as the unanimous, catholic, Christian faith and confessions of the orthodox and true church, namely, the Apostle's Creed, the Nicene Creed, and the Athanasian Creed. We pledge ourselves to these, and we hereby reject all heresies and teachings which have been introduced into the church of God contrary to them" (465:3).

7. The Lutheran Confessions, the Augsburg Confession and its Apology (1530), the Smalcald Articles (1537), the two Catechisms, and the Formula of Concord (1580) are also set forward as testimonies to the Gospel, rejection of false doctrine, and as guides to the interpretation of the Scriptures.

"With reference to the schism in matters of faith which has occurred in our times, we regard, as the unanimous consensus and exposition of our Christian faith, . . . and as the symbol of our time, the first and unaltered Augsburg Confession . . . together with the Apology thereof and the Articles drafted at Smalcald in the year 1537.

Since these matters also concern the laity and the salvation of their souls, we subscribe Dr. Luther's Small and Large Catechisms. . . . They are "the layman's Bible" and contain everything which Holy Scripture discusses at greater length and which a Christian must know for his salvation" (465:4, 5, cf. 504:5, 6; 505:7, 8).

"In this way the distinction between the Holy Scripture . . . and all other writings is maintained, and Holy Scripture remains the only judge, rule, and norm according to which as the only touchstone all doctrines should and must be understood and judged as good or evil, right or wrong.

"Other symbols and other writings are not judges like Holy Scripture, but merely witnesses and expositions of the faith, setting forth how at various times the Holy Scriptures were understood in the church by contemporaries with reference to controverted articles, and how contrary teachings were rejected and condemned (465:7, 8, cf. 506:10, 11).

8. Other aspects of tradition were accepted and indeed treasured by the Lutheran church. The liturgy, the church year, confession and absolution, are examples of this. The Reformers removed elements which seemed to them contrary to the Scriptures, but otherwise retained the practice of the Middle Ages as fully as possible.

"We . . . retain many ceremonies and traditions (such as the liturgy of the Mass and various canticles, festivals and the like) which serve to preserve order in the church" (69: 40).

"We are unjustly accused of having abolished the Mass . . . . No conspicuous changes have been made in the public ceremonies of the Mass, except that in certain places German hymns are sung in addition to the Latin responses for the instruction and exercise of the people. After all, the chief purpose of all ceremonies is to teach people what they need to know about Christ" (56:XXIV).

"Confession has not been abolished by the preachers on our side. The custom has been retained among us of not administering the sacrament to those who have not previously been examined and absolved. At the same time the people are carefully instructed concerning the consolation of the Word of absolution so that they may esteem absolution as a great and precious thing. It is not the voice or word of the man who speaks it, but it is the Word of God, who forgives sin, for it is spoken in God's stead and by God's command" (61:XXV. See also 89:53, 174:33, 215:1, 312:1).

9. Ecclesiastical order. The Lutheran Reformers had no desire to break with the traditional form of church government.

"We have given frequent testimony . . . to our deep desire to maintain the church polity and various ranks of the ecclesiastical hierarchy, although they were created by human authority. We know that the Fathers had good and useful reasons for instituting ecclesiastical discipline in the manner described by the ancient canons. . . . Furthermore, we want . . . to declare our willingness to keep the ecclesiastical and canonical polity, provided that the bishops stop raging against our churches. This willingness will be our defense, both before God and among all nations, present and future, against the charge that we have undermined the authority of the bishops" (214:1, 215:5).

"If the bishops were true bishops and were concerned about the church and the Gospel, they might be permitted (for the sake of love and unity, but not of necessity) to ordain and confirm us and our preachers, provided this could be done without pretense, humbug and unchristian ostentation" (314:1).

10. General councils. Between 1517 and 1530 there was much talk of holding a general council to overcome the differences between Catholics and Reformers. In the preface to the Augsburg Confession the Reformers express their willingness to take part in such a council (26:21). In the Smalcald Articles of 1537 Luther suggests that there are so many things wrong with the church that ten councils would have their hands full setting them right (290:10). In the Treatise on the Power and Primacy of the Pope, Melanchthon expresses some skepticism about the effectiveness of a council, since the pope does not permit anything to be decreed contrary to his will (399:55). He also points out that the decisions of the councils are decisions of the church and not of the pontiffs, and urges that kings restrain "the license of the pontiffs and see to it that the church is not deprived of the power of making judgments and decisions according to the will of God" (329:56).

11. The authority of the pope. The Lutheran Confessions are critical of papal pretensions and practices. They oppose what they consider to be his confusion of temporal and spiritual authority (326:36, 81:1ff., 172:23, 320:2,

325:31), his attempts to set up and depose kings and emperors (81:2, 320:2), his desire to extend his authority over councils (242:24, 327:40, 328:49), his craving for infallibility: "nor should that be transferred to the popes which is the prerogative of the whole church: that they are the pillars of truth and that they do not err" (173:27). They object to the bull *Unam sanctam* with its claim that "it is necessary for salvation for every human creature to be subject to the Roman pontiff" (298:4, 300:12, 320:3, 6, 326:36).

They are willing to acknowledge that the pope is "the bishop and pastor of the churches of Rome and of such other churches as have attached themselves to him" (298:1). In his subscription to the Smalcald Articles, Melanchthon adds his opinion that if the pope would allow the Gospel, "we, too, may concede to him that superiority over the bishops which he possesses by human right, making this concession for the sake of peace and general unity among the Christians who are now under him and who may be in the future" (316:5).

12. The authority of bishops. The office of bishop consists of the proclamation of the Gospel, the administration of the sacraments and church discipline.

"According to divine right, therefore, it is the office of the bishop to preach the Gospel, forgive sins, judge doctrine and condemn doctrine that is contrary to the Gospel, and exclude from the Christian community the ungodly whose wicked conduct is manifest. All this is to be done not by human power but by God's Word alone" (84:21 Cf. 81:5).

"We like the old division of power into the power of the order and the power of jurisdiction. Therefore a bishop has the power of the order, namely the ministry of Word and sacraments. He also has the power of jurisdiction, namely, the authority to excommunicate those who are guilty of public offenses or to absolve them if they are converted and ask for absolution" (283:13).

Where a bishop has temporal power as well, he has this worldly authority by human and not by divine right (83:19). "The two authorities, the spiritual and the temporal, are not to be mingled or confused, for the spiritual power has its commission to preach the Gospel and administer the sacraments. Hence it should not invade the function of the other, should not set up or depose kings, should not annul temporal laws or undermine obedience to government, should not make or prescribe to the temporal power laws concerning worldly matters" (83:12, 13).

Bishops are equal according to divine right. "The church cannot be better governed and maintained than by having all of us live under one head, Christ, and by having all bishops equal in office, however they may differ in gifts" (300:9).

13. Among the gifts of God to his church are pastors and teachers as well as apostles and prophets (324:26). The pastor proclaims the Gospel in Christ's stead (173:28), and God works through him (212:12). Even the ministry of godless men can be effectual: "They do not represent their own persons, but the person of Christ, because of the church's call, as Christ testifies (Luke 10:16), 'He who hears you hears me.' When they offer the Word of Christ or the sacraments, they do so in Christ's place" (173:28, cf. 171:19). No one should teach in the church unless he is rightly called (36, 214:1).

"If ordination is interpreted in relation to the ministry of the Word, we have no objection to calling ordination a sacrament . . . . The church has the command to appoint ministers; to this we subscribe wholeheartedly, for we know that God approves this ministry and is present in it (212:11, 12).

8

VATICAN I ON PRIMACY AND INFALLIBILITY

Maurice C. Duchaine

For an immediate setting, we shall give some information on the papal brief *Tuas Libenter* (Dec. 21, 1863; cf. Denz 1679-1684), then the development of the constitutions *Dei*

Filius and *Pastor aeternus,* of Vatican I, in the sections that immediately concern our topic.

The Papal Brief *Tuas Libenter* (Dec. 21, 1863)

Background

This is a direct result of the congress of German theologians held in Munich in 1863. Two schools are usually designated: the "German school" composed of such men as Möhler and Hefele at Tübingen and Görres and Döllinger at Munich, and the "Scholastici school" to which belonged the ultramontanes and the "orthodox" and whose proponents were Kleutgen at Mainz and Denzinger, Hettinger, Hergenrother at Würzburg, along with Schrader and Franzelin at Rome.

The main theme at the meeting was the defense of the freedom of scientific research, especially against ecclesiastical censuring. Ecclesiastical censures were not seen as useless, for no one knows where dogma begins and where science ends, but they are inopportune, especially at a time when a new synthesis between theology and philosophy was called for, and they were an obstruction to true research.

Döllinger's paper (*Rede uber Vergangenheit und Gegenwart . . .*) became the focal point of discussion. Döllinger made the following claims:

• Theology is the scientific knowledge that the church has of herself and of her past. Since this knowledge contains a divine element, it can only be a shell which contains an inexpressible core.

• Theology developed through Judaism and the Greek culture, from the time of the influence of Alexandria to the scholasticism of the thirteenth century. This development of Christian theology lacked life and a sense of history; this is the contribution that German scientific study can make.

• This study implies a freedom of research and not an atmosphere of suspicion and distrust either on the part of individuals, magazines or ecclesiastical authorities.

• Dogmas exist, but they must be given new life and explained by theology, which involves philosophy and reason. The work of elaboration should be limited only by dogma itself.

The reaction was strong both before the meeting, when the agenda was made known, and during the meeting itself:

• The theologian cannot be in conflict with defined dogma.

Since it is not clear where dogma begins and research ends, it is necessary to follow directives.

• The theologian has to keep in mind the commonly held position of the theological schools and the general consent of the faithful.

• The living magisterium of the church must be observed.

• The church has the right to recommend a theological school, not only for its doctrine but also for the school's methodology.

• When a theologian teaches a doctrine that the authorities of the church believe is contrary to Catholic doctrine, the church has the right to intervene.

• The church alone can judge when this intervention is necessary.

Pius IX, friendly at first to the Congress, had a change of heart when he received the reports from the apostolic nuncio who had attended the meetings. *Civilta Cattolica* began a series of articles on faith, knowledge, censures, etc. Cardinal Reisach composed the document which was promulgated on Dec. 21, 1863: the brief *Tuas Libenter,* sent to the Archbishop of Munich.

Statements:

• By authentic magisterium which is divinely instituted is the supreme pontiff and the bishops in union with the successor of St. Peter.

• That magisterium expresses itself not only in *definitionibus solemnibus* . . . not only in those things which must be believed because of an infallible judgment on matters that must be believed in faith and morals . . . but also in those things which the ordinary magisterium of the whole church, dispersed throughout the world, presents as divinely revealed and is therefore retained in the universal and constant consensus of Catholic theologians.

• It is also necessary to obey the decisions of the Roman congregations as regards those things which have been commonly and constantly held by Catholic consensus, such as theological truths and conclusions.

The basic point being made was that faith was not restricted to conciliar definitions; this point was repeated in the *Syllabus of Errors,* Dec. 8, 1864; cf. Denz. 1722.

Summary of the Brief:

There is a double subject of infallibility: the church, the apostolic see, the councils, the supreme pontiff, in the exercise of an official *judicium;* and the "ordinary magisterium" of the entire church dispersed throughout the world.

Infallibility can be expressed in two ways, as regards the subject of infallibility: *definire = judicium;* and *tradere =* ordinary magisterium.

The same obedience is required of both (cf. Denz. 1683).

The Constitution *Dei Filius* (April 24, 1870)

The Constitution's original schema was discussed from December 28, 1869 to January 10, 1870. The second schema came before the council from March 18 to April 12 and the result was promulgated on April 27, 1870.

The First Schema (prepared by Franzelin; see Mansi 50, 59-74).

The point was made that conciliar definitions are not the only criteria of faith; other criteria are what the church understands as an article of faith, even if no definition is involved, and Scripture as universally understood by the Fathers (Mansi 50, 61). The schema was rejected as too academic.

The Second Schema (prepared by Bishop Martin of Paderborn; see Mansi 51, 31-38). Discussion centered on the object of faith (during the council meetings and was worked upon by the Commission on Faith, *Deputatio Fidei*).

The discussions repeated the points that had been made in that of the first schema, namely that the object of faith includes more than just conciliar definitions and that one has to consider that which is accepted unanimously by the church (e.g., love of enemies).

A development of terminology emerged:

Fide divina et catholica credenda sunt, quae sive judicis dogmaticis sive universali et ordinaria doctrina et praedicatione credenda proponuntur.

The second aspect *sive universali et . . .* does not speak of the manner the object of faith is enunciated. Also, there is the problem of determining that which is of the universal magisterium. Because this second aspect is more vague and difficult to make precise, the tendency was to put it aside and give it less importance in the discussions.

Solemni judicio became identified with *ecclesia coadunate* or the church come together, while *ordinario magisterio* was applied to the *ecclesia dispersa credenda proponuntur,* that which the dispersed church proposed to be believed.

The *solemni* added nothing new to *judicium,* already a technical term; *magisterium ordinarium* meant the bishops dispersed throughout the world. The Commission on Faith made the same observations while discussing the problem of the development of dogma (Mansi 51, 36 D).

Bishop Simor as the *relator deputationis Fidei* presented the text of the final draft of the Second Schema, *Dei Filius,* on March 18 (Mansi 57, 47 C). He pointed out that papal infallibility was not the point at issue here and repeated that the document aimed especially at answering those who limited the *assensu fidei* to official conciliar definitions (Simor cited *Tuas Libenter*), as opposed to the teaching church dispersed throughout the world and teaching in unanimity.

The following points of Bishop Meurin, bishop of Ascalon, probably summarize best that which came to be generally accepted:

There is one single infallibility, but different subjects: the pope and the magisterium in a general sense;

This magisterium is double: the solemn magisterium (the councils) and the "perpetual" magisterium (or ordinary), which would be the subject of a whole gamut of non-defined truths that are the object of faith (Mansi 51, 234 B-C).

On April 6, in the course of the final deliberations, Bishop Martin spoke basically in the above terms:

Porro fide divina et catholica ea omnia credenda sunt quae in Verbo Dei scripto vel tradito continentur et ab Ecclesia *sive solemni judicio sive ordinario et universali magisterio* tamquam divinitus revelata credenda propununtur (my italics).

and presented the same explanations.

Once again we note that the understanding of magisterium and infallibility developed in a very particular and restricted context, with the element of the *fides fidelium* and a number of other questions and problems forgotten in the background under a central focal point of authority.

We presented the above developments because as is obvious the stage was set when the questions of papal primacy and infallibility were presented to the council.

The Constitution *Pastor Aeternus* (July 18, 1870)

The discussion on the primacy and infallibility of the pope appeared at the moment that the council was deliberating on the nature of the church. On Jan. 21, 1870, the dogmatic constitution *De Ecclesia Christi* was distributed. This schema contained 15 chapters:

1. *Ecclesiam esse corpus Christi mysticum*
2. *Christianam religionem nonnisi in Ecclesia et per Ecclesiam a Christo fundatam excoli posse*
3. *Ecclesiam esse societatem perfectam, spiritualem et spirituralem*
4. *Ecclesiam esse societatem visibilem*
5. *De visibili Ecclesiae unitate*
6. *Ecclesiam esse societatem ad salutem consequendam omnino necessariam*
7. *Extra Ecclesiam salvari neminem posse*
8. *De Ecclesiae indefectibilitate*
9. *De Ecclesiae infallibilitate*
10. *De Ecclesiae potestate*
11. *De Romani pontificis primatu*
12. *De temporali sanctae Sedis dominio*
13. *De concordia inter Ecclesiam et societatem civilem*
14. *De iure et usu potestatis civilis secundum Ecclesiae catholicae doctrinam*
15. *De specialibus quibusdam Ecclesiae iuribus in relatione ad societatem civilem* (see Mansi 51, 539-551)

In the midst of the May, 1870 discussions of the above schema, a new section was introduced. This section was to be added to chapter 11 on *De Primatu* and both were to become a new document entitled *Constitutio La De Ecclesia Pastor aeternus* (or as it was also called *De Primatu et Infallibilitate Romani Pontificis*. Discussion was to center on *Pastor aeternus* while Kleutgen was commissioned to take the rest of the material from the original schema on the church and to draw up *Constitutio IIa De Ecclesia*. Unfortunately, the council had to terminate its sessions before this new constitution could be brought on the council floor and the discussions on it help to balance off the one-sided and harshly sounding statements of *Constitutio Ia*.

The following are a collection of seven areas that are meant to indicate the tenor of the discussions that took place.

1. *In Primo Schemate De Ecclesia* (Mansi 51, 539-553)

This first schema on the church was prepared by Perrone on the infallibility of the church in general and Cardoni on papal infallibility (Mansi 49, 619 C). Both of these men belonged to the theological commission, which had decided to use the syllabus as the starting point. Among the materials they used were the following three questions that had been distributed:

- Whether the infallibility of the pope is different from that of the church? The answer of all was a resounding no.
- Whether the infallibility of the pope is basically and principally the infallibility of the church? The answer of all: yes. They all agreed there is only one infallibility, but there was no explanation of what was meant by "principally."
- Whether the infallibility of the pope is destructive of the infallibility of the bishops? All answered no.

In the text, we notice the following two combinations: *episcopi coadunati* and the pope and *episcopi dispersi et coadunati*.

2. Addition to Chapter 11 of the *De Ecclesia* Schema

This is the addition that with Chapter 11 was to become *Pastor aeternus*. It was only about 20 lines long in its original length and was entitled *Decretum de Summi Pontificis Primatu*. It had been prepared long before the council and among some of its statements were

- The infallibility of the pope is not to be compared with that of the bishops;
- The promise of Jesus Christ is permanent and is effective each time the pope speaks *de auctoritate sua*.

3. Discussions of May 5-7, 1870 of the Commission on Faith (Mansi 53, 248-255)

Among the questions that arose was that of the single or double subject of infallibility. At first the commission favored *unicitas subjecti*, but from May 5 on the new text spoke of one infallibility with two subjects, *sive in Ecclesiae capite, sive in toto magisterio*. The fathers of the council were clearly aware that *Pastor aeternus* presented only one aspect of the magisterium in its statements on papal infallibility.

4. The Constitution *Pastor aeternus* (Mansi 53, 240-244; 252-256)

In the course of the discussions, the following distinction emerged:

- Passive infallibility, *universalitas fidelium*, the infallibility of the church, which was based on St. Paul's *Ecclesia est columna et fundamentum veritatis*. The *corpus fidelium* cannot be led into error or be deceived when the condition of infallibility are fulfilled.

- Active infallibility or the power of the magisterium in its *actus docendi;* this power was for the benefit of the faithful.

We can conclude that infallibility of the faithful was not a point at issue in these exchanges; it was not discussed explicitly, but neither was it rejected. Rather, it was agreed upon and fell into the background.

5. *Constitutio IIa De Ecclesia* (Mansi 53, 308-317)

This schema, written by J. Kleutgen, was quoted during the discussions but never saw daylight on the council floor itself. The text spoke of the double subject of infallibility, but used a variety of expressions: *cum, sub* and *ex sancto Pontifice.* It also contained the distinction between *infallibilitas in credendo* (the faithful) and *in docendo* (the magisterium).

6. Report of the Commission on Faith by Bishop Gasser, July 11, 1870

In his report, Bishop Gasser gave the following explanations to the questions that had been submitted by some of the council bishops:

- Is papal infallibility personal? Yes, since they wanted to exclude the distinction between the *Sedes* and the *Sedens,* but no if the question means a private infallibility.
- Is papal infallibility a separate thing in itself? We can answer yes if it is meant that the pope receives a special help from the Holy Spirit because of the special promise of Jesus Christ; no, if one means that the pope does not have to act within the church.
- Is the papal infallibility absolute? No, absolute infallibility belongs to God alone.

7. Final *Relatio* by Bishop Zinelli (see Mansi 52, 1310)

In his final explanation before the vote, Bishop Zinelli insisted that the document at issue did not answer the question: Does infallibility pass from the pope to the body of bishops or does God also give the power of infallibility immediately to the body of bishops (of whom the pope is the head)? Vatican I did not treat of this question.

Terminology of Vatican I on Primacy and Infallibility

The theologians who had prepared the *De Ecclesia Christi* schema indicated very early in the game what they had in mind as regards papal primacy; the council was asked to affirm that papal jurisdiction was "authentic," "universal," "episcopal," "ordinary," and "immediate." There was an insistence on the part of the leadership to have as strong and clear a definition as possible. The following is a summary of the meaning of some of the major terms that either appear in the final text or else were objects of major discussion.

Authentic jurisdiction (chap. 3, Canon, 3064; chap. 4, 3065; numbers are from *Denziger-Schönmetzer* given in Document 1)

The pope is not a mere observer, a spectator; he has the power of governing, the full and supreme power of jurisdiction over the church (*jurisdictio plena et suprema super Ecclesiam,* see references given above). It was also true that the body of bishops had this power *etiam et eamdem jurisdictionem plenam et supremam super Ecclesiam* (see Mansi 52, 1108-1109). The relationship between the powers of jurisdiction of the pope and of the bishops was never clarified, although the question was often raised.

universalis (chap. 3, 3059, Canon, 3064; 3063). This was used in terms of emphasizing power over the entire church.

episcopalis (chap. 3, 3060). In authentic jurisdiction over the whole church, the pope had the three-fold power of teaching, ruling and ministering.

ordinaria (chap. 3, 3060, 3064). The pope has jurisdiction through the power of his office, *adnexum officio,* as opposed to delegated authority. There was much debate on this word because *ordinarie* could also be used in contrast to extraordinary (*in casibus extraordinarius*) when describing the exercise of jurisdiction. Ordinary could then have meant habitual jurisdiction in local churches.

When the word was first understood as *ordinarie* or habitual exercise, two major dangers were brought up with this word: This could effectively destroy the jurisdiction of a bishop in his diocese; would he become a delegate of the pope? The long-standing rights of the oriental patriarchs would be threatened if this power were attributed to the pope.

As the meaning of the word was clarified, it became clear that the word *ordinaria* was used in terms of *non est delegata* and in reaction to those who would restrict the exercise of papal jurisdiction to extraordinary cases, thereby effectively reducing his ministry to extraordinary cases. In his *relatio,* Bishop Zinelli (Mansi 52, 1100 B-1119 A) insisted that *Pastor aeternus* was concerned with the pope only; there was to be a chapter in *Constitutio IIa De Ecclesia,* chap. 4: *De ecclesiastica hierarchia,* where the principle was to be enunciated that the jurisdiction of bishops is also *de iure divino* and cannot be eliminated either by the pope or the councils. As regards the rights of the patriarchs, these are to be respected, as in the past, but these are a matter of discipline or ecclesiastical right (Mansi 52, 1103).

immediata (chap. 3, 3060, 3064). The pope's power was capable of being exercised directly on all the faithful without having to pass through the bishops.

ex cathedra (chap. 4, definition, 3074). Four conditions are given for an *ex cathedra* statement:

- When the pope fulfills his role as pastor and teacher of all Christians, as the universal head (using his supreme apostolic authority);
- The definition concerns doctrine of faith and morals of a revealed truth or one closely connected to it;
- He intends to bind the whole church;
- (seen later as a condition) it has to be known that he is defining (it is another question how this is to be determined).

When the above four conditions are fulfilled, the pope enjoys by divine assistance, as promised to him in the person of Peter the infallibility that Jesus desired his church to have. This is not a personal "privilege," nor is this power unconditioned or absolute (only God has absolute power).

Divine Assistance (*per assistentiam divinam,* chap. 4, 3074). The source of papal infallibility is not simply through his pontifical authority, but through a special divine assistance for an act (Mansi 52, 1213 A). This is not a power "possessed" permanently by him; the person of the pope is not changed. It is described by Cardinal Guido as an *auxilium actuale,* a *lux transiens* or an intellectual light in the functioning of his office when he is acting *ex cathedra,* that is, defining. Gustave Thils, after reading Bishop Gasser's report along with the rest of the discussion, states ". . . we believe that we should defend the doctrine that the pope enjoys divine assistance which preserves his dogmatic judgment from error *only when he speaks ex cathedra . . .*" (my italics; *L'infaillibilité* pontificale, Ed. Duculot, 1969, p. 185; see pp. 176-185).

ex sese, non autem ex consensu Ecclesiae (chap. 4, 3074). The definitions of the Roman pontiff who defines *ex cathedra* are irreformable *ex sese* and not because of the consent of the church. He does not have this absolutely, only God has absolute power; once again this statement is made; he has this power as he *represents* the church (Mansi 52, 1213 B-C, 1214 B). His power is not separate from the infallibility of the church, since there is only one infallibility and Christ promised infallibility to the entire magisterium of the church, to the apostles united to Peter (see Bishop Gasser, Mansi 52, 1216 B-C).

In giving the *relatio* on the above phrase, Zinelli explained *. . . ut coarctari non possit sed a iure tantum naturali et divino . . .* (Mansi 52, 1108 D-1109 A). *. . . a iure . . . divino . . .,* what Christ wanted for Peter and his successors. Infallibility was not divided up, partly held by the pope and partly by the bishops together with the pope. He exercised the whole power of infallibility when he spoke *ex cathedra*.

In his report, Bishop Gasser explained that the statement was intended to be a rejection of the opinion that the aid and counsel of the bishops were a strict and absolute necessity for any infallible dogmatic judgment of the pope (see Mansi 52, 1215 D). One could allow for a relative necessity, but that belongs to the conscience of the pope and is not to be incorporated in a dogmatic statement. The phrase is a rejection that all infallible judgments as a necessary and absolute condition must have an antecedent, concomitant and subsequent agreement.

Object of infallibility: The pope has the same sources as the church (Scripture, tradition and the unanimous accord of the current preaching of the whole magisterium of the church. The purpose of the power of infallibility is to protect revelation and the deposit of faith (see chap. 4, 3070). The object of infallibility is revealed truths. How about truths closely connected to these revealed truths? The answer given was in the affirmative, but the problem persisted of explaining this adequately. Finally, unable to come to any satisfactory explanation, the council fathers resorted to the principle: the object is the same as that of the magisterium of the general church and that which current theology teaches about this (see the discussions from May 8 on, Mansi 53, 258 D; see chap. 3, 3060).

A good case can be made of the current theology of that time: it is *de fide* that all revealed truths can be taught infallibly by the church; as regards non-revealed truths which are closely connected with the revealed truths, it is merely theologically certain. It is hard to see how they would be considered the objects of infallible teaching (see Hans Küng, *Infallible?*, 1971, p. 69, also p. 100).

The Declaration of German Bishops, 1875

This is a response of 23 German bishops to a newspaper article which published a dispatch from Chancellor Bismarck to the effect that Vatican I had practically eliminated the power of the bishops. These were bishops who had attended Vatican I. Their declaration was approved by Pius IX on March 2, 1875 (see Irénikon, 1956, pp. 143-149 for the two documents). We shall translate sections that might be of interest.

. . . we cannot call the pope's power over ecclesiastical matters an absolute monarchy. He is subject to divine law and to that which Jesus Christ had in mind for his church. He cannot modify the church's constitution which was given to it by its Founder . . .

. . . the bishops are not the simple instruments of the pope, nor his mere functionaries without personal responsibility . . .

. . . the statement that the pope has become as a result of his infallibility a perfect absolute monarch rests on a completely false idea of the dogma of papal infallibility. As Vatican Council declared in clear and exact terms, infallibility belongs exclusively to the *teaching power* of the pope and this power extends exactly over the same area as the infallible teaching of the church. This power is bound by the content of sacred scripture and tradition, as well as to doctrinal decisions that have been made by the church in the past . . . Thus, *nothing has changed as regards the exercise of papal power.*

9

COMMUNION, COUNCILS, AND COLLEGIALITY: SOME CATHOLIC REFLECTIONS

Patrick J. Burns

Since 1960 Catholic theologians have produced a flood of historical and systematic studies on the collegial structure of the church and the collegial nature of ecclesial ministry. Chapter Three of *Lumen Gentium* is the result of some of these studies and the point of departure for others. The present paper offers some brief observations on several of the problems discussed in this recent Catholic literature on collegiality. Some of the points touched upon involve established Catholic doctrine. Others treat historical and dogmatic questions still disputed among Catholic theologians. The criterion of selection has been the significance of the material discussed for current ecumenical dialogue on 'the Petrine function,' i.e., Christian ministry on the level of the church universal.

My remarks will be grouped under three headings: (1) the notion of *communio* as the matrix for episcopal collegiality and expressions of that collegiality in ecumenical councils; (2) the relevance of historical conciliarism for contemporary Catholic ecclesiology; and (3) the relationship between the juridically unlimited papal primacy of jurisdiction taught by Vatican I (and Vatican II) and current Catholic reflection on the essentially collegial dimension of the Petrine office.

In general, the positions advanced in this paper are advanced as Catholic positions, not necessarily as *the* Catholic positions—if for no other reason than that *the* Catholic position on a number of the points discussed does not exist.

Collegiality in Communion

A striking development in recent Catholic ecclesiology has been a shift from the church universal to the communion of local churches as the starting point of theological reflection. This *communio*-ecclesiology provides a different perspective on the collegial dimension of episcopal office, including its expression in an ecumenical council. It also provides the context for a more nuanced interpretation of the relationship between papal office and the episcopal college.

Church as Communion of Local Churches

Building on the work of Congar,[1] Lécuyer,[2] Le Guillou,[3] Hamer,[4] and others,[5] Joseph Ratzinger has recently summarized the historical evolution of reflection on the church universal as a communion of local churches.[6] The basic unity of the church in the third century was the local eucharistic congregation, united under one bishop and the college of presbyters and college of deacons who assisted him in his pastoral ministry. Such local churches were not substations of the church universal or branch offices of a world-wide organization. Rather the local Christian community, united in faith in the saving word and in eucharistic fellowship in the body of the Lord, *was* the church of God for its locality, the effective presence of the whole Christ in its concrete life and worship. Yet precisely the principle of unity of this local church, the saving presence of Christ in word and sacrament, made it aware of its essential relationship to the other local Christian communities throughout the world (where the same Lord and the same Spirit brought about the same ecclesial reality). The local church, without ceasing to be fully church, existed only in a world-wide communion of churches which constituted the church universal. Moreover, this communion was expressed concretely, "sacramentally," through exchanges of letters of communion, eucharistic fellowship, mutual care and concern.

The agents of this communion were the *bishops* of the local churches, assisting at one another's consecration, gathering in local synods, and eventually grouped together in regional patriarchates. As leaders of the local churches and agents of *communio* between these churches, the bishops became conscious of constituting a communion of their own. They spoke

of themselves as a fraternity, an order, a body, and finally
(with Cyprian) a college.[7] Before Nicaea, consciousness of
this episcopal collegiality seems to have been primarily in
terms of patriarchal centers (Rome, Antioch, Alexandria)
insuring regional unity in diversity and in turn in communion
with one another.[8] Only with the ecumenical councils of the
fourth and fifth centuries did the *universal* episcopal college
express itself concretely and actively. After Nicaea, however,
consciousness of episcopal collegiality within the church universal became well established, though always in terms of a
communio of regional and local bishops who were both leaders in their own churches and jointly responsible for the unity
of faith and love in the church universal. Regional synods
and especially ecumenical councils continued, in this historical, largely implicit *communio*-ecclesiology, to constitute the
most complete expression of the bishops' collegial ministry
within the church universal, just as the local eucharistic communities of which the bishops were the pastors continued to
constitute the most concrete realization of the church of
God.

What was the place of the church of Rome (and the
bishop of Rome) in this ancient *communio* ecclesiology? Ratzinger again provides a useful summary of recent research.[9]
Before Nicaea Rome is established as the most important
patriarchal center within the world-wide Christian communion. Its Petrine origin, its preservation of pure apostolic
tradition, and its central position in a hostile pagan world
(*analogous* to the place of Jerusalem in the primitive
church[10]) are universally acknowledged. During the third century its bishops identify themselves as occupying the chair of
Peter. But clear claims on the part of the bishops of Rome
to a more-than-patriarchal primacy in the church universal
appear to have been made only in the fourth and fifth centuries.[11] Like reflection on the universal episcopal college,
papal claims to ultimate authority and responsibility in the
universal church emerge only as concrete manifestations of
the church universal come into being at Nicaea and the
later ecumenical councils. With Damasus, Innocent, Boniface, Celestine, Leo, and Gelasius, however, all the essential
elements of the doctrine of papal primacy in the universal
church are developed and, to a considerable extent, put into
practice throughout the Christian *communio*.[12] What is significant in this development is that reflection on both the
church universal and Roman primacy within that church

universal continued to be located within a *communio*-ecclesiology. Leo's consciousness of being not only the Western patriarch but, as bishop of Rome in succession to Peter, the occupant of a central office within the world-wide *corpus Christianorum* was much less an assertion of juridical authority than a confession of ultimate responsibility for peace, unity, and purity of faith in the ecumenical Christian *communio*. And that *communio* existed concretely only in the unity-in-diversity of local and regional eucharistic communities which, through their bishops, were in communion with one another *and* with the *communio*'s central church in Rome and its bishop. Later juridical specifications of this Roman primacy were inevitable. What was not inevitable was a shift in the *starting point* of such developments from a *communio* matrix to the notion of a universal church centered in its hierarchical head.

Papal Primacy and Episcopal Collegiality in a Universalist Ecclesiology

Yves Congar has devoted his life to examining these developments and to exploring the possibility of restoring the original *communio* context of the doctrine and practice of papal primacy without ignoring later doctrinal advances or the vast cultural changes that have intervened over the centuries. His *L'église de saint Augustin à l'époque moderne* is an outstanding Catholic summary of ecclesiological developments in the West since the fifth century.[13] A detailed analysis is impossible here, but several points should be noted.

The ancient *communio*-ecclesiology, still strong in the time of Gregory the Great, continued to be influential in the West throughout the early Middle Ages. Changing cultural and political conditions in the Carolingian era, however, led to the beginnings of a monarchist ecclesiology under popes like Leo IV, Nicholas I, and John VIII—in spite of the vigorous protests of metropolitans like Hincmar of Reims. In the eleventh century, supported by the Cluniac reformers, a resurgent papacy under Leo IX, Nicholas II, Alexander II, Gregory VII, and Urban II initiated the administrative centralization, clerical dominance, and canonical reforms which were to determine the shape of the medieval church and decisively influence Catholic ecclesiology for almost a thousand years. Consciousness of episcopal collegiality decreased sharply under strong post-Gregorian popes like Innocent III, Gregory IX, and Innocent IV.[14] The distinction between Rome's patriarchal privileges and its ecumenical primacy was largely forgotten in an effectively isolated Western Christendom.[15] Not *communio* but juridical concepts like *plenitudo potestatis* constituted the central concern of the canonists, papal and anti-papal, who now became so influential in the concrete life of the church. Not only the question of papal primacy but the basic context for all ecclesiological reflection was dominated by a universalist perspective that tended to reduce the individual local churches to mere units in an administrative whole.

The schism, councils, and reform movements of the late fourteenth and early fifteenth centuries did not effectively challenge this basic perspective.[16] Neither did the Catholic response to the Reformation in the sixteenth century and after, in spite of continuing traditions of episcopalism in anti-Roman circles and of universal episcopal collegiality in Roman circles.[17] Successful post-Tridentine reform encouraged still more Roman centralization. Almost a century elapsed between Vatican I's definition of papal primacy and Vatican II's complementary doctrine on the episcopacy, and even Vatican II was *largely* concerned with episcopal collegiality in the context of a universalist ecclesiology.[18] Though practically all the basic elements of the ancient *communio*-ecclesiology are explicitly mentioned somewhere in the documents of Vatican II,[19] its crucial statements on episcopal collegiality and papal primacy are often poorly integrated with its remarks on the local churches and *their* collegial bonds within the ecumenical Christian communion. With the resources at its disposal, the council made room for the communion of local churches in a predominately universalist ecclesiology. Without trying to turn back the cultural clock fifteen hundred years or minimize the current need for Christian ministry at the level of the church universal, Catholic theology must now attempt to locate that ministry more clearly in the underlying *communio* of local and regional churches so prominent in ancient Christian tradition.

Systematic Comments from an Ecumenical Perspective

In the light of the historical developments just indicated, what difference can a recovery of the *communio* matrix of ministry in the church universal be expected to make in the shape of Catholic ecclesiology? The following propositions indicate the bare bones of such an ecclesiological shift. Obviously what is at work here is more a change of focus than a change of content, but I suspect that the long-range pastoral consequences of such a change of focus within Catholicism could have important ecumenical implications as well.

(1) Episcopal collegiality (and the primacy of the bishop of Rome as head of the episcopal college) is grounded in the communion of local and regional churches which constitute the concrete reality of the church universal.

(2) Though neither the bishop of Rome nor the other bishops "represent" their churches in the modern sense of being their democratically authorized delegates, in another sense they do possess their office and exercise their functions on the level of the church universal precisely because they are the pastors of local and regional churches and agents of their communion.[20] Historically, papal primacy within the episcopal college is rooted in the position of the church of Rome as the center of the ecumenical Christian communion.[21] Historically, the bishops' collegial authority in the universal church is rooted in the collegiality of the individual churches of which they are the pastors, whose authentic faith they express, and whose ecumenical unity they preserve.

(3) The living, day-to-day unity-in-diversity among the local and regional churches is the care and concern of the bishops in a much more pervasive way than is episcopal collegiality as expressed in an ecumenical council. The same is true of relationships between the bishop of the center of the Christian *communio* in the church of Rome and the bishops of the other local and regional churches throughout the Christian communion. Informal exchanges (in *both* directions), ordinary business, regular consultation, local and regional episcopal conferences, occasional or regular Roman synods, etc. are all important and normal means of maintaining peace, unity, and purity of faith in the world-wide Christian *communio*. The church is truly church and truly one outside of an ecumenical council. It is not a "continuing council" in the sense of a standing parliament permanently convoked.[22]

(4) A ecumenical council remains, however, the most complete expression of the basic collegiality of the Christian communion of local and regional churches and, *within* that communion, of the episcopal college together with its head. Councils should be convoked as often as they are necessary or useful for the good of the universal church. In an age of rapid change and powerful centrifugal forces like the present, they might even be convoked on a regular basis. But they are purposeful gatherings, a supplement to rather than a

substitute for the ordinary ways of maintaining peace, unity, and purity of faith in the church universal.

(5) The cardinal rule for Christian ministry within the universal church is the "principle of subsidiarity."[23] Only those matters of doctrine and discipline should be treated at the level of the church universal which cannot be better handled at a lower level (i.e., at the level of the patriarchate, national or regional episcopal conference, local diocese, etc.). The purpose of ministry within the ecumenical Christian communion is peace, unity, and purity of faith, not worldwide uniformity of liturgical norms, doctrinal formulations, or church discipline. Ratzinger's call for new patriarchates within the Catholic communion should be implemented.[24] The argument that local churches need Rome's protection against the tyranny of local bishops is specious; there are much more effective ways of dealing with such abuses on a lower level. The historical *Verschmelzung* of Rome's patriarchal privileges and its primatial responsibility within the church universal continues, to a considerable extent, even after Vatican Two's brave statements on diversity of rites and discipline and the importance of the local church. The Council's doctrine of collegiality in communion will not become practically credible, even for Catholic Christians (and especially for non-Catholic Christians), until further reform occurs in this area.

(6) The other side of the coin is equally important: corresponding to the principle of subsidiarity is the principle of universal communion. The local or regional church is wholly church but not the whole church. It is never completely autonomous or a law unto itself, without responsibility to and for the other Christian churches throughout the world. It is fully church only in *communio* with the ecumenical Christian communion and with the center of that communion, the church of Rome, just as its bishop or patriarch is fully pastor on the local or regional level only in communion (in council or out of council) with the universal episcopal college and with its head, the bishop of Rome.

(7) Finally, the specifically theological basis for this unique Christian *communio* must be constantly emphasized. Changing patterns of civil government, formal organizations, and sociological structures can and should influence the concrete shape of the ecumenical Christian communion, just as they have done so abundantly in the past. But the controlling vision of the church as a sacramental faith community called into

being by the Father's deed in Christ and preserved in its authentic mission, functions, and structures by the Spirit's continuing presence must remain decisive.

Relevant Research on Conciliarism

Before discussing some of the more technical aspects of papal primacy and episcopal collegiality against the background of the *communio*-ecclesiology outlined above, it may be well to indicate the systematic import of some recent research on conciliarism. Conciliarism is an ambiguous word, and recent research has concentrated on 'conciliar' notions in several different periods: the roots of conciliarism in early medieval canon law, the various conciliar ideas abroad during the Western Schism and the councils of Constance and Basel, and the later history of political and theological conciliarism from Basel to Vatican I. There is no possibility of summarizing all the literature here, but three points are worth considering in the present context: (1) medieval canonical opinions on 'emergency' procedures in church government; (2) the notion of a college of counselors for the pope; and (3) the decree *Haec Sancta* of the Council of Constance.

Emergency Procedures in Church Government

At least until Torquemada, technical ecclesiological questions remained largely the province of canon lawyers, not theologians. Practical men rather than system builders, these medieval canonists produced what seems to the uninitiated a jungle of conflicting opinions with regard to papal primacy and the powers of an ecumenical council.[25] In matters of faith, the authority of a pope together with an ecumenical council is more considerable than his authority apart from a council, but what did this mean in canonical terms? Here the canonists could not agree. The primacy (and indefectibility in the faith) of the *ecclesia romana* was universally maintained, but *ecclesia romana* could mean the pope alone, the pope and his college of cardinals, the entire Christian community at Rome, the universal church, or a general council representing the universal church. Again, consensus could not be reached among the canonists. In fact, of course, papal canonical theory from Humbertus of Silva Candida (d. 1061) to Giles of Rome (d. 1316) underwent a progressive monarchical shift, corresponding to the growth of papal power (engineered largely by canonically trained popes) and compounded by anti-papal political opposition (supported sporadically by anti-papal canonists). Decretalists like Hostiensis (d. 1271) were more monarchist than decretists like Huguccio (d. 1210), just as Innocent IV (d. 1254) was more a monarch than Innocent II (d. 1143).

One canonical principle remains constant throughout the entire period: "no human juridical authority is competent to pass judgment on a legitimate pope" [*ipse (papa) a nemine est judicandus*]. One exception to this canonical principle also remains constant from Humbertus to Giles of Rome: "unless he is found to deviate from the faith" [*nisi deprehendatur a fide devius*].[26] The principle would be equivalently canonized as papal primacy of jurisdiction at II Lyons, Florence, ·Vatican I, and Vatican II.[27] The exception would provoke endless controversy, occasion the Council of Constance, but never be officially denied.[28] Presumably both the principle and the exception are still valid in contemporary Catholicism.

Interpretations of the exception varied considerably. Did a heretical pope automatically cease to be pope (Hostiensis on merely declaratory judgment), or was he deposed by some other juridical body like the college of cardinals or a universal council (Alanus on effectively depository judgment)? Did *a fide devius* mean only public and contumacious heresy, or did it include equivalent crimes against the unity and peace of the church (i.e., obdurate schism, notorious misconduct, failure to do what was necessary to preserve the church universal)? No canonical consensus was ever reached on either of these questions, and to my knowledge no official decision has ever settled the matter within the Catholic communion. The case of a legitimate pope guilty of heresy (or its equivalent?) remains—apart from the parallel case of insanity—the single quasi-juridical exception to the *juridically* unlimited papal primacy of jurisdiction defined at Vatican I.

Papal Counselors and the Elements of a Doctrine of Collegiality

Even at the height of papal monarchist thought in the thirteenth century, one compensating consideration was the ancient tradition of papal consultation. Though the juridical implications of this tradition remained disputed (until Vatican I), it was universally acknowledged that, with regard to new legislation and particularly in matters of faith, the pope ought ordinarily to exercise his *plenitudo potestatis* only after suitable consultation with other ministers in the church universal. A power bestowed for the good of the universal church ought to be exercised in living contact with that church.[29] But what constituted suitable consultation? Sometimes a general council was mentioned, along the lines of the seven medieval papal councils from I Lateran to Vienne. More often the college of cardinals was indicated as the appropriate consulting body. This college (which consisted entirely of curial cardinals until the pontificate of Alexander III) had acquired enormous power and prestige in the church since becoming the papal electoral college under Nicholas II. The cardinals' original liturgical significance was largely forgotten as they came to constitute a standing papal senate, increasingly important in papal legislation and administration and actually governing the church universal during a papal vacancy. If the pope needed counsel, who was in a better position to fill that need than his own curia?[30]

A quite different (and ultimately irreconcilable) canonical creation was the application of the law of ecclesiastical corporations first to the church of Rome and later to the church universal. Late in the thirteenth century Hostiensis analyzed the relationship between the pope and the college of cardinals in terms of the rights and responsibilities obtaining between the head of a canonical corporation and its members. The law of canonical corporations had been previously developed by the decretalists to handle litigation between local ordinaries and the canons of their cathedral chapters, who together constituted a *corporatio*. Hostiensis now applied this body of the law to the *corpus ecclesiae romanae* and its power in the church universal. To their considerable satisfaction, the cardinals in this theory were *pars corporis papae:* not the pope alone but the pope together with the curial cardinals possessed *plenitudo potestatis* in the church universal. Generations of canonists argued over Hostiensis' theory. The paplists among them often admitted his basic analogy but denied that the usual limitations on the head of a canonical corporation applied in the case of the pope. The anti-papalists among them insisted that such limitations did apply and based their conclusion on a fundamental principle of canonical corporations: authority resided in the corporation as a whole, was conferred on the corporation's head (*non dominus sed procurator*) by its members, and under certain conditions could be limited or withdrawn. Papal monarchy in this interpretation was actually Roman oligarchy, with the college of cardinals limiting as well as advising the pope. Consultation had become juridical dependence in the canonists' mind and in the long run would only provoke more one-sided assertions of papal *plenitudo potestatis.*[31]

In the fourteenth century still other canonists, not all of them anti-papal, developed a position hinted at in Hostiensis and extended the analogy of corporation law from the pope and the college of cardinals to the pope and the universal congregation of believers. John of Paris was the leading theorist of this school, but he was supported by both anti-curialists like William Duranti and pro-curialists like Frances-co Zabarella. The pope's *plenitudo potestatis,* though it was to be interfered with only in exceptional circumstances, ul-timately derived from and resided *radicaliter* in the whole congregation of believers. According to Tierney and others, it was this canonical theory (and not the anti-hierocratic position of Marsilius or Ockham's radical individualism) which provided the raw material for fifteenth-century con-ciliarism.[32]

Despairing of ending the Western Schism in any other way, pious and fundamentally conservative churchmen like Conrad of Gelnhausen, Henry of Langenstein, Dietrich of Niem, Pierre d'Ailly, Jean Gerson, and Zabarella himself turned at last to the *via concilii.* To justify this course of action in a situation where no single claimant to the chair of Peter could effectively establish his authority in the uni-versal church, certain elements in the canonical corporation theory developed a century before were appealed to. If ec-clesial authority resided at least *radicaliter* in the entire con-gregation of believers, then the present emergency situation clearly justified calling not merely a general episcopal coun-cil[33] but a general council "representing" (i.e., making pres-ent[34]) all the Christian people. Only such a council could settle the schism that was destroying the church of God. And that was exactly what was done.

What is to be said about this justification for the Council of Constance? Some distinctions have to be made. To the extent that specific *juridical* limitations on the pope's primacy of jurisdiction in the church universal were implied in this line of reasoning, later Catholic theology has dissociated it-self from the thought of the men of Constance. To the extent, however, that the radical collegiality of the whole Christian communion and its episcopal shepherds constitutes a real (though non-juridical) limitation on the exercise of papal primacy, I personally see no need to disagree with them.[35] And, on a more historical level, to the extent that the prevailing opinion at Constance reflected not even a conservative version of the thirteenth-century corporation theory but simply a passionate conviction that some effective substitute for non-existent papal authority must be found in order to reestablish that very authority, I doubt that there is any need to speak of real conciliarism being *officially* endorsed at Constance at all.

It is clear that the ancient principle of papal consultation spawned strange progeny in the fertile minds of the medieval canonists. From the perspective of Vatican I the basic distinction between moral responsibility and juridical limitation was often blurred in their unsystematic, pragmatically oriented speculation. The exaggerated claims made for the place of the college of cardinals in the universal church strike us today as somewhat quaint and curious. And the legalistic corporation analogy around which the canonists' thought revolved appears obviously inadequate in the light of our present appreciation of the true unity-in-diversity of the world-wide Christian communion. Nevertheless, this canonical reflection on the college of cardinals and the universal congregation of believers serves as a permanent reminder to Catholics that the pope never acts alone, even if his actions are not always collegial in the juridical sense of the term.

The Decree Haec Sancta *of the Council of Constance*

In spite of the enormous literature which has accumulated around the decree *Haec Sancta* in recent years,[36] its contemporary *systematic* relevance is quite limited. At least as I read the evidence, the real problems connected with *Haec Sancta* are historical rather than dogmatic—*unless* the decree is accorded the status of a strict dogmatic definition. Since these historical problems cannot be resolved here, let us simply indicate the pertinent historical data and concentrate on the systematic implications of the various interpretations currently proposed.

The basic facts are not in dispute.[37] At the insistence of Sigismund, on December 5, 1414, a general council was finally convoked at Constance to settle the Western Schism. All other approaches had been tried, and all had failed. After thirty-six years of schism, Europe was determined to have a universally recognized pope. The Pisa pope, John XXIII, at first supported the council, expecting it to confirm him as the sole legitimate pope. After he realized that he too would be forced to renounce all claims to the papacy, John fled Constance (March 20, 1415). Sigismund rallied the council. John was arrested. When the council formally deposed him (May 29, 1415), John accepted his deposition. Next the Roman pope, Gregory XII, was allowed (through his legate) to re-convoke the council and announce his abdication (July 4, 1415). That left only the Avignon pope, Benedict XIII, who steadfastly refused to cooperate with the council. Though the council only got around to deposing him officially two years later (June 26, 1417), Benedict lost any effective power after the deposition of John and the abdication of Gregory. Benedict never accepted his deposition, but that made no difference to anyone in Christendom except the faithful few who constituted his immediate entourage. After endless procedural disputes, the council approved five basic reform decrees on October 9, 1417. One of these was the decree *Frequens,* which stipulated that similar general councils be held at regular intervals in the future. The council then proceeded to elect a new pope, Martin V (November 11, 1417), and formally concluded its business some months later (April 22, 1418). The schism was over.

The decree *Haec Sancta* was approved during the council's rather tumultuous fifth session (April 4, 1415), after John's flight but before his deposition and Gregory's abdication. A weaker version of the same decree had been approved at the fourth session a week earlier. A number of the cardinals and the whole French delegation objected to the stronger version, though some of them were nevertheless present at the fifth session which approved it. The decree reads as follows:

This holy synod of Constance, constituting a general council and lawfully assembled to root out the present schism and bring about the reform of the church in head and members . . . declares that . . . representing the Catholic church militant, it holds power immediately from Christ and that anyone of whatsoever state or dignity, even if it be the papal, is bound to obey it in matters which pertain to the faith, the rooting out of the said schism, *and the general reform of the church in head and members.* Further, it declares that any person of whatsoever rank, state, or dignity, even if it be the papal, who contumaciously refuses to obey the mandates, statutes, ordinances, or instructions made or to be made by this holy synod *or by any other general council lawfully assembled concerning the aforesaid matters or matters pertaining to them* shall, unless he repents, be subjected to fitting penance and duly punished, recourse being had, if necessary, to other sanctions of the law.[38]

The italicized phrases were approved only at the fifth session and have been the object of controversy ever since.

Haec Sancta never received formal papal approval, but specific papal approval was hardly necessary. In *Inter Cunctos* (February 22, 1418) Martin V gave his general approval to whatever was done *conciliariter* at Constance. Moreover, both Martin and his successor, Eugene IV, were well aware that their own legitimacy depended on the legitimacy of Constance. Both popes consistently pursued a policy of undermining conciliarist power without ever attacking any of the *decrees* of Constance directly. However, as papal power grew, conciliarist *interpretations* of *Haec Sancta* could be repudiated. Under extreme pressure, Eugene in *Dudum Sacrum* (December 15, 1433) recognized the legitimacy of the Council of Basel—although the council had already reaffirmed *Haec Sancta* (February 15, 1432) and was to do so again (June 26, 1434) before Eugene managed to transfer it to Ferrara (September 18, 1437). When the rump council remaining behind at Basel later (May 5, 1439) issued the decree *Sacrosancta,* proclaiming the doctrine of *Haec Sancta* a defined dogma of faith, it lost what little support it had left. Eugene, in Florence, reacted vigorously, branding the *conciliabulum* as illegitimate in *Moyses Vir Dei* (September 4, 1439) and its conciliarist interpretation of *Haec Sancta* as erroneous in *Etsi Non Dubitemus* (April 20, 1441). After the debacle of the closing years of the Basel *conciliabulum,* conciliarist power was definitely broken, and Eugene's astute successor, Nicholas V, was able to reestablish traditional papal authority. The episode was ended, though (as always) the idea lived on.[39]

What is the contemporary *systematic* significance of *Haec Sancta* as it was approved at Constance (and twice reaffirmed at Basel while that council was still a legitimate general council)? Very little, I would say, as long as the decree is not regarded as a strict dogmatic definition. Nevertheless, its systematic relevance depends to a considerable extent on how one interprets the decree historically.

There are three general approaches represented among contemporary historians. One, the "traditional" Catholic approach, sees no problem at all. *Haec Sancta* has no dogmatic force because the Roman pope, Gregory XII, was the legitimate pope in 1415 and Constance therefore became a legitimate ecumenical council (at the earliest) only after its convocation by Gregory. *Haec Sancta,* approved three months before this event, is not a legitimate conciliar document. Martin V's general approbation of all that was done *conciliariter* at Constance can refer only to the council's transactions after Gregory's official convocation. Eugene IV's approbation of Basel as a legitimate council did not include any approval of its reaffirmations of *Haec Sancta,* as his later condemnation of conciliarism in *Etsi Non Dubitemus* proves. Whatever its historical significance, *Haec Sancta* can be safely ignored by Catholic dogmatic theologians.[40] This interpretation still has some support in Catholic circles,[41] but I would predict a rapid decline in that support in the years to come. The legitimacy of Grègory XII is the cornerstone of this position, and more and more historians are convinced that there was in 1415 and is today simply no way of determining which of the contending obediences in the Western Schism was legitimate. The actual situation was one of three plausible claimants, none of whom could establish his claim in the universal church, each of whom had a duty to do 'whatever was necessary' to settle the schism (under pain of losing the very papal office he claimed as equivalently *a fide devius* if he persisted in a course of conduct that was destroying the peace and unity of the church universal). I seriously doubt that the illegitimacy of Constance at the time of *Haec Sancta* can be historically established.

A second approach accepts *Haec Sancta* as a legitimate decree of a legitimate council but interprets it as an emergency response to a concrete impasse in church government. With no pope who could effectively establish his claim in the universal church, something had to be done, and the council did it. The reaffirmations of *Haec Sancta* at Basel (during its legitimate period) add nothing to the decree of Constance. In other words, the authority ascribed to a general council in *Haec Sancta* must be interpreted in terms of a council *without* a legitimate pope, not a council *against* a legitimate pope. Similarly, the reference to future councils must envisage either a continuation of the same situation (i.e., another council without a legitimate pope) or mean a council which *includes* the pope as head of the college of bishops. Genuinely conciliarist sentiments lay behind the reference to "reform of the church in head and members" included in the final text of the decree, but these notions were never officially endorsed by the majority at either Constance or Basel when they approved *Haec Sancta*. Again, whatever its importance as a historical precedent for emergency procedures in church government, *Haec Sancta* does not contradict Vatican I's definition of papal primacy of jurisdiction (even in the matter of church reform). The decree does not subordinate a legitimate pope to the authority of an ecumenical council.[42] I personally believe this interpretation comes closest to capturing the general intent of the Council of Constance when it approved *Haec Sancta*. However, the reform clause and the reference to future councils are part of the official text, and it is difficult to establish beyond doubt that they do not represent a limited victory for genuine conciliarist thought, if not at Constance, at least later on at Basel.

A third approach interprets *Haec Sancta* not only as a legitimate decree of a legitimate council but as a strict dogmatic doctrinal definition, as irreformable as the dogmas of Vatican I.[43] This was certainly the intent of the illegitimate *conciliabulum* of Basel which issued *Sacrosancta:* by making the doctrine of *Haec Sancta* (interpreted in a conciliarist sense) a matter of faith, the rump council wished to brand Eugene IV as a formal heretic, liable to deposition. However, there appears to be no compelling evidence that the earlier, legitimate conciliar approvals of *Haec Sancta* at Constance and Basel intended to define its doctrine (however interpreted) as a dogma of faith.[44] Some of those who consider *Haec Sancta* a dogmatic definition interpret it in a nonconciliarist sense and hence have no problem reconciling it with *Pastor aeternus*. Others, however, emphasizing the reform clause and the reference to future councils, interpret it in a conciliarist sense and claim radical discontinuity between Constance and Vatican I. Even if one is convinced that a limited conciliarism is implied in the text of *Haec Sancta*, such doctrinal discontinuity becomes a dogmatic issue only if the decree is accorded strict dogmatic status. Unless such dogmatic status can be established, and I seriously doubt that it can, the *most* that can be claimed is that Vatican I corrects any (non-defined) conciliarist elements in *Haec Sancta* when it defines the pope's juridically unlimited primacy of jurisdiction in the universal church. At least that is how I would assess the whole complex problem as it is presently debated within Catholic theology.

Primacy and Collegiality: Vatican I and After

If recent research on Constance indicates it was not as conciliarist as we have thought, recent research on Vatican I indicates it was not as papalist as we once believed. Historical studies of Vatican I[45] have established that practically every element in Vatican II's doctrine on the episcopacy was explicitly affirmed either in the text of *Pastor Aeternus* itself,[46] the official *relationes* of Zinelli and Gasser on the last two chapters of the constitution,[47] the complete schema on the church prepared by Schrader and revised by Kleutgen,[48] or the 1875 collective declaration of the German bishops approved by Pius IX.[49] The doctrine on the episcopacy developed in *Lumen Gentium* 18-27 was really not new. What was new was the juxtaposition in one official document of traditional Catholic doctrine on the *suprema potestas* of the episcopal college in the church universal[50] and equally traditional Catholic doctrine on the *suprema potestas* of the Roman pontiff, head of that episcopal college as bishop of Rome.[51]

Lumen Gentium clearly locates the ministry of both the pope and the episcopal college *within* the one people of God, and its statements on the full ecclesial reality of the local church are open to a thoroughgoing *communio*-ecclesiology as the basic framework for this papal and episcopal ministry on the level of the universal church—appropriately limited by the principle of subsidiarity to matters not better handled by the patriarchates, national episcopal conferences, etc. The real theological problem lies in specifying the exact relationship between the episcopal college (including its head, the bishop of the central local church in the ecumenical Christian communion) and the pope acting without *juridical* dependence on the college of which he is the head or the communion of local churches of which his is the center. Vatican II juxtaposed two statements on *suprema potestas* in the church universal, emphasized the juridical independence of the pope within this collegial ministry, and left further discussion to the theologians.

In my opinion, Karl Rahner's treatment of the problem is the most staisfactory.[52] According to Rahner, there can only be *one* organ possessing *suprema potestas* in the church universal: the universal episcopal college with its head, the bishop of Rome. It is contradictory to speak of two distinct

organs of such *suprema potestas:* either one would in fact
derive its authority from the other, or neither would be
really supreme. In Rahner's analysis, the episcopal college
can never exercise its *suprema potestas* except in union with
its head (i.e., at least never in formal opposition to a legitimate pope), but neither can the pope ever exercise *suprema
potestas* in the universal church except *as* head of the episcopal college (though there are no *juridical* limitations on
the exercise of this primatial power and no *juridical* recourse from the decisions of the legitimate pope). "Ontologically," every exercise of papal primacy is really collegial in
nature (i.e., the action of the head of the episcopal college
as head); "juridically," not every exercise of papal primacy is
collegial in the formal sense of the word. An arrangement
without exact parallel in civil government, this traditional
Catholic way of affirming effective headship without denying
genuine collegiality is presented as a necessary institutionalization of collegial Christian ministry on the level of the universal church.

Rahner sees no other way of relating papal primacy and
the authority of the episcopal college as both are developed
in the documents of Vatican II. Those who speak of two
inadequately distinct organs of *suprema potestas* in the
church universal can defend their position only in terms of a
juridically unlimited papal primacy, not in terms of a papal
ministry in the universal church that would be ontologically
independent of the episcopal college of which the pope is
the head.[53] For Rahner, the "Petrine function" of preserving
peace, unity, and purity of faith in the church universal is
institutionalized in an office which is essentially collegial even
when its *suprema potestas* is exercised by the pope without
any juridical dependence on the universal episcopal college.

Vatican I's emphasis on the pope's juridical independence
(and Vatican II's almost verbatim repetition of this doctrine)
deserve further examination. It is remarkable how much of
the debate at both Vatican I and Vatican II centered around
this single point. At Vatican I, for instance, even the minority's opposition to the definition of papal infallibility was
concerned largely with the juridical independence of this particular exercise of papal primacy in the area of doctrinal
authority. There was no substantial opposition to the notion
of the infallibility of the church universal or of the college of
bishops in union with its head. As has been pointed out so
often, the phrase *ex sese, non autem ex consensu ecclesiae*

was inserted into the final text of *Pastor Aeternus* (and repeated in *Lumen Gentium* 25) precisely to exclude even a weak Gallican version of episcopal reception as a juridical limitation on papal infallibility.[54] Similarly, the controversial *Nota Praevia* was attached by papal authority to the text of *Lumen Gentium* to allay the fears of those who thought the statements on episcopal collegiality in the text of that constitution could somehow be interpreted in terms of a juridical limitation on papal primacy of jurisdiction.[55]

This insistence on a juridically unlimited papal primacy was balanced at both Vatican I and Vatican II by the free admission of non-juridical limitations on that same primacy. Bishop Salas of Conception, Chile, summarized the attitude of the majority in his speech of June 10, 1870:

> The power of the supreme pontiff is limited by natural and divine law. It is limited by the precepts and teachings of Jesus Christ our Lord. It is limited by the common good of the church. It is limited by the voice of conscience. It is limited by right reason and by common sense. It is limited by the rule of faith and discipline, etc. . . . But it cannot be limited or restricted by the bishops, either individually or corporately, either in council or out of council.[56]

In his official *relatio* on chapter three of *Pastor Aeternus* (July 5, 1870), Bishop Zinelli of Treviso insisted that the proposed definition of papal primacy did not make the pope an absolute monarch in the church or absolve him of moral responsibility toward church law and church tradition; it did, however, assert his juridical independence and deny the juridical superiority of any other authority in the church, including the bishops assembled in council apart from the pope.[57] Similarly, in his official *relatio* on chapter four of *Pastor Aeternus* (July 11, 1870), Bishop Gasser of Brixen admitted the pope's moral obligation to use all appropriate means to inform himself of the faith of the church before making use of his supreme doctrinal authority to express that faith. What the pope taught infallibly was the consensus of the congregation of believers and the universal episcopate. What the proposed definition wished to exclude was simply any *absoluta necessitas*, in juridical terms, of prior consultation or subsequent approbation.[58] The same position was expressed at Vatican II, this time in a conciliar text (*Lumen Gentium* 25).[59] It should be noted that an amendment proposed by Pope Paul to the effect that the pope is "answerable to the Lord alone" in the exercise of his office was rejected on the grounds that "the Roman Pontiff is also bound to revelation itself, to the fundamental structure of the church, to the sacraments, to the definitions of earlier councils and other obligations too numerous to mention."[60] According to Catholic doctrine, papal primacy in the church universal is a primacy limited by the mission, functions, and structures of the ecumenical Christian *communio,* and the pope is morally bound to exercise his primatial office in accord with these limitations. What is formally excluded by both Vatican I and Vatican II is any *juridical* limitation on this papal primacy of jurisdiction in either its disciplinary or doctrinal exercise.[61]

It is quite important to locate this Catholic doctrine on the pope's juridically unlimited primacy of jurisdiction in the context of a comprehensive *communio*-ecclesiology and the moral responsibilities implied in such an ecclesiology. In Catholic tradition the local church of Rome constitutes a true center of the ecumenical Christian communion, and the bishop of Rome is a true head of the universal episcopal college. His office is one of maintaining peace, unity, and purity of faith in the church universal, *as* head of the college of bishops and *in communion with* the world-wide *communio* of local and regional churches. Papal actions which violate this basic arrangement do not contribute to the good of the universal church and inevitably provoke prophetic protest within the Christian communion and the universal episopal college.[62] As the continuing Catholic discussion of emergency procedures for church government indicates, even juridically unlimited papal primacy of jurisdiction does not ultimately trap the church universal in an absolutized juridical system. Nevertheless, as history indicates, quasi-juridical procedures against heretical popes are in no sense the primary Catholic defense against abuse of primatial authority. Rather, Catholicism relies primarily on Christian prophetic protest to compensate for the lack of juridical limitations on the exercise of papal primacy. I suppose the question is debatable, but I would personally view such public criticism *within* the church —the new creation of the Spirit whose unique fellowship can never be adequately institutionalized—as ultimately a much more effective protection against the abuse of papal power than any conceivable juridical system. I believe prophetic protest is particularly effective in a 'post-Constantinian' era like our own, when neither popes nor papal critics have any

significant secular forces at their disposal.[63] Certainly more
official acknowledgment of the moral limitations on the exercise of papal authority is needed, together with practical
demonstrations of the power of prophetic protest to correct
abuses of that authority without destroying ecumenical communion. Nevertheless, I suspect that Christians, like other
people, ultimately get the leaders they deserve.

A final theological problem with important ecumenical implications is the Catholic claim that the official ministry in
the church universal outlined above is of divine law, necessary for a fully structured church, an essential (if *relatively*
peripheral) component of the Christian reality revealed by
God and responded to by the community of believers. Although it involves the area of church government, the doctrine of Vatican I and Vatican II on the college of bishops
and its primatial head has dogmatic rather than disciplinary
status in Catholic theology. At least the canons of *Pastor
Aeternus* are regarded as strict dogmatic definitions.

All sorts of questions arise in connection with this Catholic
claim, all of which need further investigation. Perhaps it
would be appropriate to conclude this study by indicating
some of them. What can be said historically, for instance,
about the continuity between whatever ministry existed on
the level of the church universal in the apostolic age and
later institutionalization of that ministry in the Catholic
communion? Dogmatic documents which make historical
assertions are necessarily open to historical criticism. Current
historical research on the origins of Roman primacy and
episcopal collegiality will inevitably produce more qualified
Catholic interpretations of the canons of Vatican I. Similarly,
in the light of our present appreciation of human historicality,
how are we to interpret dogmatic statements concerning the
juris divini status of particular church structures and sacramental practices? All admit that God's will in these areas is
always mediated by human arrangements which concretize
divine law in human law, but how can we distinguish one
from the other? Even in the area of divine law, does the will
of God for a structured sacramental church *in* history necessarily preclude real change at a later period of history and
in a different cultural context?[64]

Finally, on a more specific point, in what sense is the
current Catholic institutionalization of a juridically unlimited
but ontologically collegial papal primacy a *necessary and irreversible* concretization of effective headship within the col-

lege which fulfils the Petrine function in the church universal?
I would anticipate considerable ecumenical interest in examining Catholic tradition on this point.

Dogmatically, can a valid distinction be made between the "essential" Catholic doctrine on papal primacy and its present juridical concretization—in spite of the specific stress on precisely this juridical arrangement at both Vatican I and Vatican II? I do not know, but in the years to come Catholic theologians will either have to work out such a distinction or provide more justification for the dogmatic necessity of this particular institutionalization of effective headship within the episcopal college.

Pastorally, even if the dogmatic possibility of alternate juridical arrangements can be established, are any viable alternatives available to the present Catholic arrangement (particularly as interpreted in the *communio*-ecclesiology outlined above)? In other words, granting the vast gap that exists between Catholic theory and Catholic practice, are further juridical provisions for the Petrine office really what is needed? A number have been suggested, including a division of powers on the primatial level.[65] I personally would not place too much emphasis on such juridical changes. Undoubtedly some structural adjustments are in order; but I am inclined to believe that internal reform and renewal, more diversity on the regional level, and regular informal consultation at the level of the universal church are really what is needed.[66]

Catholics have traditionally claimed that the Petrine function requires a truly collegial office with a personal (and juridically unlimited) head at its center if Christian ministry within the world-wide Christian communion is to be fully institutionalized. I suspect that no one will take seriously the Catholic claim that this is how things *have* to be until Catholics themselves give more practical proof that this is how things *can* be in the one church of God. In the long run, effective maintenance of peace, unity, and purity of faith in the church universal is the most compelling evidence for the Catholic position we have been discussing.

10

PAPAL PRIMACY:
DEVELOPMENT, CENTRALIZATION, AND
CHANGING STYLES

Kilian McDonnell

Jesus worked within the framework of Israel where he called God's people to reform. He made no attempt to break with Israel. Indeed, he attended the temple and synagogue services, as did his followers after his death and resurrection. The followers of Jesus considered themselves to be true Israelites and wished to go on being Israel.[1] They did not aspire to be an elite, withdrawn from the rest of Israel, nor did they feel themselves called to establish new offices and structures. The Christian community was Israel called to enter the kingdom by accepting the words of Jesus. Therefore, the idea of a community or a church did not necessarily separate the followers of Jesus from Israel. It is not a matter of surprise, then, that there are not recorded in the oldest New Testament traditions any church-founding words which envisage a community separate from Israel, with its own offices, ministries and structures. This makes it understandable that Jesus did not leave a ministerial blueprint which had only to be executed.[2] There are no recorded words of Jesus about successors of the apostles, who were to carry on the ministry of the apostles. The same holds true with regard to Peter. There is considerable evidence that Peter played a special role among the disciples of Jesus during Jesus' lifetime and ministry. There is even stronger evidence of his prominence among the Twelve at Jerusalem after Jesus' death.[3] Such a leadership role for Peter is seen in various

173

New Testament writings as reflecting the will of Jesus. But Jesus is not said to have laid down precise forms for a continuing Petrine ministry.

The historical evidence for Peter's career after the death of Jesus is limited. Therefore a study of these New Testament texts alone yields meagre results. The question is not only of the Petrine ministry as seen in the New Testament. There is a further question. Is there a historical, constitutional continuity, of a linear kind, between the New Testament ministry of Peter and the later Petrine ministry, that is the papacy itself? The present stage of studies in this area does not seem to show that this continuity is historically demonstrable. That at the present the continuity is not demonstrable does not, of course, mean that it is non-existent.

I personally believe that what has come to be called the Petrine office exercised by the popes was given by Christ in Peter. Though not emphasized in this paper it is a working supposition to what follows. The problem is how does one arrive, taking the New Testament evidence for a Petrine ministry, which is admittedly difficult to interpret, at the Petrine office as the church has experienced it from the time, say of Pope Leo the Great, if not earlier. Because of the paucity of historical evidence for Peter's career after the death of Jesus, a study of the New Testament texts referring to Peter in the post-resurrection community does not give the kind of clear picture one would hope to have. Like the evidence for other New Testament ministries, the evidence for the Petrine ministry must be interpreted within the ongoing life of the faith community. The patterns of ministry which emerge in this community do so under the stimulus of a number of factors, not all of them theological.

The Petrine ministry as exercised by the popes today is the product not only of the roles Peter played in the New Testament but also is the produce of a long process of development, a development which can be studied in some still existing religious documents. But the study of the documentary evidence is not by itself sufficient to understand the historical development of the papacy. The primary focus of the investigation must be the on-going life of the community, as that community is affected by the totality of human experience. The focus, therefore, is on the history of the pilgrim people of God, a people whose attitudes and ministries are formed by the scriptures, but also by a whole spectrum of secular forces: political, economic, social, geographical. The emergence and development of the Petrine office is seen as the end result of the inter-action over an extended period of time of both theological and non-theological factors.

Though the development of the Petrine ministry in post-biblical times is not here identified as part of revelation, narrowly conceived, this development is in keeping with the developmental nature of religious institutions and revelation in both the Old and New Testaments. It is also in keeping with the developmental character of revelation itself.[4] God gradually unfolds his revelation in the historical events of a pilgrim people. The formation of the canon of the Old and New Testaments was also an expression of the principle of development. There was a gradual awareness of what belonged to the canon. From this gradual awareness developed a profession of faith, initially around the year 400 and definitely at the Council of Trent. The Spirit guides the church into all truth, including the truth of the profession of the canon. The certainty which the church has with regard to the canon surpasses a merely historical certainty, because she acts in relation to the Spirit's witness.[5] Within the Calvinist tradition this development of the canon was connected with a special form of God's providence (*providentia specialissima*) or with a peculiar divine activity concerning the canon (*actio Dei circa canonem*), or with a clear interior witness of the Spirit (*testimonium internun sancti Spiritus*).[6] Or a Protestant scholar talks about the developmental process and its end, the canon, as being related "to a special, direct intervention or inspiration of God."[7] This special activity of God or witness of the Spirit, does not exclude non-theological factors in the development, but presupposes them. It is because the Word of God reaches man in his human environment and in his human witness that the development of the canon needs the kind of special intervention, inspiration or guidance. Development is both a revelational and a canonical principle and is therefore normative. Normative is here understood not as a tool for validating doctrine but as a principle by which the community of faith understands itself and its on-going history.

The ministry of Peter recorded in the New Testament was continued and developed in post-biblical times in the Petrine ministry which becomes the Petrine office. Because it was developmental it took on a variety of forms. Further, the full Petrine nature of papal ministry was only gradually recognized. This development is under the gospel and is authentic only in so far as it proceeds in fidelity to the biblical witness. The confrontation of the historical developments with the gospel is a never-ending process, because there is an innate tendency to look upon theological development as good. One could hardly hold in principle that all development is necessarily good or desirable. Even granted the legitimacy of the development of the Petrine office, not all the powers now exercised by the pope (appointing bishops, convoking councils) represent powers necessary to and inherent in the Petrine role which the pope exercises. There is not only a development of the essential ministry but a parallel development in non-essentials.

When we approach the development of any Christian ministry we are faced with the presence of both human and divine factors. Though we know that both kinds of factors are present and operative, it is not possible clearly and precisely to separate the one from the other on the supposition that what is more manifestly human is to that degree less obviously divine.[8] The human factors in the life of the community, on the one hand, and, on the other hand, God's will and power, are not separable. Herman Fortmann once wrote that "God never acts in anything really from outside, because he is present in everything that exists distinct from him as the deepest foundation of that existence, as Creator".[9] This does not mean that an intervention by God is ruled out. What is ruled out is intervention from the outside, not intervention from within.

In making a judgment on how the church adapts itself to the changing patterns and situations, it is not possible to say that a given socio-cultural situation is the purely human element and the church's response the divine element. In Acts 6:1-6 the economic situation of the Hellenist widows was responded to by the church in the institution of leaders for the Hellenist group of Christians. The early community saw in the institution of this new leadership role a response in the Holy Spirit to the economic plight of the widows. This was a response which touched the interior life of the church through a ministry of economic relief, preaching and baptism. The human and the divine are not separable in the evolution of ministries. "No concrete frontier can be drawn between nature and grace. It does not exclude the fact that grace remains a gift."[10]

Besides the Petrine texts and the leadership role exercised

by Peter, there are human factors which contributed to the evolution of the doctrine of papal primacy. There was a widespread conviction in antiquity that Rome was accorded special honor because it was the first city of the empire. Canon 28 of Chalcedon said that "to the throne of the elder Rome, because that was the imperial city, the fathers naturally rendered the first honors." Whatever the disputes over this canon it does witness to the belief that Rome was first because of her place as the capital city of the empire.[11] Rome herself had from the beginning the consciousness that she was distinctive among all the churches because both Peter and Paul had suffered as martyrs in Rome, and in that city were to be found the "trophies" of the apostles.[12] Thus a major factor in the emergence of the bishop of Rome was the tradition that Peter and Paul were martyred and had their graves in the capital city of the empire. This can be seen as something more than a fact of political history, devoid of all divine impulse or content. The border between what is of divine will and what is of man's making cannot be defined, "and indeed cannot be defined in principle."[13] The presence of political facts and the operation of human laws of social organization do not postulate the absence of divine intent.

The church is continuously making judgments on the interaction of human and divine elements in the ministry of the church. In regard to the continuing Petrine function the church looks to New Testament evidence. But the church does not depend only on the words of the historical Jesus, even though the function he seems to have assigned to Peter is an important factor in the later development of the Petrine office. Much less is the church dependent for the structures of her ministry merely on the socio-political environment in which the church finds herself. Decisive in the structuring of the ministry is the Holy Spirit. The Spirit is not an anti-institutional moment but is constitutive of the church. The Spirit is also constitutive of her ministries both in their givenness and in their changing styles. It is then because of the constitutive nature of the Spirit that the church is able to maintain herself as a divine givenness in history and at the same time make judgments on the interaction of human and divine elements in her history.

If a special form of God's providence, or a peculiar divine activity, or an interior witness of the Spirit was present in that all important development of the canon of the Scrip-

tures, and in the decision which the church took with regard
to the canon (a decision which the church has felt she is free
to extend but not to repudiate), could not such a special
form of God's providence (*providentia specialissima*), or a
specific divine activity concerning the papacy (*actio Dei
circa . . .*), or a clear witness of the Spirit (*testimonium
internum sancti Spiritus*) also be present in the development
of the Petrine ministry into the Petrine office. The church's
judgment on the contents of the canon is not based on any
precise evidence coming from the historical Jesus. If a
"special direct intervention" of God is seen in the formation of the canon, and if the decision as to its contents is
not based on specific evidence coming from Jesus, could not
the same "special direct intervention" account for the
emergence of the Petrine office, for which there is some
evidence in the leadership role assigned to Peter in the New
Testament witness.

Since the emergence of the Petrine office took place de-
velopmentally, as a growth experience in the life of a community unfolding in history, the later historical features must
not uncritically be read back into the earlier experience. In
a developmental growth process what is true at one stage of
life may not be true of another. For instance from the
fifth to the tenth centuries the primacy was not "confessed" in the formal-juristic sense but more in a religious
sense. It was in Rome that Peter was martyred because of
his faith. His grave was there. To strengthen their faith
in times of difficulties people turned to Rome and to the
successors of Peter. From this situation Rome derived a
large amount of factual authority, which was not founded
on purely juridic considerations.[14] The historicity of the
Petrine office must be kept in mind. The more canonical
developments of papal power were not present in the earliest
periods when authority was seen less in canonical terms and
more in religious terms. One would not want to read back
papal centralism or the canonical structures of papal control into those centuries when Rome acted as a moderator.
Though the present role of the holy see could not be described as that of a moderator, article 14 of the *Decree on
Ecumenism* contends that "for many centuries . . . the
Roman see acted by common sent as moderator." Given the
historicity of the Petrine office and its developmental nature one could ask whether in response to an historically
different pastoral theology and to historically different pat-

terns of exercising authority, the Holy Spirit is not inviting the church to make the papacy a more effective instrument for unity by making it function in a simpler style which typified its earlier period. There is no theological reason why the papacy could not again assume the role of moderator as long as it is not reduced to the function of a mere chairman. In suggesting this one would not wish to deprive the Roman see either of the initiative or authority it needs to fulfill its unitive function. Nor would it deprive the Roman see of all teaching responsibility. In this too it would retain a preeminent responsibility, but it would be collegially shared. Such a development would correspond to the collegial patterns of apostolic life within the church and to the dominant patterns of society.

Something should be said about the development of the Petrine office from that of a moderator to that which is more properly monarchical, or at least highly centralized. One should not isolate the process of centralization in a manner which would indicate that it was peculiar to Rome. The kind of centralization which took place in regard to Rome also took place in regard to other churches. It was not unusual for a small individual church to cede some of its independence to the bishops of near-by major cities. This was especially the case in the development of the patriarchates. This centralization was not based simply on usurpation from above. Concession from below was also operative.[15] The Council of Nicaea which approved of this development in canon 4 speaks of the practice as an ancient custom already in 325.[16] In matters of discipline and liturgy this arrangement safeguarded regional differences and avoided the kind of fragmentation and confusion which obtains when even the smallest diocese has its own particular liturgy and discipline.

The same kind of centralization went on in regard to Rome. Papal centralism, however, has often obscured the broader notion of the papacy. Primacy is not to be identified with the specific kind of administrative centralization which has developed in the West. Yet primacy did take on the structures of administrative centralization. One should be cautioned against the supposition that in all circumstances papal centralization is an evil to be avoided. There have been times in the history of the church when papal centralization was both a necessary and effective tool of reform. Papal centralization is frequently looked upon as usurpation and oppression. Though there is enough of both of these in papal history, one cannot categorize centralization as usurpation or oppression in this simplistic manner. There are enough appeals to Rome to show that the kind of centralization which took place was not always the proud assumption of power, but rather, in a goodly number of cases, a ceding to the wishes of petitioners. During the schism of Acadius and during the period of the iconoclast emperors appeal was made to Rome by Eastern bishops.[17] More precisely the Byzantine prelates, who were so determined to defend the autonomy of their church in the course of the Acacian schism, all signed the Libellus Hormisdae of Pope Hormisdas (514-523), "the document which defined clearly the primacy of the Roman see."[18] Their appeal to Rome was a way of healing the schism.

Gregory VII's claims in *Dictatus Papae* (1075) are most certainly extensive. "The Roman church was founded by the Lord alone. . . . By law only the Roman pontiff is called universal (pontiff). . . . Only the pope's feet are to be kissed by all the princes . . . His name alone is recited in the churches. . . . It is allowed to him to depose emperors . . . He is to be judged by no one. . . . He is not catholic who does not have communion (*concordat*) with the Roman church."[19] There is little doubt, however, that Gregory's purposes were reform.[20] He saw the church in a state of corruption and he intended to free the church from the domination of the state in order to reform her. The only possible way to reform the church and make her effective was to make her free.[21] To do this the church had to have a strong centralized authority, the spiritual equivalent of the powerful imperial state. Most importantly, the church had to retain the right to make her own appointments. If bishops could ignore the decrees against simony and clerical concubinage, it was because episcopal appointments were not in the control of the church but had fallen into the hands of the lay lords. The erection of a centralized ecclesiastical authority, an organization parallel to that of the state, was rooted in a genuine desire for reform. Only in this way could the church deal with the state. Centralization in this case was an instrument of reform not a will-to-power.

Canon law was enlisted as an ally of reform. Though the church in subsequent centuries suffered from the effects of this development because of the large influence of canon law in ecclesiology and sacramental theology, during the investiture controversy canon law became a primary tool of reform. It was used to free the church from the dominion of the state, and, to say the whole truth, in some cases to subject the empire to the church. *Ius divinum* was only one of the many ways in which the canonical claims of the papacy were supported. "The whole struggle between emperor and pope centered on law."[22]

The system of holding titles to property demanded that a reform movement have large powers concentrated in the papacy. Germanic conceptions of real property made it difficult for them to conceive of real estate being owned by an institution. In this Germanic view, the man who built a building could be the only true owner. This made it difficult for the church to manage her own affairs. Throughout Germany and France there was a system of privately owned churches. In France the system was extended to privately owned abbeys and bishoprics.[23] As a result there emerged in the eleventh century a collection of autonomous and national churches, over which princes (who were thought of as "kings and priests") claimed both ownership and administration. This situation made any reform of the church beyond all likelihood, as the church was helpless to get at such problem areas as simony, lay investiture, clerical concubinage, and the poor state of preaching. Once again, a large measure of centralized authority was seen as the basis of reform. Only in this way could the church deal with the centralized authority of the empire and the state.

Both during the Council of Trent and after, the direction was toward centralization as an instrument of reform. Pius IV confirmed and promulgated the decrees of Trent unchanged, but reserved their authentic interpretation to the pope. Pius IV's successors, most especially Pius V, Gregory XII and Sixtus V, continued the reform movement by strengthening the position of the pope. Both the French revolution and the secularization of 1803 prompted, if not a reform movement, then a defense movement. In the 19th century the national churches in France, Belgium and the German-speaking countries themselves sought closer ties with Rome in order to protect themselves against the interference of the state in the matters of the church.[24]

Centralization can be an instrument of reform not only over against an absolute state, but also within the total life of the church. A measure of papal power can be an effective instrument against the vindictive and arbitrary action on the part of local churches, or the oppression of smaller dioceses by larger metropolitan churches. In our own day one could ask what would have happened to the liturgical reform of Vatican II proposed in the *Constitution of the Liturgy* had it not been for papal centralization. It would surely have been one more conciliar constitution solemnly promulgated and promptly forgotten. It was the centralized authority of Rome which made the liturgical reform of Vatican II effective.

Though papal centralism can be an instrument of reform the new accents in *The Constitution on the Church* on the local church, *communio*, and collegiality would confirm that the contemporary trend, for very good historical, cultural and pastoral reasons, is away from a style of ecclesial life which is characterized by centralization.

There is a tendency in all offices, especially those which are conferred or recognized within a liturgical context,[25] to transform facts into essences, historical conditions into metaphysical conditions.[26] What the pope can do in certain determined circumstances and under certain conditions becomes the proper and exclusive right of the pope. What was susceptible of change come to be presented as immutable, and this mutability can gradually become a matter of divine law.[27] When a pope of the middle ages justified an intervention in matters belonging to a metropolitan or a bishop, he did so by invoking certain objective criterions of intervention, such as "evident utility" and "the necessity of the church" (*ecclesiae necessitas, evidens utilitas*). In this way the pope avoided the appearance of acting at his good pleasure or arbitrarily. Even Gregory VII, never one to be modest about papal power, justified the right of the pope to transfer bishops from one see to another because of "urgent necessity" (*necessitate congente*).[28] That his language was lost can be seen by the first schema of *De Ecclesia* of Vatican II, which stated that the authority of the episcopal college could be exercised by the pope "when, how, how often it appears to him in the Lord to be expedient."[29]

The pope did not, during the first ten centuries, suggest that they had the right to nominate bishops, except in their own entourage, and later in the Western church. In spite of this *communio* was maintained with the African and oriental bishops. The system according to which the pope conferred jurisdiction was not used before the scholastics developed the distinction between the power of order and the power of jurisdiction from the popes.[30] Yet in 1943 F.X. Wernz could write that "the proper right of instituting bishops belongs by nature to the Roman Pontiff."[31] This is admittedly an extreme opinion, but the attitude is not.[32] Obviously papal centralism should not be erected into a principle. Historically it would be impossible to assert centralism as an essential element in papal primacy. The experience of the church in the first centuries would indicate that the early exercise of the Petrine office was in the context of a religious authority which did not see itself in centralized, juridical or jurisdictional categories. At this early state there did not exist the possibility of a centralized exercise of what was seen as a predominatly non-juridical religious authority. Even when Rome assumed greater importance in the life of the church the Petrine function was not exercised by the see of Rome in a manner which could be characterized as papal monarchical centralism. Article 14 of the *Decree on Ecumenism*, when speaking of those centuries before the break between the East and the West said that "if disagreements in belief and discipline arouse among them (the churches of the East and West), the Roman see acted by common consent as moderator."

As the decree indicates, the relation of the other churches to Rome was not always seen in relation to the person of the pope, but rather to the see of Rome. The consensus that within the *communio* of churches the Roman see had a special function, rested on, among other things, the tradition that at Rome were to be found the graves of Peter and Paul (with Peter always mentioned first) and on the primacy of Rome in civil terms as the capital and first city of the empire.[33] Gregory VII was generally correct when he wrote that "he is not Catholic who does not have communion with the Roman Church."

However in the earliest centuries it is possible that the Roman see did not appeal to the Petrine texts to vindicate the authenticity of her authority.[43] Up until the fourth century it was sufficient that the Roman see had its *sedes* in the capital of the empire.[35] Nor does it seem that in the earliest centuries the Petrine texts were used as tools of either Roman or papal centralism. That no appeal was made to the Petrine texts does not deprive them of significance for the Petrine office. If one invokes the principle of development to explain the importance for the Petrine office of such socio-cultural factors as Rome being the capital of the empire, one cannot scorn the principle of development when applied to the Petrine texts. One cannot suppose that only what was immediately evident as the will of Christ for his church was as a matter of fact the intent of Christ. Though to explain all development as an unfolding of a meaning previously not evident is to embrace an impoverished developmental theory, there is some such unfolding present in even highly nuanced theories of development.

The lack of evidence that the Petrine texts were cited by the early popes, however, points to one of the major ecumenical problems: How does one arrive at the later papacy when one uses Peter's role in the primitive church as the point of departure? As was said it does not seem possible to demonstrate a linear continuity in the stages of development from the Petrine ministry in the early church to the papacy of later centuries. Again that the continuity is not demonstrable from written documents does not prove it never existed. The study *Peter in the New Testament,* commissioned by the Lutheran-Catholic dialogue and published separately, is especially interesting in this regard. It distinguishes between the limited information available from our sources about the historical career of Peter, and the trajectory that the image of Peter traveled in New Testament thought: missionary fisherman, pastoral shepherd, martyr, recipient of special revelation, confessor of the true faith, magisterial protector, and repentant sinner.[36] Many of the images of Peter in subsequent church history continue this trajectory. One would want to ask if the linear continuity, even if it exists, is really necessary to authenticate the later Petrine office. Is there not another kind of continuity, that found in the identity of functions? Finally, when the relationship of the images of Peter in the New Testament is studied in relationship to the role of the Petrine office, the question arises of the kind of authority Peter exercised over the other apostles. It would be difficult, using a purely exegetical method, to demonstrate that Peter exercised authority over the other apostles. He *may* have had it but there is no evidence that he exercised it. This raises the whole question of jurisdiction, which has been bound up with papal history. How does one explain the process by which an authority in the New Testament which was conceived essentially in religious terms, came later to be expressed in legal categories.

Peter Berger has shown that the process of becoming a man takes place in an interrelationship with an environment.[37]

It is not possible for man by himself in isolation to produce a human environment, a stable context for his behavior. A stable context is defined as a universe of social relationships, the locating of roles, the discovery and assignation of authority. This stable context is incipient in every social situation continuing in time. Men do gather for specific purposes, and when this is done over an extended period of time, then certain laws of social organization become operative, and this even if you protest against them. Values become patterned, social relationships become predictable, roles are distinguishable, and there emerges a kind of de facto authority which is simply there. It is self-evident to all concerned. When that happens an institution becomes a reality. The institution is a form of crystallized human experience, existing over and beyond the individuals who embody it at the moment. The institution has a reality of its own, a reality which confronts the individual as an external and coercive fact. The institution is a coercive fact because it is understood by all to be the instrumentality by which meaning is transmitted, and because the institution is seen as a permanent solution to a permanent problem of a given collectivity.

Authority emerges in a given collectivity as part of the permanent solution. This is true even when there was no location of authority in the first steps toward institution. In the collectivity which constituted the New Testament churches Peter was given a leadership role by Christ and the "authority" implicit in that role. Over a long period of time it is not possible for a leadership function to exist in a community without that authority taking on a degree of juridical expression. The "authority" Peter possessed was a religious fact. It was service rather than dominance and power. This should not be taken to mean that the exercise of the Petrine office, modeled on the New Testament images of Peter, should be without any legal formation. Nor should the juridic elements in the exercise of the Petrine office be ontologized, as though a particular legal formulation of Petrine ministry belongs to the nature of the Petrine function and is constitutive of the church. The legal formulation of the Petrine ministry is both an expression of its theological meaning and an accommodation to the changing historical situations. This would indicate that when the life patterns of society change, so can the legal manner in which the Petrine ministry responds to those patterns.

The changing historical situations in which the Petrine

ministry functions would suggest that there are various models for exercising that ministry. One could recall three styles of exercising the Petrine ministry: the presidency in love within the communion of a lose fellowship of churches, the communion of churches looking by common consent to the Roman see to act as moderator,[38] papal centralism on a monarchical model. Within the history of the church these and variation of these, as well as other models, have typified the exercise of the Petrine ministry. The reasons for the change from one model to another came about for pastoral and theological reasons, and because new patterns of secular life had evolved. One can see in these changes from one model to another a response in the Holy Spirit to the changed needs of various historical periods. The changed patterns of secular life, the different mode of exercising authority, and the new ecumenical situation seems to indicate that the Holy Spirit is prompting the church to seek a new style of exercising the one enduring Petrine function. Neither history nor theology postulate the necessity of the present style of exercising the Petrine ministry remaining unchanged. Neither suggest that all development has come to an end.

The manner in which the Petrine ministry is exercised should vary not only in accordance with the changing cultural patterns, but also in relation to different styles of church life found within the church universal. Vatican II spoke of the history in which "the Churches of the East and the West went their own ways."[39] Vatican II also spoke of the individual churches or rites which are to be found within "that Church, Holy and Catholic, which is the Mystical Body of Christ."[40] The plurality of ecclesial types refers here not simply to ceremonial variations but to plurality of theological ecclesial cultures which have to do with plurality of geographical origin, plurality in theology, piety, community life, law, and jurisprudence.[41] Such plurality of ecclesial types corresponds to what are weighty differences of a theological, historical, sociological, psychological and cultural nature.[42] In spite of protests that his multiformity is a treasure to be maintained, plurality in ecclesial life has not always been safeguarded.[43]

Since the pope is related to the church and to the churches under various titles, namely, bishop of the Catholic church, bishop of the "Italian" see of Rome, primate of Italy, patriarch of the West, he does not relate to the plurality of churches in the same manner. Though the Petrine function is a ministry to the whole church, the occupant of the

Roman see does not always act in terms of that papal function. He can also act as primate of Italy or bishop of the "Italian" city of Rome, or as patriarch of the West. It would be necessary in the united church to recognize the universality of the Petrine ministry and the role of the papacy in that Petrine function. However, that recognition would not imply an identical relation on the part of various churches to the bishop of the "Italian" see of Rome or to the patriarch of the West. Implicit in the variety of ecclesial cultures within one allegiance is both the recognition of the Petrine ministry to the universal church, and the responsibility of individual churches which do not belong to the patriarchate of the West to rule themselves.[44]

In the united church the churches which did not belong to the patriarchate of the West might be similar to those churches of the East about which the *Decree on the Eastern Churches* said that they "have a full right and are in duty bound (*iure pollere et officio teneri*) to rule themselves, each in accordance with its own established disciplines."[45] The council, speaking of these same churches declared that they, "while keeping in mind the necessary unity of the churches, have the power (*facultatem*, which in canonical terms means *ius et officium*) to govern themselves according to their own disciplines, since these are better suited to the character of their faithful and better adapted to foster the good of souls."[46] The power, right and duty of the churches within the one allegiance to govern themselves are not concessions or privileges granted by papal power, but are inherent in the churches. On the other hand, neither is the Petrine ministry to the universal church dependent on concessions of the local churches. It is inherent in the Petrine ministry.

The primary unity in the church is the unity of persons and local churches in the head, who is Christ. The communion with the pope is subordinate to and a function of this primary unity in Christ. The unity of the church is primarily located in the person and presence of Christ in the power of his Spirit and secondarily in ministries and structures. Though the pope has come to be recognized as possessing the authority of ruling, his primary function is to give expression to this given unity and to guard it. In the earliest centuries the function of expressing and guarding unity was exercised more often than the ruling function. In terms of visibility the pope exercises a major unitive function. The necessary communion which the local churches have with each other is concretized in the necessary communion all the local churches have with the pope, who is the head of the college of bishops and a symbol of the universal church.

In both the early church and in contemporary ecclesiology are found, among others, two ways of theologizing about the church which are important for the present discussion. The first, the universalist ecclesiology takes its point of departure from the unity of the whole church and its extension into the whole world. The second, the eucharistic *communio* ecclesiology proceeds from the experience in the local church of the fullness of the gospel in the communion of faith and the sacramental life and goes on to relate each church as a faith and eucharistic communion to other churches experiencing the same fullness of the gospel. These two ways of theologizing about the church have had a long history in the church.[47] An early exponent of the eucharistic *communio* ecclesiology was St. Ignatius, while St. Cyprian developed large elements of the universalist ecclesiology. Though the universalist ecclesiology came to dominate in the West and had great importance for the development of the doctrine of papal primacy, the eucharistic *communio* ecclesiology remained an important stream of theological thought in the West throughout the early Middle Ages. In the East it remained the dominant ecclesiological category. While both of these ecclesiologies are to be found in the documents of Vatican II the *communio* ecclesiology, with its special concern for the full actualization of the gospel in the local church, was given a new emphasis.

Whatever ecclesiology becomes dominantly operative in the church, whatever the style of exercising the Petrine ministry, the ideal relationship between pope and bishops is that of collegiality based on *communio*. In this relationship there is found both presidency and mutuality. According to the *Constitution on the Church* a man becomes a bishop by sacramental consecration and by becoming a member of the college of bishops: "One is constituted a member of the episcopal body in virtue of sacramental consecration and hierarchical communion with the head and members of the body."[48] We find this practice reflected in canon 4 of the Council of Nicaea which legislates that the ordination of a new bishop be performed during the eucharistic celebration by bishops of the province who represent the college. This practice reflects something of the eucharistic ecclesiology. Each geographical or national division has a bishop (often called archbishop, metropolitan, or primate) who is first among the bishops, and in this sense, the head. In much the same manner Pope Leo spoke of the "primacy" of the metropolitans.[49] In the college of bishops whose churches are bound together by the communion of faith and sacramental life, there is both presidency and mutuality. Ideally the bishop of each diocese should do nothing of major importance which affects the other churches without the agreement of the metropolitan and the other bishops, although each bishop manages the affairs in his own diocese and those regions which belong to it. The metropolitan (archbishop or primate) exercises a presidency in love and therefore should not do anything of major importance affecting all the dioceses of his region without the consultation and consensus of the other bishops. In this manner there is the harmony of eucharistic order, namely, presidency and mutuality. This principle of presidency and mutuality can find expression also in provincial synods and in synods of particular rites. Both presidency and mutuality, which describe the relationship of churches more directly than of bishops, find in the communion of the gospel and eucharistic communion the source of church unity.

The primatial function of the pope is best understood within the framework of such a collegiality based on *communio* in which there is presidency and mutuality. Presidency safeguards the universality of the Petrine ministry while mutuality safeguards the integrity of ecclesial life at the level of the local church. There should be the same kind of consultation, the pope not acting on issues of major importance without the consultation and consensus of the bishops of the world. Obviously this should not be interpreted so as to deprive him of all initiative.

The concept of collegiality which has had influence since Vatican II is the result of a re-evaluation of *communio* ecclesiology, with its concern for the local church, and the people of God ecclesiology, with its focus on responsibility of all members of the church for her mission. Implicit in the concept of collegiality are presidency and mutuality within the allegiance of one communion. Canon 228 of the *Codex Juris Canonici* gives a theological-canonical principle which might offer a means to a synthesis of presidency and mutuality within a universal communion.[50] "Ecumenical councils possess supreme power in the universal church." This could be interpreted to mean that there is but one bearer of the supreme authority in the church, namely the episcopal college including the pope, which, however, has two ways of exercising its authority, one collective and the other personal.[51] These two ways are interdependent. The personal manner is not a private manner. It presupposes collegial consultation. It also supposes that the pope is expressing the collective faith of the church. The *Ex sese* of Vatican I was never intended to privatize the papacy or be placed in opposition to the mutuality of communion, collegiality, co-responsibility or conciliarity. On the other hand the pope exercises presidency because he bears the responsibility of feeding the whole flock and for strengthening his brothers. This is a responsibility shared by the episcopal college; however, it belongs in a unique manner to the Petrine ministry. Though every exercise of this unique responsibility has something collegial about it, even when exercised in a personal way, the responsibility is not conferred on the pope by the college of bishops but is given to him by Christ in Peter. The mutuality of collegial life and the common consent of his brothers are not the sources of his responsibility.

The pastoral exercise of the papal office, always subject to the gospel, will have to be proportioned to the needs and possibilities of the various cultures in which the church concretely lives and works. At some periods in the past, for historical reasons, the style has been strongly juridic and sometimes autocratic. In our day the signs of the times seem to call for a return to the more consentual and participatory style of pastoral leadership that was characteristic of the *communio* ecclesiology of the early centuries.

Even with greater stress on mutuality and participatory processes it must be recognized that Lutherans may have other problems. One of these problems is the anti-Christ tradition in Lutheran writings referring to the pope and the papacy. Luther in 1518 only hesitatingly took over the tradition which referred the anti-Christ to the pope. But under the influence of Lukas Cranachs and Melanchthon he developed a rather full teaching by 1520. Luther himself never characterized the person of the pope as anti-Christ, but only the institution of the papacy in its historical development, curial dimension, and ecclesiastical effects.[52] The Lutheran confessional writings do, however, speak of the pope in relation to anti-Christ.[53] The repetition of this over four hundred years must have done something to Lutheran bones. At the level of Lutheran instincts, which are conditioned by this catechetical tradition, the problem of the papacy is not easily accessible by means of theological discourse.

The title of anti-Christ seems to be a personal title[54] and for this reason, if for no other, Roman Catholics would hesitate to apply it to an office. Though Roman Catholics would hesitate to apply the term anti-Christ to the pope or to the papacy, yet there is a general recognition that the exercise of any ministry in any ecclesiastical communion, whether that be the papal ministry or that of a president of a synod, can so deviate from apostolic life and practice that it becomes a scandal to the gospel. Jesus said to Peter: "Get behind me, Satan" (Matthew 16:23). Any ministry which at one time in history was fulfilling its true apostolic ministerial function may at another time in history become unfaithful to the apostolic life. Through reform it may return to the apostolic life, and cease to be "Satan."

It is problems like these which seem patient of a theological solution which push Lutherans and Catholics to ask the hard question: How much theological agreement is necessary for unity in faith? Here one cautions against the easy assumption of a false ironism which considers major theological differences to be superficial. On the other hand care should be taken not to demand from the respective ecclesial traditions a kind of theological agreement which in fact does not exist even within our own communions. Roman Catholics should remember that from the fourth to the sixth centuries the Christians of the East were rejecting papal claims without the Eastern Christians suggesting that such a rejection justified the breaking of a common allegiance and unity. More recently Roman Catholics should remember the great diversity of theological opinions, opinions which were at times not mutually compatible, which were expressed on the floor of Vatican II by various cardinals. It has not been possible to define the limits of this diversity with regard to the papal primacy, but it should be recalled that also on this question diversity of opinion has always existed within the Roman Catholic church.

Finally, something should be said about the rhetoric of power and the possibility of a voluntary limitation of power by the popes. Lutherans are offended by the vocabulary of power and domination which some Catholic documents, such as the *nota previa* appended to *Constitution on the Church*, use to express the Petrine ministry. Though the vocabulary of power and domination are found in papal history, note should be taken that this vocabulary also evolved out of expectations of other churches. The Roman see by common consent was asked to assume roles which were in keeping with the position as the city in which were found the graves of Peter and Paul, in keeping with her position as the capital of the empire and later in response to Rome's interpretation of the Petrine text. Further, in any ministry there is an "over-againstness" which is expressed, among other things, by proclamation of judgment. There is no teaching or prophetic ministry from which the proclamation of judgment is absent. This is also true of the Petrine ministry and any Petrine ministry which was deprived of all judgment would not be either a teaching or prophetic ministry in the Christian sense. It is easy for prophetic judgment to be interpreted as speaking the vocabulary of power and domination.

The voluntary limitation by the popes of the exercise of jurisdiction would be a gesture of great importance. Though juridically it is not possible for one pope to bind his successors, were such a voluntary limitation to take place there would be a public commitment and an evangelical imperative of great force and weight which would assure against the exercise by future popes of those powers voluntarily limited. Roman Catholics need not think that a voluntary limitation of the power of jurisdiction by individual popes in any way detracts from the Petrine ministry. The present juridical expression of the Petrine ministry evolved under the impetus of a variety of factors, theological and non-theological. One is justified in supposing that such an evolution is not at an end. For historical and pastoral reasons the papacy could take on quite a different juridical expression without diminishing its essential Petrine function. Nor is there any reason why, prompted by different patterns in society and different ways of exercising authority, the Roman see by a voluntary limitation could not evolve a juridical expression in which for instance, it acted as a moderator in disagreement in belief and discipline, a moderator who is more than a chairman, who takes initiative and who has a preeminence. As has been noted article 14 of the *Decree on Ecumenism* has called attention to the fact that such was the style of exercising the Petrine function "for many centuries". However, the ultimate reconciliation of Christians cannot be a matter of juridical limitation, however desirable that might be. More central to the reconciliation is the will to unity.

Though juridical considerations will present problems for

Lutherans and developing a new style of exercising the Petrine ministry to fit the changed situation will present problems for Roman Catholics, both of these are secondary matters in comparison to the will to unity. The will to unity is manifested in the readiness to translate the allegiance to one faith, one Lord and one baptism into a viable visibility. The ultimate reconciliation of church with church will not be possible even were true unity of faith to be achieved, if at this preliminary stage there is not the will to translate that yet to be achieved full interior faith unity into a recognizable faith visibility. What the shape of that unity will be is not now known. It is known that nothing which is of the gospel will be excluded from that unity. For the present, Lutherans and Catholics "go forward without obstructing the ways of divine Providence and without pre-judging the future inspiration of the Holy Spirit."[55] However, that future inspiration of the Holy Spirit is already now pre-judged and the way toward unity is already obstructed if there is not the firm will to unity. The will to unity is defined as the readiness to translate the allegiance to one faith, one Lord and one baptism into visible forms. The necessity of unity in faith coming to recognizable visibility is of the gospel. Finally, other than fidelity to the gospel no pre-conditions to the future inspirations of the Holy Spirit can be posited.

11

PAPACY AND *IUS DIVINUM:* A ✦ LUTHERAN VIEW[1]

George A. Lindbeck

The main purpose of this paper is to explore possible Lutheran response to newer Roman Catholic thinking on *ius divinum* especially as this applies to papal primacy. A secondary aim is to describe and analyze what is said in reference to this topic by the Report of the Joint Lutheran-Roman Catholic Study Commission on "The Gospel and the Church"[2] (commonly known as the "Malta Report"). This is a product of the international commission, sponsored by the Vatican Secretariat for Christian Unity and the Lutheran World Federation which was at work from 1967-1972. The commission report contains what is the only official or quasi-official Lutheran response to newer Catholic thinking on our subject.[3]

In addition to the Report, I shall use Carl Peter's paper, "Dimensions of *Jus divinum* in Roman Catholic Theology"[4] as my chief source of information on newer thinking. Standard Lutheran reactions to traditional Catholic positions are sufficiently outlined for our purposes in papers already presented to our group: Piepkorn's "Lutheran Attitudes towards the Papacy", "*Ius Divinum* and Adiaphoron", and Kramer's "A Lutheran Understanding of Papal Primacy".[5]

In the three sections which follow, I shall first point out, using the Report as an example, that there is in some circles a remarkable convergence in the structure of Catholic and Lutheran thinking about the papacy (as well as about ministerial orders in general). Many Catholic theologians as well as Lutherans now emphasize the primacy of the gospel and employ chiefly functional categories when dealing with these questions. This, to be sure, is not simply a matter of Catholics moving towards Protestantism, for when Reformation functionalism is combined with a modern awareness of the historical and sociological dimensions of human existence, it can be used to defend what most Lutherans would regard as surprisingly Catholic positions. Within this common functional approach, it is not the possibility of papal primacy but the question of its necessity which is the major point of dispute between the confessions.

In the second section, however, I shall argue that the necessity which Lutherans are confessionally committed to denying to the papacy is not identical to that which Catholics on a historical and functional bent attribute to it. The first type of necessity is absolute in the sense of being historically unconditioned and irreversible or permanent, while the second is relative, conditioned and possibly reversible or temporary. Furthermore, a Lutheran could grant this second kind of necessity to papal primacy. He would not contradict his Confessions in doing so, even though he would go beyond them. Indeed, it could be argued that, given the changes since the sixteenth century, confessional loyalty favors a certain reformatory papalism.

Thirdly I shall suggest that what has just been said of the necessity of papal primacy holds also for its *de iure divino* character. Some Roman Catholics now appear to interpret this latter concept functionally in such a way that it simply becomes equivalent to historically contingent and possibly reversible necessity; while others who give a stronger reading, insisting on irreversibility, would be hard put to it on their own principles to show that the more minimalistic interpretation of *ius divinum* is excluded by Roman Catholic dogma (e.g., Vatican I). As the Lutheran Confessions also do not exclude this minimalistic interpretation (for it had not yet in their day been proposed) we have a situation in which the Reformation denial and the contemporary Catholic affirmation of the *ius divinum* are not irreconcilable.

I

The Malta Report thus describes the Lutheran attitude to the question of the papacy:

(66) . . . It was recognized on the Lutheran side that no local church should exist in isolation since it is a manifestation of the universal church. In this sense the importance of a ministerial service of the communion of churches was acknowledged and at the same time reference was made to the problem raised for Lutherans by their lack of such an effective service of unity. The office of the papacy as a visible sign of the unity of the churches was therefore not excluded insofar as it is subordinated to the primacy of the gospel by theological reinterpretation and practical restructuring.

(67) The question, however, which remains controversial between Catholics and Lutherans is whether the primacy of the pope is necessary for the church, or whether it represents only a fundamentally possible function. It was nevertheless agreed that the question of altar fellowship and of a mutual recognition of ministerial offices should not be unconditionally dependent on a conseensus on the question of primacy.

Five theses or propositions important for our topic can be derived from this passage.

1. Lutherans recognize the importance of what I shall (in anticipation of certain later citations) call "the Petrine func-

tion"—i.e., the service or ministry of helping the local churches to be visibly the manifestations of, and in communion with, the universal church.

2. They are open to the possibility that this needs to be more effectively institutionalized than has been true in Lutheranism up until now.

3. They do not exclude the possibility that the papacy could rightly exercise this function.

4. In order to do this, however, it must be reformed theologically and practically in order to make clear its subordination to the primacy of the gospel.

5. Even if this were to happen, however, Lutherans do not agree that the papacy is the necessary institutionalization of the Petrine function.

These propositions, it will be observed, do not go beyond the Melancthonian position which is already present as a possible Lutheran option in the symbolical books.[6] Nor does anything in them contradict what I believe Frederick Kramer would cheerfully admit is his own rather conservative contemporary view. To be sure, his paper does not dwell on the importance of the Petrine function (Thesis 1), nor on the contemporary need for its more effective institutionalization (Thesis 2), but I doubt that he would deny either of these points. He believes that the possibilities expressed in Theses 3 and 4 are purely theoretical but the Report does not disagree—it is simply neutral on this question. In any case, Theses 4 and 5 clearly express what he, like most present-day Lutherans, consider the sum and substance of the Reformation protest against the papacy.

There is, nevertheless, something significantly new about the Lutheran attitude as described in this Report. Only the fifth thesis is said to be a matter of controversy between the confessions. In contrast to the past, Catholics and Protestants think of themselves as agreed on Thesis 4, on the need for and on the controlling principle of papal reform. The papacy must be made subordinate to the primacy of the gospel.

This is not simply an isolated accord, but rather reflects a basic convergence in the fundamental structure of thinking about, not only the papacy, but the whole ordering of the church. All offices and laws must be evaluated and reshaped, not primarily in terms of ontological considerations or the repristination of either traditional or scriptural models, but in terms of their function, their service of the whole church's witness to the gospel. I shall quote three of the passages which illustrate this.

(21) Participants on both sides agreed that the authority of the church can only be in service to the word and that it is not master of the word of the Lord. Therefore the church's tradition must remain open to the word and must transmit it in such a way that the word constantly bestows the understanding which comes from faith and freedom for Christian action.

(48) . . . The church as a whole bears witness to Christ; the church as whole is the priestly people of God. As *creatura et ministra verbi,* however, it stands under the gospel and has the gospel as its superordinate criterion. Its gospel ministry is to be carried out through the proclamation of the word, through the administration of the sacraments, and, indeed, through its total life.

(50) The correct determination of the relationship between this ministry assigned to the entire church and a special office in the church is a problem for Lutherans and Catholics alike. Both agree that the office of the ministry stands over against the community as well as within the community. Further they agree that the ministerial office represents Christ and his over-againstness to the community only insofar as it gives expression to the gospel. Both must examine themselves as to how effectively the critical superiority of the gospel is maintained in practice.

It is not our business, nor that of the Malta Report, to spell out in concrete detail how these principles should be applied to the papacy, but the Report does give some very general indications of what is implied. The view of the Catholic members of the commission is given in the sentences immediately preceding the statement on the Lutheran attitude which I have already quoted.

(66) In this connection the question of papal primacy emerges as a special problem for the relationship between Lutherans and Catholics. Catholics pointed to the beginning of this doctrine in the biblical witness concerning the special position of Peter and also to the differences in the understanding of primacy in the first and second millenia. By its doctrine of episcopal collegiality, the Second Vatican Council placed the primacy in a new interpretive framework and thereby avoided a widespread onesided and isolated way of understanding it. The primacy of jurisdiction must be understood as ministerial service to the community and as bond of

the unity of the church. This service of unity is, above all, a service of unity in faith. The office of the papacy also includes the task of caring for legitimate diversity among local churches. The concrete shape of this office may vary greatly in accordance with changing historical conditions.

No reference is made in the Report to the specific problem of the papal infallibility, but something is said of the basic nature of ecclesial infallibility in general (which, it will be recalled has never had its nature specified either at Vatican I nor anywhere else):

> (22) In spite of this historical variability of proclamation, Lutherans and Catholics are convinced that the Holy Spirit unceasingly leads and keeps the church in the truth. It is in this context that one must understand the concepts of indefectibility and infallibility which are current in the Catholic tradition. These two predominantly negative concepts are subject to misunderstanding. Although they are of late origin, that to which they refer was known in the ancient church and they are based on an interpretation of New Testament texts. [John 16:13 *inter alia*.]

> (23) Infallibility must, first of all, be understood as a gift to the entire church as the people of God. The church's abiding in the truth should not be understood in a static way but as a dynamic event which takes place with the aid of the Holy Spirit in ceaseless battle against error and sin in the church as well as in the world.

Enough has been quoted, I trust to make clear the remarkable *rapprochment* in theological perspectives and principles which this document illustrates. There is, on the one side, repeated insistence on the Reformation thesis that the authority and rights of the ecclesiastical office (and of the church as a whole) are not to be viewed in static juridical or ontological terms as attributes which it continues to possess independently of what it does, but must rather be seen as functions of "service to the word" (#21). On the other hand, the thoroughly Catholic point is also made that faithful service of the reconciling word must involve concern for fostering the visible unity of the churches, i.e., concern for the Petrine function. More than this, Lutherans as well as Catholics agree that the papacy is at least a possible institutional instrument for carrying out this function.

Thus the one remaining point of dispute on the level of

theological principle is whether it is a necessary instrument
(Thesis 5).

II

On closer inspection, however, this fifth thesis proves to be
uninformative. Depending on the context in which it is used,
the word "necessity" can have many different meanings. One
could argue, for example, that papal primacy is the contingently (and perhaps only temporarily) necessary means
for carrying out the Petrine function simply because it happens at present (and we don't know about the future) to be
the only historically available instrumentality which could
effectively do this job for the church as a whole. It is thus
"necessary for the sake of the gospel" in a real, though
limited sense. There is nothing un-Lutheran in attributing
this contingent necessity to papal primacy. Presumably
Thesis 5 denies a more unconditional necessity. But what?
And is this unconditional necessity which it denies something
which Catholics are obligated to affirm? The Report makes
no effort to deal with these problems and consequently leaves
completely open the question of whether Thesis 5 does in
fact represent an interconfessional impasse, an irresolvable
dispute.

To be sure, the context provided by the Malta Report
taken as a whole suggests that it does not. On the one
hand, as we have already observed, this context is functional, emphasizing the primacy of the gospel. It is clear
that for the Catholic as well as the Lutheran authors papal
primacy can be viewed as necessary only as a means, only
as an instrument, for the proclamation of the gospel. Furthermore, it is a secondary means, instrumental to that more
fundamental service of the word performed by the visibility
of Christian unity. This visible unity also is not an end in
itself, but rather a condition—indispensable though not sufficient—for the manifestation of the full dimensions of the
reconciliation which is in Christ. Thus the Catholic authors
of this Report join with the Lutherans in employing an
analysis which suggests that the necessity of papal primacy
is at least to some extent functionally relative or conditioned, dependent on the evangelical character of its exercise of the Petrine ministry.

This impression of relativity or conditionedness is reinforced, on the other hand, by the emphasis placed by this
Report on the historicity of all church offices, of all in-

stitutionalizations of the ministry of the word. What is allowable, desirable or necessary varies from place to place, period to period, not only because of disobedience or corruption, not only because of failures in evangelical functioning but sometimes simply because of changes in historical and cultural circumstances.

(54) We are told quite early in the New Testament period of special ministries and offices. To some extent at least they were viewed as charisms. The New Testament writings testify to the great differences in congregational functions, ministries and orders in the various areas and periods of the church. These were only partially retained in later church history and they were partially interpreted in new ways (cf. the offices of presbyter, bishop and deacon). Further, these ministries and orders were imbedded in earlier historical (Jewish, Hellenistic, etc.) structures. Thus, although there is a continuity of basic structure, it can be seen that historicity is part of the essential nature of the church's ministerial office and of its congregational ordering. The gospel as witnessed to by Scripture can be criterion for church order only when it stands in living relationship to the current social realities. Orders in the New Testament are, therefore, to be seen largely as models which are open to ever new actualizations.

Nothing (other than what we have already cited) is said directly about the implications of this for the papacy, but such texts, and others which could be quoted (e.g. #56), make one thing abundantly clear. The Catholic authors of this Report would find it difficult or impossible to identify any concretely specifiable aspect of church order, including the papacy and its primacy, as unchangably or irreversibly necessary. All of them would no doubt insist that the Petrine function is unconditionally (i.e. permanently) necessary and that, in the church's pilgrim state, this normally and in the long run requires institutionalization, not only in sporadic consultative or conciliar forms, but also in a central and continuing office. At least the *need* for such an office belongs to the abiding, fundamental structure of the church, and God will see to it that when the need is unfulfilled (as was presumably the case during the Great Schism, for example), this does not continue for so long a period that utter disaster results. But is it irreversibly necessary that the occupant of this central office be the bishop of Rome? or that it always be a single individual rather than, e.g., a troika? Or that the office resemble the historic papacy rather than an ecumenical patriarchate or executive secretaryship? On none of these questions, I suspect, would there have been unanimity among the Catholic participants. Some of these would grant that, while necessary, it is only contingently necessary to associate the Petrine function and office with the Roman pontiff.[7]

If this is so, then it seems that at least some Catholics do not attribute the kind of necessity to papal primacy which Lutherans are confessionally committed to denying. Lutherans admit the importance of the Petrine function (Thesis 1), and there is nothing to prevent them from thinking that now, and perhaps in the foreseeable, it is contingently necessary for the papacy to exercize this function if it is to be carried out effectively for the church as a whole. Most contemporary Lutherans no longer believe that the papacy is unalterably the antichrist, and this means that the contingent necessity of the papacy as we have defined it is a factual, not a confessional question which cannot be dogmatically resolved by reference to sixteenth century writings.

Indeed, one can go even farther than this. It could be argued that when read in the light of our contemporary situation, the Lutheran Confessions favor, even though they do not demand, the kind of reformatory papalism which I am describing. If they were living today, men like Melanchthon and even Luther would almost certainly lose much of their pessimism regarding the possibilities of papal reform. They would urgently demand the evangelical restructuring of papal theology and practise, not only on behalf of the Roman communion, but for the sake of Lutherans, for the sake of the whole church. Such a demand, however, implies a belief in the contingent necessity of papal primacy. It makes no sense to think that papal reform is of the utmost importance to all Christians unless one also believes in the significance of the Petrine function and suspects that it cannot be properly exercised, at least in our day, apart from the pope.

It should be noted that when looked at in this way, the necessity of papal primacy is partially independent of whether non-Catholics are obligated to join the Roman communion, i.e. "submit to the pope." The necessity is, not only historically, but, as we have observed, also functionally or evangelically conditioned. Lutherans, one might say, are conscience bound not to "submit" to the papacy until it has been so thoroughly renewed that the language of submission is totally inappropriate. In the meantime, however, granting that papal primacy is contingently necessary, they are obligated to do everything possible to contribute to that renewal, not, obviously, by destructive or purely condemnatory criticism, but by working together with Catholics to the extent that this is possible, and by seeking to change their own structures in order to facilitate reunion.

We now need to turn to the question of the *ius divinum*. Is the *de iure divino* character of papal primacy reducible to the historically and evangelically conditioned instrumental necessity which we have argued could be acceptable to Lutherans, or does it add an additional qualification?

III·

Our question in this section, then, concerns the relation between *ius divinum* and a necessity which is historically relative and conditioned, but functionally urgent, i.e., contingently but really necessary "for the sake of the gospel." According to contemporary Roman Catholic thought on the subject, is something more than this affirmed when it is said that the papacy is *de iure divino*?

The 16th century answer, both Lutheran and Catholics, is clear: something more is affirmed. For the Confessions, only that which is permanently required, at least since the closure of public revelation, is *ius divinum, mandatum dei.* Trent agreed. Carl Peter's review of the evidence shows that it is precisely this which is the difference between the *ius divinum* general obligation to confess serious sin committed after baptism (DS 1706-7) and the merely canonical status of the more specific requirement that this must if possible be done before receiving the eucharist. There was, it was argued, clear scriptural foundation for the first, but not the second.[8] Thus the interconfessional controversy in those days over what qualifies as *ius divinum* was a dispute regarding what was *explicitly* contained in the original deposit of faith, i.e., in the public revelation which closed with the death of the last apostle. The quarrel over the *de iure divino* character of the papacy was in part a dispute over the status of tradition as a source of information on this point, and in part an exegetical discussion over how to interpret passages such as Matthew 16:18.

Nowadays, however, this is no longer true. It is universally acknowledged by Catholic theologians that some *ius divinum* claims have become explicit only as the result of post-biblical historical developments. It can be argued that Lutherans are committed to the same position at least in reference to the scriptural canon (assuming that its authority can be described as *de iure divino* and not simply *de iure humano*). To be sure, all *ius divinum* is said to have roots, to be implicit, in the original deposit (and therefore for all Lutherans and many Catholics, in the scriptural testimony to revelation), but it is generally admitted that the persuasiveness with which this can be argued in any given instance is largely dependent on first accepting the *ius divinum* claim which is in question. The claim defines the hermeneutical stance which enables one to find that same claim germinally present in the scriptural and/or patristic sources.

These are commonplaces. The only reason for reviewing them here is to underline the point that, whatever *ius divinum* might be for contemporary Catholics and Protestants, it is not identical to what it was for their sixteenth century forebears.

What is it then? As far as I can see, there are now two major ways of answering this question. One is exclusively functional. Here *ius divinum* adds nothing to the historically and functionally conditioned necessity which we have suggested Lutherans can also attribute to papal primacy. The other way, while also acknowledging historical and functional conditioning, appears to go farther. A *de iure divino* structure must be irreversible or permanent. There are some post-biblical developments, such as papal primacy, which are irreversible and therefore qualify as *de iure divino*. Lutherans see no biblical grounds for asserting this irreversibility, at least not as a matter of faith, and consequently deny that the papacy is *de iure divino* in this second sense. In contrast, they have no difficulty with the functionalist interpretation of the *ius divinum* character of certain post-biblical developments, for this simply affirms that what is historically and functionally necessary for the welfare of the church is also what God wills that the church be and do. Neither the Reformers nor contemporary Lutherans would deny this.

It should be noted that functionalist interpretations, (and perhaps the "irreversibilist" ones as well) involve such radical departures from traditional usage as to make questionable the propriety of continuing to use the old terms. The distinction between divine and human right becomes variable and fluid, rather than fixed and definite. Sixteenth century *ius divinum* becomes twentieth century *adiaphoron* and *vice versa*. Perhaps some things which were prohibited by divine law in biblical and post-biblical times are now in our day commanded (e.g., the ordination of women). It is, of course, possible to restrict the notion of *ius divinum* to principles and structures which are so general (e.g., the Petrine function) that nothing empirically specifiable can ever be *de iure divino*. This, as we shall see, is what Schillebeeckx as interpreted by Carl Peter seems to do. But then one is no longer dealing with anything which could be called *ius* in an even analogical sense. Perhaps it is a recognition of these difficulties which leads those whom I call functionalists to avoid *ius divinum et humanum* terminology.

As we have already indicated, not only Lutherans, but also some Catholics espouse the functionalist view, and the Malta Report does not go beyond it (although some of the Catholic participants would no doubt have insisted on saying more if their task had been to give a full exposition of the Catholic position as they understand it):

(31) Church orders arise, above all, from that ministry of word and sacrament which is constitutive for the church. That which belongs to the proper proclamation of the gospel and proper administration of the sacraments is indispensable. The concrete shape of orders is presented in the New Testament in various forms. In subsequent history it has undergone many further changes. Greater awareness of the historicity of the church in conjunction with a new understanding of its eschatological nature, requires that in our day the concepts of *ius divinum* and *ius humanum* be thought through anew. In both concepts the word *ius* is employed in a merely analogical sense. *Ius divinum* can never be adequately distinguished from *ius humanum*. We have the *ius divinum* always only as mediated through particular historical forms. These mediating forms must be understood not only as the product of a sociological process of growth but, because of the pneumatic nature of the church, they can be experienced also as fruit of the spirit.

(33) The church is permanently bound in its ordering to the gospel which is irrevocably prior to it. It is in respect to this that Catholic tradition speaks of the *ius divinum*. The gospel, however, can be the criterion for a concrete church order only in living relationship with contemporary social realities. Just as there is a legitimate explication of the gospel in dog-

mas and confessions, so there also exists a historical actualization of law in the church. Therefore, the church must discern
the signs of the Holy Spirit in history and in the present, and
in faithfulness to the apostolic proclamation must consider
the restructuring of its orders.

Not only this statement, but also some of the authors cited
by Carl Peter do not appear to go beyond the functionalist
position. This seems to be true of Neumann, Schillebeeckx
and Küng, while Rahner, Ray Brown and Peter himself can
perhaps be classified as irreversibilists.[9]

It seems to me doubtful that the distinction between these
two groups is rooted in a different evaluation of the normative role of scripture. It is not because they accord a higher
status to scripture that the functionalists affirm that only
scriptural developments are irreversible, but rather because
they stress historicity and the primacy of the gospel to such
an extent that only the most fundamental developments (all
of which had already occurred in biblical times) can be irreversible. They are the very opposite of biblicists—even less
so than Karl Rahner *et al*—in the freedom with which they
judge many New Testament developments to be reversible.
Küng's emphasis on reversibility does not make it more difficult for him than for Rahner to recognize "the very demands of faith itself" in post-biblical developments. The
question of reversibility is irrelevant to such a recognition.
A historically and functionally (i.e., evangelically) conditioned necessity can ground moral imperatives which are no
less absolute than if the necessity were also irreversible.
The necessity of patriarchies in the East might, perhaps, be
an example of this.

Now as has already been indicated, a Catholic functionalist
would presumably have no difficulty in accepting our hypothetical Lutheran attribution of a historically contingent and
functionally conditioned necessity to papal primacy as fully
satisfactory. It would, from his point of view, be equivalent
to recognizing its *de iure divino* character.

What, however, of those who hold to an irreversibilist
position? Would our hypothetical Lutheran clearly be denying anything which they consider essential when he says
that papal primacy may be reversible? On closer examination, this becomes doubtful, and the reason for this is that
the irreversibilists insist on the difficulty of specifying exactly
what is *de iure divino* and therefore irreversible in any given
development. Thus when the Lutheran says that no post-

biblical developments are irreversible, they cannot point to any *particular* thing which they are convinced, and he is not sure, will abide until the eschaton.

> The salvific realities exist "by virtue of divine law," but their form is always at the same time "of human law" and thus alterable; the border line between both territories cannot be defined, and indeed cannot be defined in principal.[10]
> There is a dimension of Christ's Church present in the first century and in the twentieth; that abiding character may be called the Church's nature. There are also the most obvious differences of form in which the Church is realized from one period to another . . . Yet . . . it must be admitted that no theological scalpel can be applied to separate the dimension of nature from that of form in the concrete.[11]
> The difficulty theologians today experience in their efforts to isolate elements of divine right in Sacraments and Church Order from contingent, changeable factors is not new . . . *Ius divinum* claims, then as now, were shrouded in the realm of mystery. The role of the Roman Catholic theologian was to bring the light of reason to bear . . . Had that mystery not somehow transcended these efforts, then the *divinum* in *ius divinum* would have been a misnomer.[12]

This makes it difficult or impossible to specify any concrete and empirically or operationally meaningful differences between the irreversibilist and functionalist interpretations. The latter can of course admit that divine and saving mystery (i.e., *ius divinum*) is at work in all concrete developments which are profitable to the church. He can even indicate certain functions which are unalterably necessary (e.g., ministry of word and sacraments and the Petrine function) and believe that these will always "by divine right" be institutionalized in some fashion or other. The irreversibilist may be unhappy with this minimalism. He may want to limit the "in some fashion or other". He may wish to hold that however radically reinterpreted or restructured, the legitimate Petrine office will always be in visible continuity with the historic papacy. He may think it impossible that papal primacy of jurisdiction could ever become so meagre a thing as the jurisdiction possessed by—to take an extreme example—the secretary of a Quaker meeting. Yet in the light of what these passages say about mystery, it is hard to see how he could ever confidently affirm that either concretely identifiable visible continuity or a specifiable degree of jurisdiction are unalterably (and therefore, in his understanding of the term, *de iure divino*) necessary to the Petrine office.

Carl Peter's treatment of Schillebeeckx perhaps illustrates this difficulty. He appears to be unhappy with Schillebeeckx's statement that ". . . even an episcopal or presbyteral structure of the leadership of the church is not dogmatically inviolate, although the collegial unity of all the shepherds of the church, with the office-bearer who has the function of Peter in their midst, is."[13] The problem is that there is no equation between this function and the papacy.[14] Yet Peter shows no inclination to question that Schillebeeckx's position is genuinely Catholic because Schillebeeckx, whatever his deficiencies, seems to hold "that a unifying principle corresponding to Peter in the New Testament presentation of the apostles is always necessary in the church: and is of divine origin".[15]

Our hypothetical Lutheran, however, accepts the same position which Peter ascribes to Schillebeeckx. If Schillebeeckx is dogmatically acceptable even though it is the Petrine function, not its papal institutionalization which he describes as *de iure divino*, then so also is the Lutheran.

It is for Roman Catholics to decide whether this Schillebeeckxian-Lutheran position is reconcilable with Canon 2 of *Pastor aeternus* (DS 3058). Can "divine right" (with its implication of perpetuity) be applied only to the first clause, "the blessed Peter has perpetual successors in the primacy over the universal church," but not to the second, "the Roman pontiff is . . . the successor of the blessed Peter in the same primacy." This seems to be grammatically possible. Is it also theologically and dogmatically possible from a Roman Catholic perspective?

If so, there is no irresolvable contradiction between the Lutheran Confessions and Roman Catholic dogma on this point. *De iure divino* as applied to the institutionalization of the primacy in the Roman pontiff could mean for the contemporary Catholic simply "God-willed," while for the Lutheran Confessions it meant (among other things) "irreversibly" or "permanently" God-willed. The Catholic affirmation of the first meaning obviously is not logically opposed to the Lutheran denial of the second.

Because of this ambiguity, the traditional controversy over the *de iure divino* character of the papacy is now of only historical interest. The terms of the discussion have changed. When one looks at the ministerial orders of the church functionally and historically (i.e., in terms of their service of the word and of development in time), then the neat sixteenth century dichotomy between either *ius divinum* or *ius humanum* becomes impossible. Concrete post-biblical structures and offices can be inextricably both to a far greater degree than was allowed for by late medieval juridical categories.

In conclusion, then, the only meaningful contemporary manner of posing the question of papal primacy is to ask whether it is a possible—or perhaps even the best or only —way of effectively institutionalizing the Petrine function now or in the foreseeable future. On this point, at least as far as their Confessions are concerned, Lutherans are open to persuasion. Indeed, in so far as they take seriously their claim to be, not a sect, but a reform movement within the universal church, they should be delighted to recognize papal primacy to the degree that this becomes truly a servant of the gospel and of the evangelical unity of the church.

12

WHAT IS THE PETRINE FUNCTION?

George H. Tavard

There seems to be a growing ecumenical feeling that the Petrine function, whatever it may be, is of importance to the church. Yet the attempt to determine this function runs into several basic difficulties. These relate to:

- the language, which designates as Petrine both the function of Peter himself, and a remnant or continuation of this function after his death;
- the vagueness of the New Testament on the matter;
- variations in the historical implementation of a Petrine function;

- variations in the theological justifications of such a function.

In the following pages I wish to draw attention to some aspects of the problem.

I. Concerning language, an agreement may be easy on the essential difference between the task of Peter as an apostle, perhaps as chief apostle, and whatever aspect of this task should continue in the later church. The 'Petrinity' of the latter is only analogical to the former. It is not a task of Peter today. Rather it is both similar to his, and vastly dissimilar from it.

II. The texts of the New Testament in which a Petrine function has been read are particularly difficult to interpret. These are mainly Matthew 16:18-19, where the Petrine function is that of "rock" supporting the foundation of the Church; Luke 22:32, where it is that of "strengthening the brethren" after undergoing conversion; John 21:15-17, where it is that of shepherding the flock. On the meaning of these texts, see the Report of the Panel on Peter and the New Testament.

III. The variations in the historical implementation of the Petrine function are remarkable. On this point, see the patristic papers on the papacy (Godfrey Diekmann, James McCue) with the Report of the Patristics Panel, and the papers on the Middle Ages and *Unam Sanctam*. I will add the following remarks.

Before a Petrine function appears clearly, we find several images of Peter in the early church: Peter as witness to Christ, co-martyr with Paul in Rome (*Prima Clementis,* V, 2-7); Peter as co-teacher with Paul (Ignatius: *Ad Romanos,* IV, 3); Peter as a great seer (the Transfiguration, the visions in Acts, the apocalypses in the Petrine Epistles, the pseudo-Clementine literature, where Simon Peter is the true seer over against Simon the Magician, the false seer); Peter as painted in the art of the cemeteries (catacombs), where he is shown mainly in the two functions of receiving the New Law from Christ (in relation to Peter the seer and to Peter as the new Moses?) and of bringing the Gentiles to baptism (in keeping with Acts 10-11, and perhaps as indicating the contents of the New Law he has received also in relation to the new Moses).

At the same time, there emerges an image of the church in Rome ("presiding in agape": Ignatius's *Ad Romanos*; whereunto the faithful convene from everywhere: Irenaeus,

Adv. Haer., III, 1), together with an image of the bishop of Rome (intervening in the life of distant churches, like Victor in the paschal controversy; sending legates to faraway councils; taking sides in distant theological controversies; consulted by bishops on a wide range of doctrinal and moral questions). The correlation between the image of Peter and those of the Roman church and of its bishop remains unclear for a long time.

This correlation becomes explicit with Pope Leo I: Peter continues his task in the bishop of Rome; the predominance of Rome over all other churches derives from Peter's presence in his successors, the bishops of the Roman see; the text of Matthew 16:18-19 is interpreted in this sense. However, an alternative reading of the facts is contained in Canon 28 of Chalcedon, following Canon 6 of Nicaea: the authority of a bishop follows the civic importance of his see. In the light of Canon 28, the acclamations of Pope Leo after the reading of the tome seem to be rhetorical exaggerations rather than expressions of a theology: "Peter has spoken through Leo! The apostles have spoken! Leo has taught according to piety and truth! Cyril has taught so! Eternal memory to Cyril! Leo and Cyril have taught alike!" For Leo, however, the Petrine function is that of *authentic apostolic teaching*.

The growing practice of appealing to the bishop of Rome to resolve conflicts and solve problems even in distant areas shows the Petrine function as that of a *supreme court of appeals*.

In the early Middle Ages, the Petrine function is equated in Rome with a *vicariate of Christ* or even a *vicariate of God*. Meanwhile, it is understood in Gaul (Hincmar) as continuing in all the bishops: all bishops are successors of Peter and vicars of Christ. Whatever special authority is in the hands of the bishop of Rome may be lawfully exercised only insofar as the pope typifies and exemplifies *what Peter was and therefore of what all bishops ought to be*. (See my article, *Episcopacy and Apostolic Succession according to Hincmar of Reims, Theological Studies*, Dec. 1973, p. 594-623). In this line of thought, St. Bernard informs Eugene III that, as bishop of Rome, he ought to shine with all Christian virtues (*De Consideratione*, bk. II, ch. VI-XI). Savonarola's denunciation of Alexander VI as antichrist is to be seen on the background of this evangelical conception of the papacy.

With the great scholastics, writing after Innocent III, the growing claims for the bishop of Rome refer to *government,* which includes *infallible teaching* and not only discipline and organization. This line of thought culminates in the definition of papal infallibility at Vatican I, while the Hincmar line, after flourishing in medieval conciliarism and counter-reformation Gallicanism, diminishes.

Vatican II sees more features in the Petrine function than were explicit at Vatican I. The Petrine function implies heading the episcopal college (*Lumen Gentium,* n. 22), being the *unitatis, tum episcoporum tum fidelium multitudinis, perpetuum ac visibile principium et fundamentum* (n. 23), being the *supremus omnium christi fidelium pastor et doctor* (n. 25) and, as such, able to pronounce infallible definitions. IV. Theological justifications for the Petrine function seem to fall into three categories:

- the scriptural—based on the New Testament as interpreted in the light of later ecclesiological development and tradition;
- the esthetic—offered by some medieval authors, for whom all hierarchies necessarily culminate in one person endowed with supreme authority. (See my essay, *Succession et Ordre dans la Structure de l'Eglise,* in the septi-centennial work, *St. Bonaventure,* vol. III, Grottaferrata, 1974);
- the historical—seeing the Petrine function as a historical-providential development necessitated by the complexity of life in a universal church. I would personally favor this view of the question.

In the light of these remarks, it would seem that only one point remains constant in the different understandings of the Petrine function: it has something to do with the universality of the church. This is clear in the context of Vatican I and II, where the task of the pope is patterned on the episcopal model: the Petrine function in the universal church is analogical to the episcopal function in the diocese. As the episcopal function is described in terms of unity and universality, these are the two main referents of the Petrine function according to Vatican II (*Lumen Gentium,* n. 23). Other secondary aspects of the function follow: spreading "the Christian name" (n. 23); guaranteeing the legitimacy of the canonical mission (n. 24); exercising the supreme magisterium (n. 25). In other words, it includes mission, government, and teaching, although it relates primarily to the preservation of unity in universality (n. 22-23). However, this does not make the pope a bishop of bishops. For, in Vatican II, the Petrine function is fulfilled, though in different ways, by the entire episcopal college, by its head, the pope, and by each member of the college (n. 23).

Reflection on the history of the church shows that unity and universality are not constants, but variables: their forms have changed through history. It logically follows that the Petrine function must itself be a variable. Its forms have varied, and must vary, in keeping with the changing forms of universality and unity.

If this is correct, several conclusions may be suggested.

1) A definition of the Petrine function may be proposed. Its purpose is to keep the balance between the centripetal movement of the local church (at all levels of localization: eucharistic gathering, territorial or elective parish, diocese, region, nation) and the centrifugal movement of the universal church. In other words, it is to relate local unity to geographic and cultural universality, local units of the church to the church universal, so that pluralism and pluriformity do not undermine oneness, and that unity and uniformity do not destroy diversity.

2) Assignment of this function to one special office or officer is a more dubious enterprise. The exercise of this function by the bishop of Rome is too well attested to be discarded. Yet its attribution to the Roman pontiff as a distinctive mark placing him over and above all other bishops cannot be necessarily and absolutely permanent if the forms and, a fortiori, the exercise of the function are historical variables. In principle, the Petrine concern should be shared by all the faithful; the Petrine function by all those who have authority, at their level of authority. The practical means of determining the different levels of authority and the criteria of their legitimacy may evolve as the church, led by the Spirit, adjusts its life to the changing times.

3) A major source of the current Catholic-Protestant dilemma on the matter is that Catholics have been used to regard as a constant what is a variable. In opposition, Protestants have taken variations to be tokens of unauthenticity. In this, I suspect that their sin has been the same as that of Catholics: both have hankered after unattainable permanence.

13

THE PETRINE OFFICE: SOME ECUMENICAL PROJECTIONS

Joseph W. Baker

The author of *Two Centuries of Ecumenism: the Search for Unity* alluded to the neuralgic point of Roman Catholic involvement in the ecumenical movement: "Dollinger wanted unity without the bishop of Rome. He was betting against the Pope, and it seems that he lost his bet. A lesson of ecumenical importance must be learned from the failure of the Old Catholics. There will be no universal reunion without the Bishop of Rome, since there can be no Catholic unity without Roman Catholicism."[1]

The late Father H.A. Reinhold touched on the same general theme in his remarks at the Twenty-First North American Liturgical Week (1960):

As we skim over the tops of the waves of the ecumenical and liturgical movements we see the image of our Catholic selves as the world and our separated brethren see us now. I hope I have not misrepresented any aspect of this delicate subject. We must face the issue: a grudging admiration for achievement is something no Protestant or Orthodox will withhold, but will they be attracted by the rest of the image? When they discover the Roman liturgy, then will they see the Church in her most essential, most intimate, and profoundest manifestation. They are not ready for reunion with the Holy See. History, natural causes, political affairs, and long separation have built up a mentality that only a miracle could overcome. So long as we feel that the Churches separated have to "submit to the See of Peter," we need to ask ourselves whether we see and live the inward wealth of Rome and its holy liturgy. Until this day is reached no progress can be made.

Disciplines are different. There are explicit dogmatic statements on one side, where the other believes it to be more advisable to leave an issue in its present stage of acceptance without juridical decision. The first nine hundred years of patristic spirituality and biblical inspiration face an enormous corps of developed systems, schools, and methods worked out to a fine point; there are rites obsolete on one side which are in daily practice on the other, not to mention the ingrained prejudiced and bitter memories on the one side and the proud stance of right and authority on the other. These things are beyond repair, I fear. Only a new start from the present status quo, not going back to the affairs of four and nine hundred years ago, has the slightest hope of success.

Would it not be a terrible disaster if the world as we know it disappeared or a new world rose out of the present chaos, if mankind went forward towards POINT OMEGA without us? Would it not be a terrible judgment if we found all Christians reduced to the state of little branch Churches as we have seen them in the Moslem lands or tolerated by Red governments, kept by the state as another agency for the rulers to establish totalitarian control? Tolerating diversity in discipline, rite, and the degree of formulating the same dogma appears the only human way to establish the conditions of communion between the estranged brothers. The Church has shown in her religious orders how to protect and keep vigorously alive the most ancient orders, some of them in visible contrast with all the rest in their rites, their asceticism, and their discipline. With this tradition as an example, we may breathe easier. The liturgy then is the pattern upon which we hope to see consultations and discussions carried on—the great center around which a myriad of nonessential differences may turn.[3]

In our previous discussions, the pronounced emphasis given to considerations of the papacy suggest our basic concurrence with the assertion of the first quotation—that there can be no universal reunion without the bishop of Rome. The trend of our dialogue has been in the direction of formulating an acceptable solution which would reflect due consideration of viewpoints similar to those of Father Reinhold.

1) Father Carl J. Peter made an important contribution to our considerations of the papacy with his conclusion that: "The qualification *jure divino* indicates that the realities in question are held to be more than purely human in origin and more than divine in the true sense that everything else

is as well . . . ."[3] And again that: "There is no adequate study of what Roman Catholics mean when in theologizing today they refer to *jus divinum* and lay claim to it for some of their rites and institutions. . . ."[4]

Is it possible for a non-Roman Catholic theologian to conclude that *iure divino* in reference to the papacy is not reducible to an adiaphoron, but that there is some similarity between the institution and development of the papacy and a contemporary theological concept of Dominical institution of the sacraments?

2) Confronted by factual pluralism, the quest for Christian unity has begun to focus with increasing intensity on the subject of the coexistence of ecclesial *typologies* within the one church of Christ. This is a subject which has received considerable attention from the joint working group of the Roman Catholic Secretariat for Promoting Christian Unity and the Faith and Order Commission of the World Council of Churches. In this consultation, Emmanuel Lanne, O.S.B. has presented a paper on "The Possibility of a Variety of Typologies Within the Same Ecclesial Allegiance".[5] Bernard Lambert, O.P. in his work "Le Probleme Oecumenique" (translated and published in America as "Ecumenism: Theology and History") pursues the same line of thought.

Some hope for Catholic acceptance of this principle can be derived from the address of Cardinal Jan Willebrands at Cambridge, England on January 18, 1970. It may be useful to recall some of the words of Cardinal Willebrands:

> May I invite you to reflect on a notion which, it seems to me, has received much fruitful attention from theologians recently? It is that of the *typos* in its sense of general form or character, and of a plurality of *typoi* within the communion of the one and only Church of Christ.
>
> When I speak here of a *typos* of the Church, I do not mean to describe the local or the particular Church in the sense the Vatican Council has given it. In the "Decree on the Bishops'
>
> Pastoral Office in the Church" the Council describes the local Church or the diocese as "that portion of God's people which is entrusted to a bishop to be shepherded by him with the corperation of the presbytery. Adhering thus to its pastor and gathered together by him in the Holy Spirit through the gospel and the Eucharist, this portion constitutes a particular church in which the one, holy, catholic and apostolic Church of Christ is truly present and operative."

From this description it becomes clear that the local Church is not merely a part of the whole but that the fullness of the whole universal Church is present in the local Church, or if that fullness is not present in it, the local Church is not perfect and complete. Here we are not making a distinction between the essence of the Church and its empirical manifestation. The New Testament never makes this distinction when it speaks of Churches. We are talking about the universal Church which is manifest in a particular place. It is this meaning of the local Church which the Vatican Council has discovered again.

As distinct from this notion of the local Church, with all of the theological meaning it contains, the notion which I submit to your attention, that of a *typos* of a Church does not primarily designate a diocese or a national Church (although in some cases it may more or less coincide with a national Church). It is a notion which has its own phenomenological aspects, with their particular theological meaning.

In the Decree on Ecumenism we read: "For many centuries the Churches of East and West went their own ways, though a brotherly communion of faith and sacramental life bound them together" (N. 14). The theological element which must always be present and presupposed is the full "communion of faith and sacramental life." But the words "went their own ways" point in the direction of the notion which I would like to develop a little more. What are these "own ways" and when can we speak of a *typos*? A bit further on the Decree on Ecumenism explains "the heritage handed down by the apostles was received in different forms and ways, so that from the very beginnings of the Church it has had a varied development in various places, thanks to a similar variety of natural gifts and conditions of life" (N. 14).

Where there is a long coherent tradition, commanding men's love and loyalty, creating and sustaining a harmonious and organic whole of complementary elements, each of which supports and strengthens the other, you have the reality of a *typos*.

Such complementary elements are many. A characteristic theological method and approach (historical perhaps in emphasis, concrete and mistrustful of abstraction) is one of them. It is one approach among others to the understanding of the single mystery, the single faith, the single Christ.

A characteristic liturgical expression is another. It has its own psychology; here a people's distinctive experience of the one divine Mystery will be manifest—in sobriety or in splendor, inclining to tradition or eager for experiment, national or supranational in flavor. The liturgical expression is perhaps a more decisive element because "the liturgy is the summit toward which the activity of the Church is directed; at the same time it is the fountain from which her power flows" (Const. on the Liturgy, n. 10).

A spiritual and devotional tradition draws from many springs—the bible, the fathers, the monastic heritage, its own more recent classics. It meets new needs in its own way; its balance of joy and contrition, of action and contemplation, will be determined by history and temperament.

A characteristic canonical discipline, the fruit also of experience and psychology, can be present. Through the combination of all of these, a *typos* can be specified.

In the Constitution on the Church of the Second Vatican Council we read: "By divine Providence it has come about that various Churches, established in various places by the apostles and their successors, have in the course of time coalesced into several groups, organically united, which, preserving the unity of faith and the unique divine constitution of the universal Church, enjoy their own discipline, their own liturgical usage, and their own theological and spiritual heritage" (N. 23). It is through such deeply seated realities as these, and not because of mere territorial or national boundaries, that we can find the expression of a typology of Churches. Different *typoi* exist in countries where eastern and western Churches live together. If within one nation two *typoi* are so closely related, that in a situation of full communion between them, Providence draws them into coalescence, the authentic and strong elements of each will take their place in an enriched unity. Such a strengthening and enrichment will manifest itself primarily where it finds its highest motive— in a renewal of witness to Christ, a renewal of mission. A reunion which would not be a new Pentecost, a fresh manifestation of the eternal mystery to a time with its own spiritual needs, would be a nine days' wonder and little else.

It seems to me that Pope Gregory in his famous letter to Augustine, Archbishop of the English nation, opened the way for a new *typos* of the Church in western countries. He writes: "My brother, you are familiar with the usage of the Roman Church, in which you were brought up. But if you have found customs, whether in the Roman, Gallican, or any other Churches that may be more acceptable to God, I wish you to make a careful selection of them, and teach the Church of the English, which is still young in the Faith, whatever you can profitably learn from the various Churches. For things should not be loved for the sake of places, but places for the sake of good things. Therefore select from each of the Churches whatever things are devout, religious, and right; and when you have arranged them into a unified rite, let the minds of the English grow accustomed to it" (Bede, *A History of the English Church and People* 1, 27, 2).

Obviously the very existence of different *typoi* "added to

external causes and to mutual failures of understanding and charity" can also "set the stage for separations" (Decree on Ecumenism, N. 14). Through the grace of God, the ecumenical movement is creating understanding and charity and restoring unity between those who have grown asunder. The life of the Church needs a variety of *typoi* which would manifest the full catholic and apostolic character of the one and holy Church. If we are only going to fossilize, common sense would seem to suggest that it is not very important whether we do so together or separately. Unity is vital only if it is a vital unity.

None of us, I fancy, underestimates what is needed of wisdom and discernment, of strength and patience, of loyalty and flexibility, of forbearance, of willingness to teach and to learn, if we are to make progress towards this goal. Nor, happily, is any of us in doubt as to the sources whence we shall derive what we need. The movement we aspire to make together is within the one great dynamic, the *aedificatio Christi*. The tradition which is shared and enriched in a true typology is a *living* tradition—something which looks to the past only as it has vital meaning for the present and contributed dynamically to the future.

If a typology of Churches, a diversity in unity and unity in diversity, multiplies the possibilities of identifying and celebrating the presence of God in the world; if it brings nearer the hope of providing an imaginative framework within which Christian witness can transform human consciousness for today, then it has all the justification it needs. . . .[6]

Lanne sees the typologies of the church as facilitating the church's action in the world. Lanne suggests: "The Word is proclaimed in a particular way, it is incarnated in a culture—and there we have a conjunction of the divine and the human. In the same way, the sacraments, the life of the koinonia is expressed in a given place and time, and through this it manifests, expresses, makes possible the action of the universal church at all times and all places insofar as the latter is the church of Jesus Christ in the Holy Spirit."[7]

The Uniate Rites within the Roman Catholic communion, several of them organized within a patriarchal structure having considerable autonomy, suggest one form of the acceptance of typologies already existing within Roman Catholicism. At the same time, Vatican II effected profound changes in the uniatizing tendency. In particular, the Decree on Ecumenism in treating of the Eastern churches, speaks with approval of the importance of the local church; of the concept of sister churches and of the diverse ways in which the heritage handed down by the apostles was received and developed in East and West, "thanks to a similar variety of natural gifts and conditions of life."[8]

This document states that "far from being an obstacle to the church's unity, such diversity of customs and observances only adds to her (the Eastern church's) beauty and contributes greatly to carrying out her mission . . . . To remove any shadow of doubt, then, this sacred Synod solemnly declares that the churches of the East, while keeping in mind the necessary unity of the whole church, have the power to govern themselves according to their own discipline, since these are better suited to the temperament of their faithful and better adapted to foster the good of souls. Although it has not always been honored, the strict observance of this traditional principle is among the prerequisites for any restoration of unity."[9]

Given such a statement about the legitimacy of the typology of the Eastern church, one may legitimately ask if there is any essential obstacle to application of these same principles to those churches which grew out of the Reformation.

The Vatican Council's approval of the principle of diversity in unity, and the semi-official position taken by Cardinal Jan Willebrands at Cambridge would seem to establish as a position of the Roman Catholic Church that the incorporation of diverse but proven typologies of church structure within the one visible and united church would enrich all.

3) What is to be said of divergences in doctrine among the typologies of Christianity? Father Dulles has raised the question of whether the Catholic church must require "as a condition for reunion, that the other churches accept the Catholic dogmas"?[10] Resolution of the Filioque Controversy at the Council of Florence suggests that this has not always been demanded.

Attention is also called to the approval accorded diverse theological developments in the Eastern and Western churches in the Decree on Ecumenism: "In the investigation of revealed truth, East and West have used different methods and approaches in understanding and proclaiming divine things. It is hardly surprising, then, if sometimes one tradition has come nearer than the other to an apt appreciation of certain aspects of a revealed mystery, or has expressed them in a clearer manner. As a result, these various theological formulations are often to be considered as complementary rather than conflicting."[11]

And again: "After taking all these factors into consideration, this sacred Synod confirms what previous councils and
Roman pontiffs have proclaimed: In order to restore communion and unity or preserve them, one must 'impose no
burden beyond what is indispensable.' (Acts 15, 28)"[12]

The same Decree on Ecumenism stipulates that "Catholic
theologians engaged in ecumenical dialogue, while standing
fast by the teaching of the church and searching together
with separated brethren into the divine mysteries, should act
with love for truth, with charity, and with humility. When
comparing doctrines, they should remember that in Catholic
teaching there exists an order or 'hierarchy' of truths, since
they vary in their relationship to the foundation of the
Christian faith."[13]

Given the different methods and approaches in understanding and developing doctrine, is it possible for the Catholic
church to affirm that positive acceptance of the dogmas proclaimed during the period of mutual schism is not an absolute
requirement for unity? Since the definition of the Immaculate
Conception and the Assumption and papal infallibility reflect
a lived tradition quite different from that of the churches of
the Reformation, is it realistic to expect acceptance of the
conclusions without the lived-faith experience which pre-
ceded them?

On the part of the churches of the Reformation, and in
particular the Lutheran communion, can we expect them to
affirm that these doctrines are not contrary to revelation?
Further, would it be possible for them to accept a functional primacy of the Roman see? Acceptance of a de facto
primacy would seem to be in accord with the thesis once
proposed by Dr. Lindbeck that: "Developments which are
not dogmatically binding may also be binding, though in a
lesser degree, in view of not disrupting or injuring the unity
of the church or the weight of pastoral and theological considerations favoring them."[14] It can be argued that such a
mutual yielding on these questions implies confidence in and
yielding to the Holy Spirit rather than doctrinal indifference.

4) Is it possible for both sides to interpret the doctrine
of papal infallibility as relating to the basic indefectibility of
the church in proclaiming the apostolic teaching? Authentic
Roman Catholic interpretation has already so circumscribed
this dogma as to render grosser misinterpretations meaning-
less. On the only occasion on which papal infallibility has
been invoked since 1870, there was prior consultation of

all of the bishops of the Catholic church. It would be difficult to conceive of circumstances arising in the future which would be resolved solely by an infallible papal pronouncement. The principle of collegiality is assurance that even if an emergency situation evolved, consultation with the entire episcopal body through the synod of bishops would precede any decision. The deliberate reticence of the Second Vatican Council, refusing to ascribe the character of infallible pronouncements to any of its acts, suggests the pattern for the future.

A somewhat more thorny practical problem can be seen in the issuance of papal encyclicals which proclaim the teaching of the ordinary magisterium without attaching the note of infallibility. The theological aftermath of *Humanae Vitae* gives assurance that the right of dissent from non-infallible pronouncements remains.

5) In his paper, "A Lutheran Understanding of Papal Primacy."[15] Dr. Quanbeck enumerated certain characteristics which a renewed papacy ought to exhibit, which might open the way for Lutherans to see the papacy as a sign of unity for Christians outside the Catholic church. Among these are:

A. *Conformity to the servant-form manifested in the minister of Jesus Christ.* The Constitution on the Church in the Modern World and the efforts of the episcopate together with the Holy Father showed that an honest effort in this direction is being made.

B. *Authority in the church, whether of pope or pastor, is the authority of Christ, that is, of the Word of God.* Catholic teaching agrees that authority in the church, whether of pope or pastor, is the authority of Christ, the word of God. As Dr. Quanbeck states, there is a growing consensus among the churches on certain aspects of the understanding of this principle that:

1) *Teaching in the church be in accordance with the word of God. The church always stands under the authority of Christ.*
2) *There is a range of great variety of theologies within the scriptures.* Diverse theologies operating within the range of scriptural theologies have a legitimate place in the church.
3) *Proclamation of the gospel requires the adoption of the language and conceptuality of the people addressed.* This is an echo of the words of Pope John XXIII at the opening of the Second Vatican Council: "The substance of

the ancient doctrine of the deposit of faith is one thing, and the way in which it is presented is another. And it is the latter that must be taken into great consideration with patience if necessary, everything being measured in the forms and proportions of a magisterium which is predominantly pastoral in character." (October 11, 1962)

C. *Collegial exercise of authority.* Perhaps the most concrete example of the development of the principle of collegiality within Roman Catholicism is the institution of the Synod of Bishops. The decision of Pope Paul VI to convene these synods every two years (in response to a vote of the bishops gathered in the synod of 1969) indicates the firm establishment of this institution. The broadening of the base for collegial decision-making is a matter of gradual yet certain development, but this problem is common to all of the Christian churches.

D. *Exercise of authority in the church must make room for the initiatives and freedom of the Holy Spirit.* Again, this is a problem common to all Christian denominations. The abolition of the Index, the reform of methods by which controversial writings are to be examined, and the tolerance shown to Catholic Pentecostals may be cited as examples of the Roman Catholic Church's desire to avoid circumscribing the work of the Holy Spirit.

E. *Exercise of authority should lead, not drive; encourage rather than restrict; motivate rather than dominate.* It is to be hoped that this is the ideal and goal of anyone having a position of authority in any of the Christian churches. At the same time, there is no way of construing any meaningful authority which cannot be abused. Where this occurs, it is not a sign of the failure of the church, but a failure of human beings. We recognize that the church is made up of sinful men and that failure is to be found at every level within the church.

F. *Exercise of authority in the church should mediate between contending parties so that the energies of the community may be used for their true end, the building up of the body of Christ. Special concern should be given to minorities, especially those who lack the resources or the eloquence to present their own case persuasively.* In our country, the concern to give voice to the poor, the aged, to the young and to the unborn, to the black and Spanish-speaking minorities is common to most churches.

6) It may be in order to reflect upon the stipulations for an acceptable papacy in the paper of Dr. Fred Kramer.[16]

A. While Roman Catholic theologians may acknowledge that the term *de iure divino* applied to the papacy requires explanation, very few would be willing to relegate the papacy to the status of a merely *de iure humano* institution, and the members of the Roman Catholic Church at any level would reject this concept.

B. While it is conceivable that the papacy could be altered, so that the holder of this office would be pope for a specified number of years, or be required to retire at a certain mandatory age, we may ask if the statement in Dr. Kramer's paper that "the individual pope's position would depend on the good will of those who elected him, and who could also depose him" is seen as representing some necessary and irreducible evangelical principle?

It is true that Catholic theologians have taught that a pope ceases to be pope if he falls into public heresy. It would seem to be in order to derive some method of determining this and of taking action. By the same token, Catholic theologians teach that mental illness can deprive a pope of his ability to fulfill his office. Removal of an incumbent pope might be a difficult process to institutionalize, but it would seem proper to expect each pope upon assuming office to establish an understanding in case of such eventuality, much as American presidents in recent years have arrived at understandings with their vice-presidents. Since the office of the cardinal secretary of state under Pope Paul VI has been defined as akin to that of a prime minister, the understanding might be between a pope and his cardinal secretary of state.

7) In an attempt to project steps towards union between the Roman Catholic and the Lutheran communities, it appears that the first requisite would be a declaration by each of the communions that it recognizes the other as faithful to the apostolic teaching. This could include a mutual recognition of orders and sacraments, as recommended at an earlier stage of this dialogue. There should be on the part of the Lutheran communions, an acceptance of the position that a functional papal primacy is not contrary to the gospel. The Roman Catholic Church would acknowledge the legitimate autonomy of the Lutheran communions and the right of their leadership to participate in the collegial decision-

making of the whole church, as well as in the election of future popes.

8. Preliminary steps which might ease transition to a unified church might include:

- A mutual declaration on the validity of orders as proposed earlier by this group;
- The Roman Catholic extension of the provisions for sacramental sharing with the Eastern Orthodox Churches[17] to communicants of the Lutheran Synods;
- Roman Catholic recognition of mixed marriages between Lutherans and Catholics witnessed by Lutheran pastors as valid, extending the same recognition to these marriages as given to Orthodox-Roman Catholic marriages witnessed by an Orthodox priest as determined in 1967;[18]
- Approval of some form of altar and pulpit fellowship between Lutherans and Catholics;
- Initiation of projects of preaching and teaching in both communions aimed at deepening the sense of the unity already existing through faith and baptism.

NOTES

1. Differing Attitudes Toward Papal Primacy

Part I   Common Statement

1. It should be noted that we shall in this report follow the practice established in Volume IV of employing the term "ministry" to refer to the task or service which devolves on the whole church in distinction from the (or a) Ministry (or Minister) which performs a particular form of service—specific order, function or gift (charism) within and for the sake of Christ's church and its mission in the world. "This Ministry has the two-fold task of proclaiming the Gospel to the world—evangelizing, witnessing, serving—and of building up in Christ those who already believe—teaching, exhorting, reproving, and sanctifying by word and sacrament. For this two-fold work, the Spirit endows the Ministry with varieties of gifts, and thus helped the church to meet new situations in its pilgrimage. Through proclamation of

the word and administration of the sacraments, this Ministry serves to unify and order the church in a special way for its ministry," *Lutherans and Catholics in Dialogue IV: Eucharist and Ministry,* p. 11; see also p. 9.

2. Martin Luther, "On Councils and the Church," Luther's Works, vol. 41, pp. 9-178. For a commentary, see Jaroslav Pelikan, "Luther's Attitude Towards Church Councils," *The Papal Council and the Gospel* (ed. K. E. Skydsgaard ed.) Minneapolis: Augsburg, 1961, pp. 37-60, and for a full treatment, Ch. Tecklenburg-Johns, *Luthers Konzilsidee in ihrer historischen Bedingtheit und ihrem reformatorischen Neuansatz.* Berlin: Topelmann, 1966.

3. See above, note 1.

4. Cf. *Peter in the New Testament,* Raymond E. Brown, Karl P. Donfried, John Reumann, eds. Minneapolis and New York, Augsburg Publishing House, and Paulist Press, 1973, pp. 162ff.

5. Thus, Melanchthon noted in signing the Smalcald Articles with their anti-papal polemics that if the Pope "would allow the Gospel, we, too, may concede to him that superiority over the bishops which he possesses by human right, making this concession for the sake of peace and general unity among the Christians who are now under him and may be in the future." T. G. Tappert, ed., *The Book of Concord* (Philadelphia: Fortress Press, 1959) pp. 316-317.

6. *The Book of Concord,* p. 298.

7. Carl Peter, "Dimensions of *Jus Divinum* in Roman Catholic Theology," and George A. Lindbeck, "Papacy and *Ius Divinum,* A Lutheran View," see below.

8. Maurice C. Duchaine, "Vatican I on Primacy and Infallibility."

9. The Theological Commission of Vatican Council II rejected a proposed amendment to the effect that the pope, calling the bishops to collegial action, is "bound to the Lord alone" (*uni Domino devinctus*). In support of this reflection, the Commission wrote that such a formula was "oversimplified: for the Roman Pontiff is also bound to adhere to the revelation itself, to the fundamental structure of the Church, to the sacraments, to the definitions of former Councils, etc." (*Schema Constitutionis De Ecclesia,* MCMLXIV, p. 93).

10. *Peter in the New Testament,* pp. 8f.

11. *Ibid.,* pp. 158-68 with detailed discussion in previous chapters of the book. See also "Procedures of the New Testament and Patristics Task Forces.

12. *Ibid.,* p. 166. Cf. Oscar Cullman, *Peter-Disciple, Apostle, Martyr.* Philadelphia: Westminster Press, 2nd ed., 1962.

13. James F. McCue, "The Roman Primacy in the Patristic Era: I. The Beginnings Through Nicaea," see below.

14. George H. Tavard, "The Papacy in the Middle Ages," see below.

15. Denzinger-Schonmetzer, *Enchiridion Symbolorum.* 33rd ed.

(hereafter cited as DS) (Freiburg: Herder, 1965), 1307 and 3059.

16. DS 3059-3065

17. *Lumen Gentium*, Chapter III.

18. *Guadium et Spes*, 4.

19. *Dei Verbum*, 10.

20. *Lumen Gentium*, 25

21. *Book of Concord*, Article 14, pp. 214f.

22. *Lutherans and Catholics in Dialogue IV, Eucharist and Ministry*, pp. 19, 20. See also note 5 above.

23. The expressions, "legitimate traditions" and "spiritual heritage", are meant to include the broad span of all the elements that Lutherans have experienced as being the ways in which they and their ancestors have lived the gospel. These ways pertain to different though related levels that may be called, customs and faith, discipline and doctrine, canon law and teaching, etc. The intention of the text is to suggest that structures of reconciliation should extend further than the central patrimony of faith, in order to include also the *adiaphora* that usage has legitimized.

Part II   Reflections of the Lutheran Participants

1. *Lutherans and Catholics in Dialogue IV: Eucharist and Ministry*, 1970, p. 11.

2. *Apology of the Augsburg Confession* 7:20. Theodore G. Tappert ed. *The Book of Concord*, Philadelphia: Fortress Press, 1959, p. 171.

3. *Lutherans and Catholics in Dialogue III: The Eucharist as Sacrifice*, 1967, *IV: Eucharist and Ministry*, 1970.

4. *Lutherans and Catholics in Dialogue IV: Eucharist and Ministry*, p. 19.

5. *Ibid.*, p. 20.

6. *Ibid.*, p. 11

7. *Schaff-Herzog. Encyclopedia of Religious Knowledge.* New York and London; Funk and Wagnalls, 1908. Vo. II pp 76, 260-262; Vol. XII p. 2

8. Tappert, *op. cit.* pp. 298,299

9. It was this statement that provoked the assertion of the Smalcald Articles that the pope is the real antichrist: Part II, Article IV, 10, 11. Tappert, *op. cit.*, p. 300.

10. For a modern Roman Catholic interpretation and critique of this document, see G. Tavard, *"The Papacy in the Middle Ages,"* below.

11. Smalcald Articles Part II, Article IV, 1; Treatise on the Power and Primacy of the Pope, 1-4. Tappert, *op. cit.* pp. 298, 320.

12. Tappert, *op. cit.* pp. 325, 326.

13. See his note in signing the Smalcald Articles, Tappert, *op. cit.* pp. 316, 317.

14. Smalcald Articles Part Two, 4, 1. Tappert, *op. cit.* p. 298.

15. Treatise 25, Tappert, *op. cit.* p. 324.

16. So, for example, Balthasar Meisnerus. *Disputatio decima de distinctis gradibus ministrorum et usu templorum*, thesis XIII, in his *Collegium adiaphoristicum*, editio altera (Wittenberg: Haeredes D. Tobiae Mevii et Elerdus Schumacherus Johannes Borckardus, 1653), p. 198.

17. For one of the fullest discussions of the question of papal primacy by a 17th century Lutheran author, see Johannes Gerhardus: *Confessio Catholica*, liber II, articulus III, "De pontifice Romano", (Frankfurt und Liepzig: Christianus Genschius Johannes Andreae, 1679), pp. 523-675, especially chapters 1 through 5, pp. 523-581.

18. Such contacts recurred, e.g., at Augsburg during the diet of 1530, at the Leipzig Colloquies of 1534 and 1539, at the Colloquy of Hagenau of 1540, at the Colloquy of Worms in 1540-1541, and at the Colloquies of Regensburg of 1541 and 1546.

19. Hans Preuss. *Die Vorstellungen vom Antichrist im späterem Mittelalter, bei Luther und in der konfessionalen Polemik*, Leipzig, 1906. Bishop Arnulf of Orleans protested (ca. 991) against the misuse of the papal office in his time, denouncing the cruelty, concupiscence, and violence of a succession of popes, and asking, "Are any bold enough to maintain that the priests of the Lord all over the world are to take their law from monsters of guilt like these—men branded with ignominy, illiterate men, and ignorant alike of things human and divine? If, holy fathers, we are bound to weigh in the balance the lives, the morals, and the attainments of the humblest candidate for the priestly office, how much more ought we to look to the fitness of him who aspires to be the Lord and Master of all priests! Yet how would it fare with us, if it should happen that the man the most deficient in all these virtues, unworthy of the lowest place in the priesthood, should be chosen to fill the highest place of all? What would you say of such a one, when you see him sitting upon the throne glittering in purple and gold? Must he not be the 'Antichrist, sitting in the temple of God, and showing himself as God'?" Philip Schaff, *History of the Christian Church*, New York: Scribner and Sons, 1899. Vol. IV pp. 290-292.

20. We may mention the abortive Colloquy of Regensburg in 1557, the Colloquies of Zabern in Alsace in 1562, of Baden (1589), Emmendingen (1590), Aegensburg (1601), and at Torum in Poland (1645).

21. The course that the discussions took in one series of exchanges is instructive. In 1691 the Lutheran Abbot Gerard I of Loccum (Gerard Walter Molanus) in his *Cogitationes privatae de methodo reunionis ecclesiae protestantium cum ecclesia romano-catholica* stated that the Lutherans are willing to concede that by positive ecclesiastical law the bishop of Rome is the first patriarch, the first bishop of the church, and as such entitled to obedience in

spiritual matters. If the bishop of Rome wants recognition of his status as of divine right he must be ready to prove it to a general council from sacred scripture. In a later exposition, Gerard sees the primacy of the pope by divine right as one of the nineteen issues that make up the "irreconcilable" controversies. In his detailed discussion he quotes the Roman Catholic theologians of the Sorbonne against the primacy of the pope by divine right, against infallibility, and against the pope's authority to adjudicate controversies inside or outside of a general council. If these views should find acceptance in the rest of the Roman Catholic Community, Molanus holds that the entire business would be resolved, These views, however, did not find much acceptance; indeed, the documents that Molanus quotes were placed on the index of forbidden books.

22. See the recent book by Manfred P. Fleischer, *Katholische und Lutherische Ireniker unter besonderer Berucksichtigung des 19. Jahrhunderts,* (Göttingen: Musterschmidt Verlag), 1968.

23. Cf. *Lumen Gentium* 18, 22, 24, 25; the *Addenda* of November 16, 1964; *Christus Dominus* 2, 4, 8. Declaration in Defense of the Catholic Doctrine of the Church against Certain Errors of the Present Day: 3. (1973)

24. For example, the reservation of the question of birth control during Vatican II, and, the encyclical *Humanae Vitae* which ignored the advice of a majority of the special advisory commission.

25. Published in 1973 by Augsburg Publishing House, and Paulist Press, cited above Chapter 1, Note 4.

26. See the studies by McCue and Piepkorn in this volume.

27. *Peter in the New Testament,* p. 8.

28. The terminology here takes up a suggestion made by J. M. Robinson and H. Koester in their book, *Trajectories through Early Christianity,* (Philadelphia, Fortress Press), 1971.

29. *Peter in the New Testament,* pp. 23-28, esp. 29f., and passim.

30. See the study by James F. McCue in this volume.

31. See the Common Statement above.

32. See Carl Peter, "Dimensions of *Jus Divinum* in Roman Catholic Theology," in *Theological Studies* XXXIV (1973) pp. 227-250; and A. C. Piepkorn, "Ius Divinum and Adiaphoron in Relation to Structural Problems in the Church: the Position of the Lutheran Symbolical Books," below.

33. Peter, *passim.*

34. e. g. The encyclicals of Pope Leo XII (notably *Rerum Novarum*), as well as those of Pope Pius XI (*Quadragesimo Anno*) and Pope John XXIII (*Mater et Magistra, Pacem in Terris*).

35. The encyclical *Divino Afflante Spiritu* of Pope Pius XII, 1943, gave papal sanction to the use of historical-critical methods in the study of scriptures. This approval is made more explicit in the instruction *Holy Mother Church* (prepared by the Pon-

tifical Commission for the Promotion of Bible Studies, 1964) and by the dogmatic constitution of Vatican II *Dei Verbum*
36. Tappert, *op. cit.* pp. 316-317.

Part III Reflections of the Roman Catholic Participants

1. *Acta Apostolicae Sedis* 65 (1973), 402-403.
2. *Ibid.*, p. 403.
3. DS 3054-3055.

2. The Roman Primacy in the Patristic Era

Part I The Beginnings Through Nicaea

1. See L. Brun, "Der kirchliche Einheitsgedanke im Urchristentum" *ZST*, 14 (1937), 86-127; Jean Daniélou " 'mia Ekkleskia' chez les Pères grecs des premiers siècles," *L'Eglise et les églises*, 1954, I, 129-139.

2. Walter Bauer, *Rechtgläubigheit und Ketzerei im ältesten Christentum*, (1934), 2nd ed. 1964, ET 1971. For a criticism of Bauer see H. E. W. Turner, *Pattern of Christian Truth*, London, 1954. For a review of the reactions to Bauer, see the appendix by G. Strecker in the second edition of *Rechtgläubigkeit*.

3. Irenaeus informs us that the Valentinians speak of the orthodox as the common people and the people of the church (*quos communes et ecclesiasticos ipsi dicunt—A.H.* 3.15.2). In the same section Irenaeus presents the treacherous Valentinians as leading the crowd to ask the Valentinians "de nobis, quod cum similia sentiunt, sine causa abstineamus nos a communicatione eorum; et cum eadem dicant et eandem habeant doctrinam, vocemus illos haereticos." Irenaeus is not here presenting his own views, but rather a criticism made against the orthodox. But this criticism presupposes a state of affairs that gives considerably more support to the traditional view than to Bauer's proposal. Moreover, we get similar results from Clement of Alexandria (*Strom.* 2.3; 4.13; 5.1) and from the 37th fragment of Heracleon: the terms used by the gnostics clearly suggest that the church constitutes the mass over against an elite group.

4. On Jewish-Christianity see H. J. Schoeps, *Jewish Christianity*, 1969; Jean Daniélou, *La Théologie du Judéo-Christianisme*, Paris, 1958. The two books differ considerably.

5. See the collection of similar assertions from a variety of sources in A. Harnack, *Mission and Expansion of Christianity*, 1908, II, 1ff.

6. 16:2 is taken by many to be non-original, in part because it

requires a more polemical understanding of "catholic church"—i.e. "catholic" as opposed to heretical.

7. Such at least appears to be the implication of *Trall.* 3:1: "Without these (i.e., deacons, bishop, and presbyters) it is not called 'church.' "

This, however, raises the vexing question of the significance of Ignatius' silence about a bishop at Rome. Some would interpret the silence as indicating that Ignatius knew that there was no bishop at Rome. Others interpret the silence as indicating that Ignatius wasn't familiar enough with the Roman situation to know whether or not Rome had a bishop. Others argue from the *Trall.* 3 text that Ignatius must have thought that there was a single bishop at Rome.

8. See G. F. Snyder, *The Apostolic Fathers*, vol. 6: *The Shepherd of Hermas*, 1968, p. 19. On the division into sections and the dating of these sections, see pp. 3-7, 22-24. S. Giet, *Hermas et les pasteurs*, Paris, 1963, 283-284, accepts a late first or early second century dating, and is not impressed with arguments made for a more precise dating.

9. The dating of Polycarp is disputed. Some have seen in the letter a reaction to Marcion (Harrison, Quasten) and have accordingly dated the main body of the letter near mid-century. Others (e.g., William Schoedel, *Apostolic Fathers*, vol. 5: *Polycarp*, pp. 37-40) reject the anti-Marcion interpretation and theory of a composite letter and date the whole fairly close to the time of Ignatius.

10. Alexandria might be considered an exception here. Demetrius (189-231) is the first clearly visible bishop in the monepiscopal sense, so that in the 190s monepiscopacy may not have been all that "self-evident." And whether anyone before Heraclas, Demetrius' successor, was consecrated by other bishops is moot.

11. See Schoedel, *ibid.* p. 78n.

12. It should be noted that some would interpret the materials in Eusebius as referring exclusively to a dispute between Rome and Asia Minor, and not also to a local problem.

13. See G. LaPiana, "The Roman Church at the End of the Second Century," *Harvard Theological Review*, 18 (1925), 201-277.

14. Again Alexandria may not fit the generalization until slightly later.

15. For the problem of the early understanding of "apostle," see J. McCue, "Apostles and Apostolic Succession in the Patristic Era," in *Lutherans and Catholics in Dialogue*, IV, 1970, 138-148 and the literature noted there.

16. For details and literature, see J. McCue "Apostles and Apostolic Succession in the Patristic Era" in *Lutherans and Catholics in Dialogue*, IV, 1970, 161-165.

17. See *ibid.* 145

18. The *Epistula Apostolorum* is dated in the early second century in Hennecke-Schneemelcher, I, 191.

19. The document is third century. Greater precision in dating seems impossible. See Hennecke-Schneemelcher, II, 110-111.

20. *Ibid.* I, 484-488. On the position of Peter, see pp. 492f. The relevant Greek texts are in A. De Santos Otero, *Los evangelios apocrifos*, Madrid, 1963, pp. 549-552.

21. There is less general agreement as to the Petrine or non-Petrine authorship of 1 Peter. Whichever position one takes will not substantially affect the assertion that "in the course of the second century a large body of writing came to be associated with Peter."

22. It has long been noted (cf. A. Harnack, *Geschichte der altchristlichen Literatur bis Eusebius;* II: *Die Chronologie*, I, 1897, 703-707) that whereas Rome is originally identified as the church of the *two* apostles *par excellence*, Peter and Paul, the latter gradually falls into the background and Rome becomes the *ecclesia Petri*.

23. For a more detailed portrayal of the various apostles in second and third century apocryphal material, see W. Bauer in Hennecke-Schneemelcher, II, 35-73.

24. For an analysis of the various kinds of regional leadership that emerge in the church during this time, see Clemens Bauer, *Bild der Kirche, Abbild der Gesellschaft*, 1963; F. Dvornik, *Byzantium and the Roman Primacy*, New York, 1966, 27-39; K. Lübeck, *Reichseinteilung und kirchliche Hierarchie des Orients bis zum Ausgang des vierten Jahrhunderts*, Munster, 1901.

25. See H.J.W. Drijvers, *Bardaisan of Edessa*, Assen, 1966, 214-217, for the argument that at the time of which Eusebius writes there existed at Edessa no ecclesiastically organized Christianity.

26. For a more detailed analysis of Irenaeus' text see J. McCue, "Roman Primacy in the Second Century and the Problem of the Development of Dogma," *TS*, 25 (1964), 175-179.

27. It is assumed here that the *pontifex maximus* and *episcopus episcoporum* referred to by Tertullian in *De pudicitia* is the Catholic bishop of Carthage and not the bishop of Rome. See J. Quasten, *Patrology*, II, 312-314.

28. See *De unitate*, 4. I. On either of the two readings, *Unitas sacerdotalis* refers to unity among the bishops, not to unity within a single church of the presbyters with the bishop. See Bayard, *Saint Cyprien: Correspondence*, Paris, 1961, II, 183, n. 1.

29. The text was written without knowledge of Ulrich Wickert's *Sacramentum Unitatis, Ein Beitrag zum Verständnis der Kirche bei Cyprian*, Berlin, 1971, BZNW, vol. 41. Because at least one English language review (M. Fahey, in *JBL* 91 [1972], 582-583) suggests that that work constitutes a massive refutation of a non-primatial interpretation of Cyprian, several comments should perhaps be made here.

1) First, whatever else Wickert is saying, and whatever his disagreement with Hugo Koch and the older Protestant literature, he is *not* arguing for a Roman primatial interpretation: *"Dass Cyprian, wenn man es so nennen dürfte, 'Episkopalist,' nicht 'Papalist' gewesen ist, hat Hugo Koch unwiderleglich dargetan."* (Wickert, *TLZ* 92 [1967], 257; Fahey cites this article as a summary of Wickert's views.)

2) Wickert's complex interpretation of the *ecclesia principalis* of *Ep.* 59:14 runs approximately as follows: the *ecclesia principalis* exists in every local church, and yet is not perfectly realized in any such church. Peter brings the *ecclesia principalis* to Rome (but then the other apostles bring it elsewhere); and inasmuch as Peter is associated in a unique way with the *ecclesia principalis* through having been for a brief time its unique embodiment prior to the calling of the entire twelve, it is especially repugnant that the schismatics should go to Rome for support in their church-rending ways. Rome should be especially mindful of its responsibility to preserve unity by not contravening the decisions of the African bishops.

3) It has not been possible to work this interpretation through the committee. If accepted it would provide a way of harmonizing Cyprian's reference to the *ecclesia principalis* and his "episkopalist" ecclesiology. It might however be objected that it goes too far in attenuating the link between Rome and the *ecclesia principalis,* since in principle the term could be connected with any church. In either case, the interpretation of Cyprian's views on the status of the church and the bishop of Rome given in the text would not be decisively affected.

Part II   From Nicaea to Leo the Great

1. The drafter of this part gratefully acknowledges the helpful criticism and suggestions of the Reverend Monsignor John P. Sankovitz of The Saint Paul Seminary, Saint Paul, Minnesota, and of the Reverend John E. Lynch of The Catholic University of America, Washington, D. C.—To make the documentation as readily accessible as possible, the references in this part are normally to Carl Mirbt, *Quellen zur Geschichte des Papsttums und des Römischen Katholizismus,* 6th edition completely reworked by Kurt Aland, 1 (Tübingen: J. C. B. Mohr [Paul Siebeck], 1967), cited as Mirbt-Aland; the Greek and Latin *Patrologiae* edited by Jacques Paul Migne, cited respectively as MPG and MPL; and *Acta Conciliorum Oecumenicorum,* edited by Eduard Schwartz, cited as ACO.

2. Constantine's conception of his position vis-á-vis the church

has been the subject of much debate. See Francis Dvornik, *Early Christian and Byzantine Political Philosophy* (Washington, D. C.: The Dumbarton Oaks Center for Byzantine Studies, 1966), 2, 753-757.

3. See Perikles-Petros Joannou, *Die Ostkirche und die Cathedra Petri im 4. Jahrhundert,* posthumously edited by Georg Denzler (Stuttgart: Anton Hiersemann, 1972), pp. 71-77. Joannou, a Greek philologist, belonged to the Roman Catholic Byzantine Rite.

4. In this connection it should be noted that Canon 35 (33) of the fourth century Apostolic Canons prescribed merely that the "bishops of each nation must recognize and acknowledge as head him who is first among them and do nothing extraordinary without his consent" (Mirbt-Aland, no. 329). The ninth canon of a synod of Antioch which was long confused with the Dedication Synod of 341 but probably was held within a year or two of Nicaea makes it clear that the presiding bishop of the province is the one who has his seat in the civil provincial capital.

5. The Greek text explicitly names Julius in canon 3 and canon 9 (Mirbt-Aland, no. 273). In their letter to Julius, the Sardican bishops say: "This will appear best and most fitting, if the priests of the Lord from each of the various provinces report to the head, that is, to the seat of Peter the Apostle" (Mirbt-Aland, no. 274).

6. The creed which Liberius subscribed has been variously identified as (a) the First Creed of Sirmium (351), an Eastern statement that reproduces the "Fourth Creed" of the Dedication Council of Antioch in 341 (an attribution that is traditional but dubious), expanded by the addition of 26 anathemas, most of them addressed against the positions associated with Marcellus and Photinus; (b) the "Blasphemy" (Second Creed) of Sirmium (357), a Latin Anomaean document of Western authorship that explicitly forbids the use of both *homoousios* and *homoiousios;* and (c) the homoeusian Formula of Sirmium of 358. See Joannou, pp. 124-130.

7. The four "letters from exile" which document the "apostasy" of Liberius are now generally considered genuine.

8. The schism of Felix contributed to a second schism (366-367), when the followers of Felix chose Ursinus (366-367) to oppose Damasus as bishop after the death of Liberius. A brief third schism unrelated to the two earlier ones took place in 418-419, when Eulalius opposed Boniface.

9. Jerome's links to the Roman church were close—indeed, he regarded himself as a potential successor to Damasus, who employed Jerome as secretary—and he felt himself as a Western Christian even when he was in the East. Writing to Damasus in 375, he saw the chair of Peter as Damasus himself. "I know that the church is built on that rock. Whoever shall eat the Lamb outside this house is profane. If anyone is not with Noah in the ark, he shall perish in the dominating flood" (Mirbt-Aland, no. 359).

He regarded Damasus as competent to order the compilation of a new creed to replace that of Nicaea and to tell Jerome with which of the three Antiochene parties, all of whom claim to be in communion with Rome, to communicate (Mirbt-Aland, no. 360). In 382 Gregory of Nazianzus in the *Carmen de vita sua* spoke appreciatively of the ancient Rome that "binds together the whole West by saving teaching, as is just, since it presides over all, and cultivating God's universal harmony" (MPG, 37, 1068).

10. See J. Macdonald, "Who Instituted the Papal Vicariate of Thessalonica?," in F. L. Cross (editor), *Studia Patristica*, 4 (Berlin: Akademie-Verlag, 1961), 478-482. Macdonald argues that the formal initiation of the vicariate goes back no earlier than to Innocent.

11. A more generalized parallel occurs in the letter of the Council of Arles to Sylvester: *"Partibus . . . in quibus et apostoli cotidie sedent"* (Mirbt-Aland, no. 239).

12. In the *Explanatio symboli ad initiandos* Ambrose noted that the creed that he was setting forth is "the creed which the Roman church holds, where Peter, the first of the apostles, sat, and to which he brought the common decision" (MPL, 17, 1196). On Ambrose's view of Peter as the paradigm of the penitent restored to service and as the "vicar of Christ's love," see Mirbt-Aland, nos. 317 and 318 respectively.

Optatus of Mileve (fl. 365-385) in *De schismate Donatistarum* asserts that "the episcopal chair was conferred on Peter first in the city of Rome, [the chair] on which Peter, the head of all the apostles, sat, for which reason he is called Cephas," a play on the Greek *kephalē* and the Latin *caput.* In the chair of Peter "unity was to be preserved by all, lest the apostles might uphold each for himself separate chairs, so that he who should set up a second chair against the unique chair would already be a schismatic and a sinner." Optatus notes with satisfaction that Siricius is his colleague and that "he with the whole world agrees with us in one bond of communion through the intercourse of letters of peace" (Mirbt-Aland, nos. 287-288). For Optatus, whose bête noire is Donatism, the bishop of Rome is the symbol of unity in a Catholic community that embraces the whole West and is in communion with the historic East as well. In "The Work of Optatus as a Turning-Point in the African Ecclesiology," in *The Thomist*, vol. 37, no. 4 (October 1973), Robert B. Eno sees the new element in Optatus as the "transfer of the Petrine-Unity symbolism from the local level to the world level of the universal church or at least of the western church."

13. The meaning of the final phrase is debated. It can be read to suggest that the bishops in council expect the bishop of Rome to condemn the heresy of Pelagius on biblical grounds. It can also be read to indicate that the bishops in council saw the authority of the bishop of Rome as based on the written word of God.

14. Augustine's view of the place and function of the bishop of

Rome within the church is too complex to be sketched in a brief summary. It is worth remembering, however, that Augustine saw Peter as the *typus* of the church (MPL, 38, 479) and as bearing the *figura* in whom the church is signified (MPL, 38, 479). Against the Donatists Augustine asserted that "the primacy of the apostolic chair always flourished" in the Roman church (MPL, 33, 163). But he sees a general council and the consent of the universal church as the right way to establish the best opinion in a controversy and to remove all doubts.—For a recent discussion of the relationship between Rome and North Africa from Tertullian into the seventh century, see Werner Marschall, *Karthago und Rom: Die Stellung der nordafrikanischen Kirche zum Apostolischen Stuhl in Rom* (Stuttgart: Anton Hiersemann, 1971), especially chapters 3 (Augustine), 4 (Optatus), 6 (Donatism), 7 (Pelagianism), and 8 (the Apiarius affair).

15. Jaroslav Pelikan, *The Emergence of the Catholic Tradition (100-600)* (Chicago: The University of Chicago Press, 1971), p. 316, notes that both the tradition and the Eastern theology of the time supported Celestius' views; that Celestius professed "an impeccable trinitarian orthodoxy"; and that the issues still lay in the realm of tolerable differences in teaching and not in the realm of officially defined dogma.

16. When Zosimus condemned Pelagius and Celestius, Prosper of Aquitaine (390?-463?) observed that now the sword of Peter had been given "to all the bishops of the church for the striking down of the impious" (MPL, 51, 271).

17. Writing his *Vita Augustini* around 437, Possidius clearly taught that Innocent and Zosimus, as bishops of Rome, effectively cut the Pelagian heretics off from the church, instructing the churches of the West and East by letter that all Catholics were to anathematize and avoid the Pelagians, and therein pronounced on them the judgment of God's Catholic church (MPL, 32, 48-49). About the same time (between 432 and 440), the unreliable and anonymously circulated *Praedestinatus,* which Altaner links with Arnobious the Younger (fl. 432-455), equates the condemnation of Pelagius and Celestius by Innocent with the condemnation of the universal church (MPL, 53, 618).

18. The edict of Theodosius was nevertheless incorporated into the Codex Theodosianus and the Codex Justinianus and thus became part of the canon law of the Byzantine empire.

19. Augustine's words are: *"Existunt exempla, ipsa sede apostolica judicante vel aliorum judicata firmante, quosdam pro culpis quibusdam, nec episcopali spoliatos honore nec relictos omnimodis impunitos. Quae ut a nostris temporibus remotissima non requiram, recentia memorabo."* There is no way of knowing what concrete cases from "very remote" times Augustine may have had in mind.

20. Of interest is the statement of Cyril in a letter to Nestorius: "Peter and John are equal in honor in that they are apostles and holy disciples" (MPG, 77, 112).

21. See in this connection Michele Maccarone, "L'antico titolo papale *Vicarius Petri,*" *Divinitas,* 1 (1957), 365-371, as well as his "'Cathedra Petri' und die Entwicklung der Idee des päpstlichen Primats vom 2. bis 4. Jahrhundert," *Saeculum,* 13 (1963), 278-292.

22. Wilhelm de Vries sees Leo as providing a "more precise jurisdical definition for the idea of succession" ("Theoretical and Practical Renewals of the Primacy of Rome," in Hans Küng, editor, *Papal Ministry in the Church* [Concilium; 64] [New York: Herder and Herder, 1971], p. 46). Not all scholars agree that Leo operates with a "juristic theology."

23. Leo's contemporary, Peter Chrysologus of Ravenna (400?-450), also affirmed that Peter "lives and presides in his own see. . . . We cannot decide questions of faith apart from the consent of the bishop of Rome" (MPL, 54, 753). Socrates (380?-450), writing his *Church History* around 439, in describing the Dedication Synod of Antioch in 341 reflected his own belief when he noted that the synod had no representatives of the Roman see and added: "Although the ecclesiastical canon forbids the churches to make ordinances against the mind of the bishop of Rome" (MPG, 67, 196). Like Socrates, Sozomen (fl. 439-450), writing his *Church History* about 450, looked back and saw Julius restoring Athanasius, Marcellus, Asclepas of Gaza, and Lucian of Adrianople to their own sees, "asserting that he has the solicitude for all because of the dignity of his see." Sozomen also cites "a priestly law, annulling whatever is done against the mind of the bishop of Rome" (MPG, 67, 1052-1057).

24. After Hilary's death, Leo in 450 partially restored certain metropolitical rights to the see.

25. On the basis of Theodoret's restoration to his see by Leo, the former was tentatively allowed to sit in the Council of Chalcedon, but he received final recognition only after the council had compelled him formally to abjure Nestorianism (ACO, II/I, iii, 9 [368]).

26. Similarly, Rufinus accounts for the fact that the creed of the church at Rome does not add anything to the clause, "I believe in God the Father the almighty," by suggesting that "no heresy has ever had its origin there" (Mirbt-Aland, no. 367). Joseph Ratzinger bases the special primacy of Rome over Antioch and Alexandria in the early church not on the third century idea (still unknown even to Augustine) "that the bishop of Rome was the successor of Peter the apostle with the prerogatives mentioned in Matthew 16:17-19," but on three other grounds. The first was that "it was agreed in the fourth and fifth centuries that Rome had kept itself from heresies and that, as the home of an inviolate tradition, it could be called upon in special measure as the guardian of correct belief." The second was that "as the see of the apostles Peter and Paul Rome stood in an especially strong and immediate apostolic tradition. It was therefore an apostolic see— not that its bishop had a special office but that the *ecclesia* of

Rome had a special significance for the entire church." The third was that "the church of Rome was successor to the special place held by the Jerusalem community in the primitive church. The migration of Peter to Rome was viewed by the infant church as the definitive act by which it gave up trying to be the church of the Jews and became the church of the gentiles" "Primacy and Episcopacy," *Theology Digest,* 19 [1971], 202).

27. Timothy was driven out only a few years later.

28. For Leo's letter of May 22, 452, to Anatolius and the latter's reply, deliberately delayed for nearly two years, see MPL, 54, 1001-1010; 1082-1084.

29. See, for example, his letter of around 446 (MPL, 54, 645-663).

4. The Bull "Unam Sanctam" of Boniface VIII

1. H. Bettenson: *Documents of the Christian Church,* Oxford, 1953, p. 161-163.

2. See Henri de Lubac: *La Foi Chrétienne. Essai sur la Structure du Symbole des Apôtres,* Paris, 1969, p. 169-222.

3. For some of the following points I draw on Yves Congar: *L'Eglise, de saint Augustin à l'Epoque Moderne,* Paris, 1970.

4. See Louis Bouyer: *L'Eglise de Dieu,* Paris, 1970, p. 61.

5. The conflict over the king's sources of income, which came to a head under Philip the Fair, was already well under way at the time of Louis IX, later canonized as St Louis.

6. Jean Rivière: *Le Problème de l'Eglise et de l'Etat au temps de Philippe le Bel,* Louvain, 1926.

7. Congar, p. 277.

8. DS, p. 279.

9. Congar, pp. 271-290.

10. *Ibid.,* p. 276, n. 15.

11. Charles Journet: *L'Eglise du Verbe Incarné,* vol. 2, Paris, 1951, p. 1094.

12. *Ibid.,* p. 275.

13. Preface to Jean-Marie Paupert: *Pour une Politique Evangélique,* Paris, 1965, p. 11; see "Dogme et Théologie dans la Bulle *Unam Sanctam*" (*La Foi dans l'Intelligence,* Paris, 1964, pp. 361-369).

14. *Documentation Catholique,* 1955, 1209, col. 1223.

15. This distinction was made in the address by which John XXIII opened Vatican Council II.

16. I use the term 'archeological', here, in the sense of Michel Foucault: *L'Archéologie du Savoir,* Paris, 1969.

5. "Ius Divinum" and "Adiaphoron"

1. In this connection Hans Volz calls attention to the very early formulation of Martin Luther: "Sacra scriptura, quae est proprie jus divinum" (WA 2, 279, 23-24).

2. There are a number of occurrences of *ius divinum* or a synonym in the Lutheran symbolical books that do not shed additional light on the meaning of the term. By accommodation, Apology, 7, 23, differentiates *leges divinae, canonicae, et civiles*. In the careful distinction that Boniface VIII made in *Unam sanctam* (1302) between *potestas humana* and *potestas divina* (DS 874), the Smalcald Articles see the origin of the papal claim to be called by divine right the highest officer (*der Oberste*) over the Catholic church (Part Two, 4, 13). The Treatise on the Authority and Primacy of the Pope charges the bishop of Rome with claiming by divine right to "be above all bishops and pastors" and to "have both swords" (1-2.5); from paragraphs 3 and 6 it is clear that the Treatise too has *Unam sanctam* in mind. The papal claim to superiority by divine right is referred to without comment in paragraphs 12, 20, 38, and 57. Paragraph 65 declares that the primitive differentiation between presbyter and *episcopos* is not by divine right.

6. A Lutheran Understanding of Papal Primacy

1. Henry Denzinger, "The Sources of Catholic Dogma," in *Enchiridion Symbolorum* (B. Herder, 1957) pp. 451ff.

2. *Ibid.*, p. 452.3.

3. *Ibid.*, p. 454.

4. Tappert, pp. 217, 300, 301, 327, 330.

5. *Ibid.*, pp. 316f.

9. Communion, Councils, and Collegiality

1. Yves Congar, "Conclusion," *Le concile et les conciles* (Cerf, 1960), pp. 300-334; "De la communion des églises à une ecclésiologie de l'église universelle," *L'épiscopat et l'église universelle* (Yves Congar & B.-D. Dupuy; Cerf, 1962), pp. 227-260; "Konzil als Versammlung und grundsätzliche Konziliarität der Kirche," *Gott in Welt: Festgabe für Karl Rahner* (H. Vorgrimler; Herder, 1964), v. 2, pp. 135-165.

2. J. Lécuyer, *Études sur la collégialité épiscopale* (Mappus, 1964).

3. M.-J. Le Guillou, *Mission et unité. Les exigences de la communion*, I & II (Cerf, 1960).

4. J. Hamer, *L'église est une communion* (Cerf, 1962).

5. L. Hertling, *Communio: Church and Papacy in Early Christianity* (Loyola University Press, 1972); J. Colson, *L'épiscopat catholique. Collégialité et primauté dans les trois premiers siècles de l'église* (Cerf, 1963); G. Dejaifve, "Les douze apôtres et leur unité dans le tradition catholique," *Ephemerides Theologicae Lovanienses* 39 (1963) 760-778.

6. Joseph Ratzinger, *Das neue Volk Gottes: Entwürfe zur Ekklesiologie* (Patmos, 1969), especially pp. 121-224. The following paragraphs draw heavily on Ratzinger's analysis.

7. *Ibid.*, pp. 171-174 and 207-210.

8. *Ibid.*, pp. 132 and 185-187.

9. *Ibid.*, pp. 126-134.

10. *Ibid.*, pp. 128-130.

11. *Ibid.*, pp. 131-132. Ratzinger (*ibid.*, p. 122) treats the earlier exchange between Stephen and Cyprian as an intra-patriarchal conflict, not as a Roman claim to ecumenical primacy.

12. Included here is the papal claim to be *caput* of the ecumenical Christian *corpus:* the center of the horizontal ecumenical *communio* is also its "hierarchical" head, though the term is not yet used and its later juridical implications are only imperfectly perceived.

13. Yves Congar, *L'église de saint Augustin à l'époque moderne* (Cerf, 1970). Cf. also his *L'ecclésiologie du haut moyen âge* (Cerf, 1968) and "La collégialité de l'épiscopat et la primauté de l'évêque de Rome dans l'histoire," *Angelicum* 47 (1970) 403-427. G. Dejaifve offers a shorter survey of much the same material in "La collégialité épiscopale dans la tradition latine," *L'église de Vatican II* (G. Baraúna; Cerf, 1966), v. 3, pp. 871-890.

14. Cf. Yves Congar, *L'église de saint Augustin à l'époque moderne, op. cit.*, pp. 260 and 337, and "Notes sur le destin de l'idée de collégialité épiscopale en Occident au moyen âge," *La collégialité épiscopale* (Y. Congar; Cerf, 1965), pp. 99-130.

15. Cf. J. Ratzinger, *Das neue Volk Gottes, op. cit.*, pp. 135-138.

16. Cf. below, pp. 8-17.

17. Cf. G. Alberigo, "La collégialité épiscopale selon quelques théologiens de la papauté," *La collégialité épiscopale, op. cit.*, pp. 183-222.

18. Cf. J. Ratzinger, *Das neue Volk Gottes, op. cit.*, pp. 184-187; H.-M. Legrand, "The Revaluation of Local Churches: Some Theological Implications," *Concilium* 74 (1972) 53-64; B. Lambert, "La constitution du point de vue catholique de l'oecuménisme," *L'église de Vatican II, op. cit.*, v. 3, pp. 169-173.

19. In addition to the fundamental statements in *Lumen*

Gentium 13, 23, and 25-27, cf. *Unitatis Redintegratio* [Decree on Ecumenism] 16-18; *Orientalium Ecclesiarum* [Decree on Eastern Catholic Churches] *passim; Christus Dominus* [Decree on the Bishops' Pastoral Office in the Church] 3, 11-24, and 36-43; and *Ad Gentes* [Decree on the Church's Missionary Activity] 19-22 and 37-38.

20. A surprising adversary of this position within contemporary Catholic theology is Karl Rahner. Though Rahner has written extensively on the bishop's role in the local church, he maintains that (at least from one point of view) a man becomes bishop of Rome by becoming head of the college of bishops and a man becomes a bishop period by being coopted into the college of bishops. Cf. Karl Rahner, *Theology of Pastoral Action* (Herder & Herder, 1968), pp. 83 and 87, and *Bishops: Their Status and Function* (Helicon, 1964), pp. 17-19. This thesis allows Rahner to explain the membership of non-diocesan bishops in the episcopal college— though there are simpler ways of doing that. Cf. Ratzinger's comments in *Das neue Volk Bottes, op. cit.*, pp. 184-187. A much more impassioned defense of the priority of the bishop's role in the local church is given by T. Strotmann, "Primauté et céphalisation. A propos d'une étude du P. Karl Rahner," *Irénikon* 37 (1964) 186-197.

21. This does not settle dogmatic speculation about the possibility of transferring the Petrine title to some other local church. The chances of such a transference actually occurring are, however, almost non-existent. Moreover it is difficult to see how a primatial church in Mexico City or Manila would solve any problems in the long run.

22. Cf. Ratzinger's criticism of such a politicized notion of church-as-continuing-council in *Das neue Volk Gottes, op. cit.*, pp. 155-161.

23. This principle, taken from Catholic social philosophy, must itself be applied analogously to the church.

24. Cf. J. Ratzinger, *Das neue Volk Gottes, op. cit.*, pp. 141-145. The ecumenical implications of the distinction between papal primacy within the church universal and patriarchal primacy within the Latin patriarchate are obvious. Surely one of the conditions for restoring full communion between Catholic and non-Catholic Christians in the West will be the acknowledgment of each confession's right to retain its traditional liturgical, doctrinal, and disciplinary "way of life," perhaps on the analogy of a non-territorial patriarchate.

25. The best path through this jungle remains the work of Brian Tierney: *Foundations of the Conciliar Theory* (Cambridge University Press, 1955); "Pope and Council: Some New Decretist Texts," *Mediaeval Studies* 19 (1957) 198-218; "Collegiality in the Middle Ages," *Concilium* 7 (1965) 5-14; "Canon Law and Western Constitutionalism," *Catholic Historical Review* 52 (1966) 1-17; "Roots of Western Constitutionalism in the Church's Own

Tradition," *We, the People of God* (J. Coriden; Canon Law Society of America, 1968), pp. 113-128; "Hermeneutics and History: The Problem of *Haec Sancta*," *Essays in Medieval History for Presentation to Bertie Wilkinson* (T. Sandquist & M. Powicke; University of Toronto Press, 1969), pp. 355-370.

26. For the early history and later interpretation of this quotation, with its exceptive clause, from Gratian (*Decretum* 40, 6), cf. (in addition to Tierney) August Franzen, "The Council of Constance: Present State of the Problem," *Concilium* 7 (1965) 37-41 and 48; Hans Küng, *Structures of the Church* (University of Notre Dame Press, 1968), pp. 224-240, 264-265, and 270-278; Harald Zimmermann, "Die Absetzung der Päpste auf dem Konstanzer Konzil: Theorie und Praxis," *Das Konzil von Konstanz* (A. Franzen & W. Müller; Herder, 1964), pp. 113-137.

27. *DS* 861, 1307, 3059-3064, and *Lumen Gentium* 18 and 22.

28. The competence of any juridical body to judge the pope was explicitly denied by Vatican I (*DS* 3063). Nevertheless, in his official *relatio* clarifying the meaning of papal primacy in *Pastor Aeternus*, Bishop Zinelli discussed the possibility of an heretical pope in the following terms: *Nec validum pondus habent hypothetici prorsus casus de pontifice in haeresim ut privata persona lapso aut incorrigibili, qui casus aequiparari possunt aliis de pontifice habitualiter in dementiam lapso, etc. Haec, providentiae supernaturali confisi, satis probabiliter existimamus numquam eventura. At Deus in necessariis non deest; ac proinde si ipse permitteret tantum malum, non deerunt media ad providendum, quin propter hos casus hypotheticos doctrina de vere plena et suprema potestate Romani pontificis infirmetur* (Mansi, v. 52, col. 1109). Bishop Gasser, discussing a similar situation in connection with papal infallibility a few days later, seems simply to deny that what is a juridical possibility will ever actually occur: *Sed ideo nil timendum, ac si per malam fidem et negligentiam pontificis universalis ecclesia in errorem circa fidem induci posset. Nam tutela Christi et assistentia divina Petri successoribus promissa est causa ita efficax, ut judicium summi pontificis, si esset erroneum et ecclesiae destructivum, impediratur; aut, si reapse pontifex ad definitionem deveniat, illa infallibiliter vera existat* (Mansi, v. 52, col. 1214).

29. Cf. Yves Congar, *L'église de saint Augustin à l'èpoque moderne, op. cit.,* pp. 260-263.

30. Cf. Klaus Mörsdorf, "Cardinal," *Sacramentum Mundi* (Herder & Herder, 1968), v. 1, pp. 259-262, and Brian Tierney, *Foundations of the Conciliar Theory, op. cit.* pp. 68-84.

31. Cf. Brian Tierney, *Foundations of the Conciliar Theory, op. cit.,* pp. 149-153; J. Watt, "The Medieval Canonists and the Formation of Conciliar Theory," *Irish Theological Quarterly* 24 (1957) 13-27; J. Lecler, *"Pars corporis papae.* Le sacré collège dans l'ecclésiologie médiévale," *L'homme devant Dieu* (Editions Monlaigne, 1964), v. 2, pp. 183-198. [In a sense this thirteenth-

century canonical speculation anticipated contemporary reflection on the possibility of institutionalizing the primatial office in more than one person. From the viewpoint of a *communio*-ecclesiology, the traditional connection between papal primacy in the church universal and the pope's office as the monarchical bishop of a central local church would weigh against such a development.]

32. This is the basic thesis of Tierney's *Foundations of the Conciliar Theory, op. cit.;* cf. especially pp. 157-247. Francis Oakley, *Council over Pope?* (Herder & Herder, 1969) and "The New Conciliarism and Its Implications," *Journal of Ecumenical Studies* 8 (1971) 815-840, seems to support Tierney's analysis, though (because of his reading of *Haec Sancta* as a strict dogmatic definition) Oakley himself believes it is necessary to admit a radical discontinuity in the development of Catholic ecclesiology and calls for an appropriate "provisional" ecclesiology to handle such discontinuity. Cf. also Hans Küng, *Structures of the Church, op. cit.,* pp. 258-270, and August Franzen, "Council of Constance: Present State of the Problem," *op. cit.,* pp. 45-55. Paul de Vooght's most recent statements on the question can be found in *Les pouvoirs du concile et l'autorité du pape au Concile de Constance* (Cerf, 1965) and "Les controverses sur les pouvoirs du concile et l'autorité du pape au Concile de Constance," *Revue Théologique de Louvain* 1 (1970) 45-75.

33. Whatever "conciliarism" was at work at the councils of Constance and Basel had little to do with the later episcopalism characteristic of theological Gallicanism and its Germanic counterparts. There were few bishops present at Basel and, though a considerable number of bishops participated in the Council of Constance, voting took place by "nations" (i.e., according to the pattern of the medieval universities, not by country). In contrast to previous and subsequent ecumenical councils, this arrangement gave non-bishops the same right of suffrage as the bishops themselves. Though there may be grounds for broadening the base of participation in future ecumenical councils, the point here is that fifteenth century conciliarist thought paid little specific attention to *episcopal* collegiality. A natural link exists, of course, between the notion of "representing" the universal congregation of believers who constitute the local churches of the ecumenical Christian *communio* on the one hand and the collegial activities of their bishops in council on the other; but at Constance and Basel consciousness of this episcopal collegiality was not strong. Cf. Charles Moeller, "La collégialité au Concile de Constance," *La collégialité épiscopale, op. cit.,* pp. 131-150. This lack of focus on episcopal collegiality as such also seems to characterize the slightly later conciliarist reflections of Nicholas of Cusa, Nicholas of Tudeschi, and Enea Silvio Piccolomini. To my knowledge, it is still unclear exactly how this fifteenth century "representative" conciliarism crystallized into the episcopalism which so complicated the third session of the Council of Trent [cf. Hubert Jedin,

Krisis und Abschluss des Trienter Konzils. 1562/1563 (Herder, 1964)] and persisted, in a ever more qualified form, from Richer to Bossuet to Tournély to Maret and Vatican I. Much more research is needed along the lines of Olivier de la Brosse, *Le pape et le concile. La comparaison de leurs pouvoirs à la veille de la Réforme* (Cerf, 1965). Historically the *political* implications of Gallicanism and Josephinism constituted an enormously complicating factor; theologically that factor can today for all practical purposes be ignored.

34. On the notion of "representation" at Constance and Basel, cf. Hubert Jedin, *Bischöfliches Konzil oder Kirchenparlament?* (Basel: Helbing & Lichtenhahn, 1965²), pp. 8-9. Certainly no fifteenth century populism was at work at either Constance or Basel. Any parliamentary tendencies were decidedly aristocratic: the princes and above all the professors wanted a say along with the cardinals and bishops.

35. Cf. below, pp. 18-22. Historically, the crucial question about the interpretation of *Haec Sancta* is to what extent the genuinely conciliarist notions of Zabarella, d'Ailly, Gerson, and the German reformers (i.e., at least some *juridical* limitations on papal primacy by a general "representative" council) received the Council's official approval at its fifth session. As far as I can determine, that historical question is still unresolved.

36. For a general orientation, cf. E. Delaruelle, E. Labande, and P. Ourliac, *L'église au temps du grand schisme et de la crise conciliarie, 1378-1449* (A. Fliche & V. Martin, *Histoire de l'église* XIV/1-2; Bloud & Gay, 1962-1964); K. Fink, "Zur Beurteilung des Grossen Abendländischen Schismas," *Zeitschrift für Kirchengeschichte* 73 (1962) 335-343; H. Hürten, "Zur Ekklesiologie der Konzilien von Konstanz und Basel," *Theologische Revue* 59 (1963) 362-371; *Das Konzil von Konstanz, op. cit.;* Joseph Gill, *Constance et Bâle-Florence* (*Histoire des conciles oecuméniques* 9; l'Orante, 1965); P. de Vooght, *Les pouvoirs du concile et l'autorité du pape au concile de Constance, op. cit.;* August Franzen, "Council of Constance: Present State of the Problem," *op. cit.,* pp. 29-68.

37. Cf. A. Franzen, "Council of Constance: Present State of the Problem," *op. cit.,* and the following articles in *Das Konzil von Konstanz, op. cit.:* August Franzen, "Zur Vorgeschichte des Konstanzer Konzils," pp. 3-35; Josef Lenzenweger, "Von Pisa nach Konstanz," pp. 36-54; August Franzen, "Das Konzil der Einheit: Einigungsbemühungen und konziliare Gedanken auf dem Konstanzer Konzil," pp. 69-112; Harald Zimmermann, "Die Absetzung der Päpste auf dem Konstanzer Konzil: Theorie und Praxis," pp. 113-137; Karl Fink, "Die Wahl Martins V.," pp. 138-151; Remigius Bäumer, "Das Verbot der Konzilsappellation Martins V. in Konstanz," pp. 187-213; and Remigius Bäumer, "Die Stellungnahme Eugens IV. zum Konstanzer Superioritätsdekret in der Bulle *Etsi non dubitemus,*" pp. 337-356.

38. *Haec sancta synodus Constantiensis, generale concilium faciens, pro extirpatione praesentis schismatis et unione ac reformatione ecclesiae Dei in capite et membris . . . legitime congregata . . . declarat quod . . . ecclesiam catholicam repraesentans, potestatem a Christo immediate habet, cui quilibet cujuscumque status vel dignitatis, etiamsi papalis existat, obedire tenetur in his quae pertinent ad fidem et extirpationem dicti schismatis et reformationem dictae ecclesiae in capite et in membris. Item declarat quod quicumque cujuscumque conditionis, status, dignitatis, etiam si papalis, qui mandatis, statutis seu ordinationibus aut praeceptis hujus sacrae synodi et seu cujuscumque alterius concilii generalis legitime congregati, super praemissis seu ad ea pertinentibus, factis vel faciendis, obedire contumaciter contempserit, nisi resipuerit, condignae paenitentiae subjiciatur et debite puniatur, etiam ad alia juris subsidia, si opus fuerit, recurrendo'* (Mansi, v. 27, col. 585).

39. Cf. Yves Congar, *L'église de saint Augustin à l'époque moderne, op. cit.,* pp. 339 ff. and 390 ff.

40. The best-known representative of this approach is Joseph Gill; cf. "The Fifth Session of the Council of Constance," *Heythrop Journal* 5 (1964) 131-143, and *Constance et Bâle-Florence, op. cit.*

41. *Haec Sancta,* for instance, is not included even in the latest editions of Denzinger; cf. the editors' note, *Enchiridion Symbolorum* (Herder, 1963[32]), pp. 315-316.

42. This position is defended, with slight variations, by the following Catholic scholars: August Franzen, "Einigungsbemühungen und konziliare Gedanken auf dem Konstanzer Konzil," *op. cit.* [cf. also his "Council of Constance: Present State of the Problem," *op. cit.,* pp. 57-59]; Helmut Riedlinger, "Hermeneutische Überlegungen zu den Konstanzer Dekreten," *Das Konzil von Konstanz, op. cit.,* pp. 214-238 [with several qualifications]; Brian Tierney," "Hermeneutics and History: The Problem of *Haec Sancta," op. cit.;* Hubert Jedin, *Bischöfliches Konzil oder Kirchenparlament? op. cit.;* and Yves Congar, *L'église de saint Augustin à lépoque moderne, op. cit.,* pp. 300-338. All of these men recognize the legitimacy of the decree *and* deny its strict dogmatic character; they differ slightly in their interpretations of the content of the degree. In my opinion they constitute the best contemporary authorities on the problem.

43. Cf., for example, Hans Küng, *Structures of the Church, op. cit.,* pp. 240-258, and Francis Oakley, "The New Conciliarism and Its Implications," *op. cit.*

44. Though it is an anachronism to apply contemporary canonical *norms of legitimacy* to the earlier councils, contemporary notions of *what is required for a strict dogmatic definition* certainly can be used to evaluate the dogmatic status of past conciliar pronouncements.

45. A representative selection would include the following: Roger Aubert, "L'ecclésiologie au concile du Vatican," *Le concile*

et les conciles, op. cit., pp. 245-284, and *Vatican I (Histoire des conciles oecuméniques* 12; l'Orante, 1964); G. Dejaifve, "Le premier des évêques," *Nouvelle Revue Théologique* 82 (1960) 561-579, "Conciliarité au Concile du Vatican," *Nouvelle Revue Théologique* 82 (1960) 785-802, and "Primauté et collégialité au Premier Concile du Vatican," *L'épiscopat et l'église universelle, op. cit.,* pp. 639-660; J. Hamer, "Le corps épiscopal uni au pape . . . d'après les documents du Premier Concile du Vatican," *Revue des Sciences Philosophiques et Théologiques* 45 (1961) 21-31; W. Kasper, "Primat und Episcopat nach dem Vatikanum I," *Theologische Quartalschrift* 142 (1962) 47-83; G. Thils, *Primauté pontificale et prérogatives épiscopales* (Warney, 1961) and *"Protestas Ordinaria," L'épiscopat et l'église universelle, op. cit.,* pp., 689-708; J.-P. Torrell, *La théologie de l'épiscopat au premier concile du Vatican* (Cerf, 1961).

46. *DS* 3061.

47. Cf. Mansi, v. 52, col. 1100-1117 and 1204-1230.

48. Cf. the study of F. Van der Horst, *Das Schema über die Kirche auf dem I. Vatikanischen Konzil* (Paderborn: Bonifacius-Druckerei, 1963).

49. Cf. *DS* 3112-3117 and O. Rousseau, "La vraie valeur de l'épiscopat dans l'église d'après d'importants documents de 1875," *L'épiscopat et l'église universelle, op. cit.,* pp. 709-736.

50. Cf. *Lumen Gentium* 22: *Ordo autem Episcoporum, qui collegio Apostolorum in magisterio et regimine pastorali succedit, immo in quo corpus apostolicum continuo perseverat, una cum Capite suo Romano Pontifice, et numquam sine hoc Capite, subjectum quoque supremae ac plenae potestatis in universam Ecclesiam exsistit. . . . Suprema in universam Ecclesiasm potestas, qua istud Collegium pollet, sollemni modo in Concilio Oecumenico exercetur. . . . Eadem potestas collegialis una cum Papa exerceri potest ab Episcopis in orbe terrarum degentibus, dummodo Caput Collegii eos ad actionem collegialem vocet, vel saltem Episcoporum dispersorum unitam actionem approbet vel libere recipiat, ita ut verus actus collegialis efficiatur.*

51. Cf. *Lumen Gentium* 22: *Romanus enim Pontifex habet in Ecclesiam, vi muneris sui, Vicarii scilicet Christi et totius Ecclesiae Pastoris, plenam, supremam, et universalem potestatem, quam semper libere exercere valet.* The complete text of chapter three of *Pastor Aeternus,* including the canon defining papal primacy, can be found in *DS* 3059-3064. As H. Ryan remarks in an unpublished paper on "The Primacy of Jurisdiction of the Roman Pontiff according to the First Vatican Council," the nature of the "jurisdiction" in question remains crucial for the interpretation of this definition. Zinelli, in his official *relatio* (Mansi, v. 52, col. 1103-1104), analyzes it in terms of an individual bishop's pastoral functions in the local church: papal jurisdiction presumably includes whatever is necessary to fulfil these same functions on the level of the church universal. As employed in *Pastor Aeternus,*

jurisdictio involves sacramental, doctrinal, and disciplinary activities. Historically the division of hierarchical ministry into three offices (*munera*) of teaching, governing, and sanctifying is a nineteenth century development in Catholic theology and difficult to coordinate with the older division of hierarchical ministry into two powers (*potestates*) of order and jurisdiction. Even this latter terminology came into use only after 1100, as absolute ordination was finally authorized and it became possible to distinguish between sacramental ordination and a subsequent *missio canonica*. Ultimately one must speak of *one* radical hierarchical power communicated to individual ministers in varying degrees and with various conditions attached. Cf. Klaus Mörsdorf, "Ecclesiastical Authority," *Sacramentum Mundi, op. cit.*, v. 2, pp. 133-139, and "Jurisdiction," *ibid.*, v. 3, pp. 229-231; Karl Rahner, *Theology of Pastoral Action, op. cit.*, pp. 36-40; and Otto Semmelroth, "Die Lehre von der kollegialen Hirtengewalt über die Gesamtkirche unter Berücksichtigung des angeführten Erklärungen," *Scholastik* 49 (1965) 161-179.

52. In addition to the works cited in note 29, cf. Rahner's commentary on *Lumen Gentium* 18-27 in H. Vorgrimler (ed.), *Commentary on the Documents of Vatican II* (Herder & Herder, 1967), v. 1, pp. 186-218. Rahner's latest essay on the subject is "Zum Verhältnis zwischen Papst und Bischofskollegium," *Schriften zur Theologie VIII* (Benziger, 1967), pp. 374-394.

53. Cf. Klaus Mörsdorf, "Ecclesiastical Authority," *op. cit.*

54. Cf. G. Dejaifve, "Ex sese, non autem ex consensu ecclesiae," *Salesianum* 25 (1962) 283-295, and Heinrich Fries, "Ex sese, non ex consensu ecclesiae," *Volk Gottes: Festgabe für J. Höfer* (R. Bäumer & H. Dolch; Herder, 1967), pp. 480-500.

55. Cf. J. Ratzinger's excellent commentary on this *Nota Praevia* in H. Vorgrimler (ed.), *Commentary on the Documents of Vatican II, op. cit.*, v. 1, pp. 297-305.

56. *Potestas summi pontificis limitature jure naturali et divino, limitatur Jesu Christi Domini nostri praeceptis et doctrinis, limitatur communi ecclesiae bono, limitatur conscientia, limitatur recta ratione et sensu communi, limitatur regula fidei et morum, etc. . . . Sed nec limitari nec restringi potest ab episcopis sive conjunctum sive separatim, sive in concilio sive extra concilium* (Mansi, v. 52, col. 579-580).

57. Cf. Mansi, v. 52, col. 1108-1110. The final text of *Pastor Aeternus*, however, is very explicit in its denial of *any* juridical limitations on papal primacy: *Et quoniam divino Apostolici primatus jure Romanus Pontifex universae Ecclesiae praeest, docemus etiam et declaramus, eum esse judicem supremum fidelium, et in omnibus causis ad examen ecclesiasticum spectantibus ad ipsius posse judicium recurri; Sedis vero Apostolicae, cujus auctoritas major non est, judicium a nemine fore retractandum, neque cuiquam de ejus licere judicare judicio. Quare a recto veritatis tramite aberrant, qui affirmant, licere ab judiciis Roma-*

norum Pontificum ad oecumenicum concilium tamquam ad auctoritatem Romano Pontifice superiorem appellare (*DS* 3063). Cf. *Lumen Gentium* 25: [*Definitiones ejus*] *nec ullam ad aliud judicium appellationem patiantur.*

58. Cf. Mansi, v. 52, col. 1213-1217.

59. *Lumen Gentium* 25: *Ad quam* [*revelationem*] *rite indagandam et apte enuntiandam, Romanus Pontifex et Episcopi, pro officio suo et rei gravitate, per media apta, sedulo operam navant. . . .*

60. Cf. Rahner's commentary on *Lumen Gentium* 18-27, cited in note 52, p. 202.

61. This juridically unlimited papal primacy of jurisdiction is predicated, of course, only of a certainly legitimate pope. The emergency procedures which would have to be invoked in the case of an insane or heretical pope are not discussed in any official Catholic document. They do, however, constitute a quasi-juridical limitation on the exercise of papal primacy in exceptional circumstances, at least according to those canonists who hold a truly depository rather than merely declarative theory of papal deposition.

62. Such prophetic protest, under certain conditions, is prefectly compatible with Catholic tradition. [It would in fact be a permanent possibility under *any* juridical arrangement for the government of the church universal: ultimately, no church structure can guarantee that Christian ministry will never be abused.] Zinelli at Vatican I remarked that no one should so absolutize papal authority *quasi praecepta evidenter injusta, nulla, et damnosa possent inducere obligationem, nisi ad scandalum vitandum* (Mansi, v. 52, col. 1109). In his commentary on *Lumen Gentium* 18-27, cited in note 52, pp. 202-203, Rahner is more explicit: "The Pope is obviously bound by the ethical norms of the gospel . . . . . And though there is no legal authority to see that these ethical norms are observed, and to question the validity of the Pope's decisions if they are not, the charismatic and prophetic quality of the Church still makes 'open opposition' (Gal. 2:11) possible. . . . . It follows also from what has been said that the ultimate maintenance of unity between the primate and a permanently effective college, that is, between the primatial and the synodal structure of the Church is not a matter of an imperative *norm* by which all dangers are averted from the start. The unity is given in the eschatological event, wrought continually and incalculably by the Spirit alone . . . . . The Protestant theologian should be particularly well equipped to recognize that Catholic theology sees and affirms that the institutional element in the Church does not ultimately function on its own." In his commentary on the *Nota Praevia,* cited in note 55, p. 304, Ratzinger makes the same point: ". . . The juridicial and the moral order by no means always coincide. Juridically speaking, there is no appeal from the Pope even when he acts without the college, and the college cannot act

without him at all; morally speaking, the Pope may have an obligation to listen to the bishops, and the bishops may have an obligation to take the initiative themselves." Ratzinger's most recent statement on the problem occurs in *Das neue Volk Gottes, op. cit.*, p. 144: *Umgekehrt wird Kritik an päpstlichen Äusserungen in dem Mass möglich und nötig sein, in dem ihnen die Deckung in Schrift und Credo bzw. im Glauben der Gesamtkirche fehlt. Wo weder Einmütigkeit der Gesamtkirche vorliegt noch ein klares Zeugnis der Quellen gegeben ist, da ist auch eine verbindliche Entscheidung nicht möglich; würde sie formal gefällt, so fehlten ihre Bedingungen, und damit müsste die Frage nach ihrer Legitimität erhoben werden.*

63. It makes sense to speak of the power of prophetic protest in a Christian communion whose sole bond of unity is mutual faith and love in the Spirit. In a free faith community it is at least possible to settle differences without denying the legitimacy of the officials involved or impugning the good faith of either side. The disputing parties can even agree to disagree for a while without rupturing the basic Christian *communio,* particularly if legitimate local diversity is acknowledged in practice as well as in theory. Prophetic protest without juridical protection was quite another matter, however, in an era of prince-bishops who wielded both swords, to say nothing of princely popes who launched crusades against other Christians and placed whole nations under interdict. Power politics and prophetic protest do not mix.

64. Very little research has been published on the whole problem of *jus divinum* in Catholic ecclesiology. In addition to the exploratory essay of Karl Rahner, "Über den Begriff des *Jus Divinum* im katholischen Verständnis," *Schriften zur Theologie V* (Benziger, 1962), pp. 249-277, cf. Piet Huizing, "Göttliches Recht und Kirchenverfassung," *Stimmen der Zeit* 183/94 (1969) 162-173, and Johannes Neumann, "Das *Jus Divinum* im Kirchenrecht," *Orientierung* 31 (1967) 5-8.

65. Cf. the sobering discussion of the complexity of the problems involved in Piet Huizing, "The Problem of the Division of Governmental Functions in the Church," *Concilium* 63 (1971) 127-134, and the essays collected in *We, the People of God, op. cit.*

66. I would stress these factors even if solutions were readily available to the dogmatic problems within Catholic theology about juridical limitations on the primatial head of the episcopal college and the separation of that primatial office in the church universal from the personal head of the central local church within the Christian communion.

10. Papal Primacy: Development, Centralization, and Changing Styles

1. Eduard Schweizer, *Church Order in the New Testament*, trans. F. Clarke (*Studies in Biblical Theology*, 32) SCM Press, London, 1961, 34-50.

2. Raymond E. Brown, "The Unity and Diversity in New Testament Ecclesiology," *Novum Testamentum*, vol. 6 (1963), 301.

3. *Peter in the New Testament*, Augsburg Publishing House, Minneapolis/Paulist Press, New York, 1973; Beda Rigaux, "St. Peter in Contemporary Exegesis," *Church History* (*Concilium*, vol. 7, no. 3), Burns and Oates, London, 1967, 78-82. This reference is to the British edition of *Concilium*.

4. Gabriel Moran, "The Continuing Revelation in the Church," *Theology of Revelation*, Burns and Oates, London, 1967, 115-130.

5. Nicolaas Appel, S.J., "The New Testament Canon: Historical Process and the Spirit's Witness," *Theological Studies*, vol. 32 (1971), 645.

6. G.C. Berkouwer, *Dogmatische Studien* (*De Heilige Schrift*, vol. 1), J.H. Kok, Kampen, 1966, 93-96.

7. Hans von Campenhausen, *The Formation of the Christian Bible*, trans. John A. Baker, Adam and Charles Black, London, 1972, x.

8. Piet Schoonenberg, S.J., *The Christ*, trans. Della Couling, Herder and Herder, New York, 1971, 16.

9. Quoted in Schoonenberg, *op. cit.*, 21.

10. *Ibid.*, 36. Cf. also Hans Urs von Balthasar, "A Theology of the Evangelical Counsels," *Cross Currents*, vol. 16 (Spring, 1966), 220, 221.

11. Anton Michel, "Der Kampf um das politische oder petrinische Prinzip der Kirchenführung *Das Konzil von Chalkedon*, Echter-Verlag, Würzburg, 1953, vol. 2, 491-562; Thomas Owen Martin, "The Twenty-Eighth Canon of Chalcedon: A Background Note," *ibid.*, 433-458. Leo rejected canon 28 even though the accompanying letters referred to the apostolic nature of Rome's ministry. Francis Dvornik thinks that if these words on apostolicity had been found in the formal text of the canon, Leo might have been satisfied. Cf. *The Idea of Apostolicity in Byzantium and the Legend of the Apostle Andrew*, Harvard University Press, Cambridge, 1958, 94.

12. Walter Bauer, *Orthodoxy and Heresy in Earliest Christianity*, eds. Robert Kraft and Gerhard Krodel, Fortress Press, Philadelphia, 1971, 112.

13. Schoonenberg, *op. cit.*, 47.

14. T. M. Schoof and B.A. Willems, "De wisselende rol van Petrus' opvolgers," *Tijdschrift voor Theologie*, vol. 9 (1969), 289.

15. John E. Lynch, "Advantages and Drawbacks of a Centre of Communications in the Church," *Papal Ministry in the Church*, ed. Hans Küng (*The New Concilium*), Herder and Herder, New York, 1971, 97.

16. "Each new bishop should be installed by the group of bishops resident in the province. If it is not possible for the bishops to come together because of pressing difficulties or because of the distances involved, then at least three bishops (of the province) shall come together and, after having obtained the written agreement of the other bishops, they shall proceed to the consecration. It belongs to the metropolitan of each province to confirm what has been done." J. D. Mansi, *Sacrorum Conciliorum Nova et Amplissima Collectio*, Antonio Zatta, Florentia, 1759, vol. 2, 669.

17. Dvornik, *Byzantium and the Roman Primacy*, Fordham University Press, New York, 1966, 95.

18. *Ibid.*, 61.

19. *Das Registers Gregors VII*, ed. Eric Caspar (*Monvmenta Germaniae Historica*), Weidmannsche Buchhandlung, Berlin, 1920, 202-208.

20. Augustin Fliche, *Saint Grégoire VII*, J. Gabalda et Fils, Paris, 1928, 81.

21. Fliche, *La Querelle des Investitures*, Editions Montaigne, Paris, 1946, 23-56.

22. Walter Ullmann, *Medieval Papalism: The Political Theories of the Medieval Canonists*, Methuen and Co., London, 1949, 1.

23. Dvornik, *Byzantium and the Roman Primacy*, 128, 129,

24. Victor Conzemius, "Why was the Primacy of the Pope Defined in 1870?" *Papal Ministry in the Church*, 77.

25. Kilian McDonnell, "Church Order and the Ontologizing Function of the Liturgy," *Worship*, vol 44 (November, 1970), 528-540.

26. Herbert Marcuse, *Eros and Civilization*, Beacon Press, Boston, 1955, 109.

27. Gustave Thils, *Choisir les Evêques? Elire le Pape?*, Gembloux, Duculot, 1970, 96.

28. *Das Registers Gregors VII*, 204.

29. The text is speaking of the college of bishops: *Potestas tamen huius Collegii, etsi ordinaria, utpote officio inhaerens, nonnisi modo extraordinario et in devota subordinatione Jesu Christi Vicario in terris quando, quomodo et quousque eidem id in Domino vedetur expedire, legitime exercetur. Schemata Constitutionum et Decretorum, De Ecclesia,* art. 16. Typis Polyglottis Vaticanis, 1962, 24. This was somewhat softened in the *nota previa*, art. 4: "The care of the whole flock of Christ has been entrusted to the Supreme Pontiff. It belongs to him, according to the changing needs of the church during the passage of time, to determine the way in which it is fitting for this care to be exercised, whether personally or collegially. The Roman Pontiff proceeds according to his own discretion and in view of the welfare

of the church in structuring, promoting and endorsing any exercise of collegiality."

30. G. Philips, *L'Eglise et son Mystère au Deuxieme Concile du Vatican,* Desclee et Cie, Tournai, 1967, vol. 1, 278.

31. *Ius canonicum,* Gregorian University, Rome, 1943, vol. 2, 725.

32. This section is indebted to G. Thils, *La primaute pontificalé. La doctrine de Vatican I. Les voies d'une révision,* Gemblous, J. Duculot, 1972.

33. On the concept of *communio* cf. Ludwig Hertling, *Communio: Church and Papacy in Early Christianity,* trans. Jared Wicks, Loyola University Press, 1972.

34. Joseph Ludwig, *Die Primatworte Mt 16, 18.19 in der altkirchlichen Exegese,* Aschendorffsche Verlagsbuchhandlung, Münster, 1952.

35. Dvornik, *Byzantium and the Roman Primacy,* 40, 41.

36. *Peter in the New Testament,* 157-168.

37. Peter L. Berger, *The Sacred Canopy,* Doubleday and Co., Garden City, New York, 1967, 3-52.

38. *Decree on Ecumenism,* art. 14.

39. *Ibid.*

40. *Decree on Eastern Catholic Churches,* art. 2.

41. *Decree on Ecumenism,* art. 14.

42. *Ibid.,* art. 19.

43. *Ibid.,* art. 16.

44. *Decree on Ecumenism,* 16; *Decree on Eastern Churches,* 5.

45. *Decree on the Eastern Churches,* art. 5.

46. *Decree on Ecumenism,* 16.

47. Nicholas Afanassieff, "The Church which Presides in Love," *The Primacy of Peter,* J. Meyendorff *et al.,* Faith Press, London, 1963, 57-110. Cf. also Alexander Schmemann, "The Idea of Primacy in Orthodox Ecclesiology," *ibid.,* 30-56.

48. art. 22.

49. Mansi, vol. 6, cols. 196f.

50. *Concilium Oecumenicum suprema pollet in universam Ecclesiam potestate.*

51. I owe this insight to Pierre Duprey.

52. W. Maurer, "Anti-Christ, II Kirchengeschichtlich," RGG³, 1957.

53. Apology, VII, 4, 23ff. 48; XV, 18; XXIV, 51; XXVI, 98. Smalcald Articles II, 4.

54. Johann Michel, "Anti-Christ," *Encyclopedia of Biblical Theology,* ed. Johannes Bauer, Sheed and Ward, London, 1970.

55. *Decree on Ecumenism,* art. 24.

11. Papacy and "Ius Divinum": A Lutheran View

1. This paper was originally delivered at the February 17-21, 1972 meeting in New Orleans. Only minor changes have been made in it.

2. Published in *Lutheran World* XIX (1972) pp. 259-273 and in *Worship* XLVI (1972) pp. 326-351. The author of the present article was a member of the commission which produced this report, and one of his contributions to its work, containing background material for the present article, has been published: "The Lutheran Doctrine of the Ministry: Catholic and Reformed," *Theological Studies* XXX (1969) pp. 588-612.

3. Since this article was written, E. Schlink has published "Zur Unterscheidung von *ius divinum* und *ius humanum*," *Begegnung* (Festschrift for Heinrich Fries, edited by M. Seckler, O. Pesch, J. Brosseder & W. Pannenberg) Graz: Verlag Styria, 1972, pp. 233-250. His conclusions regarding the Lutheran position are compatible with those of the present study.

4. Since published in *Theological Studies* XXXIV (1973) pp. 227-250.

5. The first and third of these papers are published in the present volume.

6. "Concerning the pope . . . if he would allow the Gospel, we, too, may concede to him that superiority over the bishops which he possesses by human right, making this concession for the sake of peace and general unity among Christians who are now under him and may be in the future." Smalcald Articles III.xv, *The Book of Concord* (ed. T.G. Tappert) pp. 316-317.

7. Some documentary evidence for this is provided by a paper presented to the commission by E. Schillebeeckx and since published under the title "The Catholic Understanding of Office in the Church," *Theological Studies* XXX (1969) pp. 567-587. Cf. Carl Peter, *op. cit.*, pp. 229-230 and *infra* footnotes 13-15.

8. *Op. cit.*, p. 241.

9. *Ibid.*, pp. 227-236.

10. P. Schoonenberg, *The Christ*, New York: Herder & Herder, 1971, p. 47. Quoted by C. Peter, *op. cit.*, p. 228, fn. 4.

11. C. Peter, *op. cit.*, p. 231 thus summarizes Karl Rahner's position.

12. *Ibid.*, pp. 244-245.

13. Schillebeeckx, *op. cit.*, p. 570. Quoted by Peter, *op. cit.*, p. 230.

14. *Ibid.*

15. *Ibid.*, p. 231.

13. The Petrine Office: Some Ecumenical Projections

1. *Two Centuries of Ecumenism:* The Search for Unity, (Mentor-Omega Press).

2. *Proceedings of the Twenty-First North American Liturgical Week* (1960) pp. 111-112.

3. Father Carl J. Peter, *Dimensions of Jus Divinum in Roman Catholic Theology*, p. 112.

4. *Ibid.*, p. 113.

5. Emmanuel Lanne, O.S.B., *"The Possibility of a Variety of Typologies Within the Same Ecclesial Allegiance,"* in *One in Christ*, 1970, No. 3. pp. 430-451.

6. Cardinal Willebrands' Address in Cambridge, England, January 18, 1970 A/RC DOC (USCC 1972) pp. 38-41.

7. *Ibid.*

8. *Decree on Ecumenism*, n. 14.

9. *Ibid.*, n. 16.

10. Avery Dulles, S.J., *"Dogma As An Ecumenical Problem,"* in *Theological Studies*, September, 1968, p. 398.

11. *Decree on Ecumenism*, n. 17.

12. *Ibid.*, n. 18.

13. *Ibid.*, n. 11.

14. George Lindbeck, in *One Baptism for the Remission of Sins*, p. 83.

15. Warren A. Quanbeck, "A Lutheran Understand of Papal Primacy."

16. Fred Kramer, *"A Lutheran Understanding of Papal Primacy."*

17. Decree on Eastern Churches, n. 27.

18. Decree on Catholic Orthodox Marriage, February 22, 1967.

PARTICIPANTS

Catholics:

The Most Reverend T. Austin Murphy, Auxiliary Bishop of Baltimore, Maryland

The Rev. Msgr. Joseph W. Baker, Vice-Chairman of the

Ecumenical Commission of the Archdiocese of St. Louis, Missouri

The Rev. Raymond E. Brown, S.S., Union Theological Seminary, New York, New York

The Rev. Walter Burghardt, S. J., Woodstock Center for Theological Reflection, Washington, D.C.

The Rev. Godfrey Diekmann, O.S.B., St. John's University, Collegeville, Minnesota

The Rev. Maurice C. Duchaine, S.S., St. Patrick's Seminary, Menlo Park, California

The Rev. Avery Dulles, S.J., Woodstock Center for Theological Reflection, Washington, D.C.

The Rev. Joseph Fitzmeyer, S.J., Fordham University, New York, New York

The Rev. Edward McGlynn Gaffney, formerly Assistant Director, Bishops' Committee on Ecumenical and Interreligious Affairs, Washington, D.C.

The Rev. John F. Hotchkin, Director, Bishops' Committee on Ecumenical and Interreligious Affairs, Washington, D.C.

Dr. James F. McCue, School of Religion, University of Iowa, Iowa City, Iowa

The Rev. Kilian McDonnell, O.S.B., Executive Director, Institute for Ecumenical and Cultural Research, Collegeville, Minnesota

The Rev. Carl J. Peter, Catholic University of America, Washington, D.C.

The Rev. Msgr. Jerome D. Quinn, The St. Paul Seminary, St. Paul, Minnesota

The Rev. George H. Tavard, A.A., Methodist Theological School, Delaware, Ohio

Lutherans:

Dr. Paul C. Empie, formerly General Secretary, U.S.A. National Committee of the Lutheran World Federation, New York, New York

The Rev. Joseph A. Burgess, Pastor of Faith Lutheran Church, Regent, North Dakota

Dr. Karlfried Froehlich, Associate Professor of the History of the Early and Medieval Church, Princeton Theological Seminary, Princeton, New Jersey

Dr. Eric W. Gritsch, Professor of Church History, Lutheran Theological Seminary, Gettysburg, Pennsylvania

Dr. Kent S. Knutson, now deceased (1973), formerly President of the American Lutheran Church, Minneapolis, Minnesota

Dr. Fred Kramer, Professor of Systematic Theology, Concordia Theological Seminary, Springfield, Illinois

Dr. George A. Lindbeck, Professor of Historical Theology, Yale University Divinity School, New Haven, Connecticut

Dr. Carl H. Mau, Jr., General Secretary, U.S.A. National Committee of the Lutheran World Federation, New York, New York

Dr. Paul D. Opsahl, Executive Director, Division of Theological Studies, Lutheran Council in the U.S.A., New York, New York

Dr. Arthur Carl Piepkorn, now deceased (1973), formerly Graduate Professor of Systematic Theology, Concordia Seminary, St. Louis, Missouri

Dr. Warren A. Quanbeck, Professor of Systematic Theology, Luther Theological Seminary, St. Paul, Minnesota

Dr. John Reumann, Professor of New Testament, The Lutheran Seminary at Philadelphia, Pennsylvania

Dr. William Rusch, Associate Executive Director, Division of Theological Studies, Lutheran Council in the U.S.A., New York, New York

Dr. Virgil R. Westlund, Director of Studies and International Exchange, U.S.A. National Committee of the Lutheran World Federation, New York, New York